ideals

Treasury of Budget Saving Meals COOKBOOK

From the kitchens of IDEALS, we bring you the three following best-selling cookbooks combined in a single volume for your enjoyment.

Book I   Budget Saving Meals Cookbook
by Donna M. Paananen

Book II   Meatless Meals Cookbook
by Donna M. Paananen

Book III   Ideals Family Cookbook

Bonanza Books
New York, N.Y.

CONTENTS

Book I   Budget Saving Meals Cookbook

Book II   Meatless Meals Cookbook

Book III   Ideals Family Cookbook

ISBN: 0-517-332493
BUDGET SAVING MEALS COOKBOOK
Copyright © MCMLXXX BY DONNA M. PAANANEN
MEATLESS MEALS COOKBOOK
Copyright © MCMLXXIX BY DONNA M. PAANANEN
IDEALS FAMILY COOKBOOK
Copyright © MCMLXXII BY IDEALS PUBLISHING CORPORATION
ALL RIGHTS RESERVED.

THIS EDITION IS PUBLISHED BY BONANZA BOOKS,
A DIVISION OF CROWN PUBLISHERS, INC.,
BY ARRANGEMENT WITH IDEALS PUBLISHING CORPORATION.
a b c d e f g h
BONANZA 1980 EDITION

MANUFACTURED IN THE UNITED STATES OF AMERICA

Book I
Budget Saving Meals
COOKBOOK

by Donna M. Paananen

Breakfasts and Breads

Cereals and grains are relatively low-cost additions to our diet—especially when they are homemade. Don't underestimate the importance of breads and cereals in your diet; nutritionists remind us to have four servings of these foods daily.

Braided Garlic Bread

   1 cup yogurt (or milk, soured
     with 1 tablespoon vinegar)
   2 tablespoons honey
   ¼ cup water
   ¼ cup vegetable oil
2½ cups unbleached white flour
   2 packages active dry yeast (5 tablespoons)
   1 teaspoon salt
   3 cloves garlic, minced
1½ to 2 cups whole wheat flour

Heat first four ingredients in a small pan until very warm (115°). Place white flour, yeast (at room temperature), salt, and garlic into a warmed mixing bowl and pour warm liquid over flour mixture. Blend at low speed with mixer until all ingredients are moistened. Continue to beat at medium speed for 3 minutes. Stir in whole wheat flour with a wooden spoon until soft dough is formed. Turn out onto a well-floured board and knead until smooth (8 to 10 minutes). Place dough in a greased bowl, turn once, and cover. Let dough rise in a warm place for 1 hour or until doubled in bulk. Punch down dough and divide into 3 equal parts. Form each part into long, smooth rolls. Join them securely at the top and braid carefully. Pinch ends together. Place braid on a well-greased baking sheet, cover and let rise in warm place until double, about 30 minutes. Preheat oven to 400° and bake bread for about 25 minutes or until golden. Remove from baking sheet, and, if desired, brush crust with melted butter. Yield: 1 large loaf.

Whole Wheat Sesame Seed Bread

   2 packages active dry yeast
   1 tablespoon honey
   2 cups lukewarm milk
   3 cups whole wheat flour
   1 to 1½ cups unbleached flour
   1 teaspoon salt
   ½ cup wheat germ
   ½ cup sesame seeds
   2 tablespoons vegetable oil

Dissolve yeast and honey in milk. Stir in 2 cups whole wheat flour and beat thoroughly. Stir in 1 cup of unbleached flour vigorously. Add salt, wheat germ, sesame seeds, and vegetable oil. Add the final cup of whole wheat flour and enough unbleached flour to make a workable dough. Turn onto a lightly-floured surface and knead 8 to 10 minutes or until smooth. Place dough in a greased bowl, turn to coat all sides. Cover with a towel. Let rise in a warm place (85°) for approximately 1 hour. Punch down and shape into 2 loaves. Place loaves into greased 8½ x 4½ x 2⅝-inch loaf pans. Cover and let rise in warm place for about 30 minutes or until doubled. Bake at 350° for approximately 35 minutes or until done. Yield: 2 loaves.

Super Zucchini Bread

   3 cups unbleached flour
1¼ cups raw wheat germ
   1 cup raisins
   1 cup chopped nuts (or less)
   1 tablespoon baking powder
   2 teaspoons cinnamon
   1 teaspoon salt
   2 eggs
1¼ cup brown sugar, firmly packed
⅔ cup vegetable oil
   2 teaspoons vanilla
   3 cups grated zucchini, drained

Preheat oven to 350°. In medium bowl, mix together dry ingredients. In a separate bowl, beat eggs until light colored; beat in sugar until dissolved. Add oil and vanilla. Fold in zucchini. Gradually stir in flour mixture until thoroughly blended. Pour into 2 greased 8½ x 4½ x 2⅝-inch loaf pans. Bake for 1 hour or until done. Cool in pan for 10 minutes before removing to wire racks. Yield: 2 loaves.

Hilda Blackford's Raisin-Nut Bread

    2 cups raisins
    2 teaspoons baking soda
    2 cups boiling water
    1 cup brown sugar, firmly packed
    2 tablespoons butter
    1 teaspoon salt
    3 eggs
    1 teaspoon vanilla
    4 cups unbleached flour
    1 cup chopped nuts
    1 pound fresh cranberries, chopped, optional

Mix raisins, baking soda, boiling water, brown sugar, butter, and salt together and let sit for 2 hours or overnight. Preheat oven to 350°. Add the rest of the ingredients, stirring thoroughly until well-blended. Pour into well-greased loaf pan. Bake for 1 hour or until done. Yield: 1 loaf.

Variation: Replace 2 cups flour with 2 cups rolled oats and add ½ teaspoon baking powder.

Bara Brith (Welsh tea bread)

    2 tablespoons lemon juice
    1½ cups milk
    3½ cups whole wheat flour
    1 teaspoon baking powder
    1 teaspoon baking soda
    ½ teaspoon cinnamon
    ½ teaspoon mace
    ½ teaspoon ground ginger
    ½ teaspoon ground cloves
    1 teaspoon salt
    ½ cup shortening
    ½ cup brown sugar, firmly packed
    ¾ cup currants
    ¾ cup raisins
    1 tablespoon grated lemon rind
    1 tablespoon old-fashioned molasses

Preheat oven to 350°. Stir lemon juice into milk and set aside to clabber. Stir dry ingredients together thoroughly. Cut in shortening with a pastry blender until mixture resembles crumbs. Mix in brown sugar, currants, raisins, and lemon peel thoroughly. Make a well in the center of the flour mixture and pour in the milk and molasses. Mix batter until all ingredients are well moistened and blended. Pour batter into a well-greased 9 x 5 x 3-inch loaf pan. Bake 1 hour or until pick inserted in center comes out clean. Cool in pan on wire rack for 10 minutes; before removing from pan. Serve thinly sliced and buttered. Usually better the second day. Yield: 1 loaf.

Apple Cider Bread

    1 cup apple cider
    2 eggs
    ¼ cup vegetable oil
    1 cup cooked or canned winter squash
      or pumpkin purée
    ⅔ cup brown sugar, firmly packed
    2 tablespoons grated orange rind
    1½ cups unbleached flour
    ½ cup raw wheat germ
    2 teaspoons baking powder
    ¼ teaspoon baking soda
    ½ teaspoon salt
    ¼ teaspoon cinnamon
    ¼ teaspoon nutmeg
    ¼ teaspoon cloves
    ½ cup chopped walnuts

Place apple cider in a stainless steel, glass, or enameled pan over high heat and reduce to ¼ cup. Cool. Preheat oven to 350°. Beat eggs with vegetable oil; stir in purée, sugar, rind, and cider. Mix together all dry ingredients except nuts. Fold the wet ingredients into the dry ingredients carefully until just blended. Stir in the nuts. Pour into a well-greased 8½ x 4½ x 2⅝-inch loaf pan and bake on the middle shelf for 1 hour or until tester inserted in the center comes out clean. Cool completely on a wire rack before removing from pan. Can be frozen. Yield: 1 loaf.

Too many of us continue to underestimate the importance of breakfasts—even when nutritionists stress the fact that it is the most important meal of our day.

With a little planning ahead, breakfast need not consist of expensive cereal from a box or sweet rolls wrapped in plastic. Vary food choices and still get one-third of the total protein for the day by eating a thrifty but nutritious, breakfast.

There are several methods which can be used to help bread dough rise. One method is to place the bowl over the pilot light on a gas stove. Another is to place the bowl near a radiator. Perhaps the best is to place a pan of very hot water on the lower shelf of the oven, then put the dough on the top shelf and close the door. This method promotes a steadily rising dough.

Breakfasts and Breads

Buckwheat Pancakes or Waffles

1 cup buckwheat flour
1 teaspoon baking powder
½ teaspoon salt
1 cup milk
1 egg, beaten
1 tablespoon honey
2 tablespoons melted butter or margarine

Mix dry ingredients together thoroughly. Stir in rest of ingredients in order, mixing well after each addition. Pour by ladlefuls onto greased, hot griddle or, following manufacturer's specifiations, into waffle iron. Yield: approximately 10 pancakes or 4 waffles.

Note: Extra pancakes or waffles can be frozen until needed. Toast, frozen, in toaster until heated through.

Herbed Bread

2 packages active dry yeast
2 cups lukewarm water
2 tablespoons honey
2 teaspoons salt
2 tablespoons soft butter or margarine
1½ tablespoons crumbled, dry oregano
4 to 5 cups whole wheat flour or a combination of unbleached white and whole wheat flour
Romano or Parmesan cheese

Mix yeast and water together in a large bowl. Stir in honey. Add salt, margarine, and oregano. With an electric beater, beat in 2 cups flour at low speed until thoroughly blended. Add 1 more cup; beat until smooth. With a wooden spoon, gradually beat in rest of flour until a workable dough is formed. Turn out onto a lightly floured board and knead until smooth. Place in a greased bowl; turn to grease all sides. Cover with a towel and let rise in a warm place (85°) for 1 hour or until doubled in bulk. Punch down and shape into a round loaf. Place on a well-greased baking sheet and sprinkle surface with Romano or Parmesan cheese. When nearly doubled in size, bake at 375° for approximately 1 hour or until done. Yield: 1 loaf.

"Staff" as used in "bread is the 'staff' of life" is defined by Webster as "a support." Could you call the bread your family eats the "support" of life? Make certain the bread your family eats can support life by making it of highly nutritious ingredients.

Puffed Pancakes

2 cups whole wheat or unbleached flour
¼ cup nonfat dry milk powder
2 teaspoons baking powder
1 teaspoon salt
1½ cups milk
¼ cup vegetable oil
2 egg whites, beaten until stiff

Mix dry ingredients together in a large bowl. Make a well in the center. Pour milk and oil into the well and mix until dry ingredients are just moistened. Gently fold beaten egg whites into the batter. Pour by ¼ cupfuls onto a lightly greased, hot griddle. Bake until bubbles form and begin to break on the surface and sides begin to look done. Turn and brown the other side. Yield: 16 3-inch pancakes.

Granola

6 cups rolled oats
1 cup whole wheat flour
1 cup raw wheat germ
1 cup Flaked Coconut (page 60)
½ cup sunflower seeds (or more)
½ cup soy nuts, peanuts, *or* other inexpensive nuts
½ cup vegetable oil
½ cup honey
⅓ cup water
½ teaspoon salt
1 teaspoon vanilla
1 cup raisins, prunes, dates, currants, or other fruit available

Preheat oven to 350°. In a very large bowl, mix together oats, flour, wheat germ, coconut, seeds, and nuts. In a separate container, mix together the rest of the ingredients except raisins. Pour wet ingredients over dry; mix thoroughly until well blended. Spread mixture onto two well-greased baking sheets. Bake for 30 minutes or until golden, stirring regularly. When thoroughly cool, stir in fruit. Store in an airtight container. Serve with milk, yogurt, fruit, etc., as a breakfast cereal or as an ingredient in cookies, breads, or snack items. Yield: approximately 3 quarts.

Appetizers and Savory Snacks

Packaged snack items often put a huge dent in the family food budget, so why not make your own inexpensive snacks at home and let your family share in the enjoyment. Freshly-popped popcorn, for example, is not only inexpensive, but calorie counters will be happy to know, there are only 200 calories in three cups of plain popcorn! Homemade crackers can be fun to make as well as economical. Roasted pumpkin, squash, and sunflower seeds are always a favorite with children. Take a walk in the woods and bring home nuts to munch on. Cheese makes a nutritious snack, and, bought in bulk, saves you money. Extra cheese can be frozen and used for cooking. And, vegetables from the garden always offer the best budget-saving, nutritious appetizers and snacks.

Sauerkraut Balls

　2　tablespoons butter or margarine
　1　small onion
　1　clove garlic
　¼　cup cooked ham
　¼　cup beef stock or bouillon
　2　tablespoons whole wheat flour
1½　cups sauerkraut, well drained
　1　tablespoon fresh parsley
　1　egg
⅔　cup milk
　¼　cup non-instant powdered milk
　　　Extra whole wheat flour
　　　Raw wheat germ
　　　Vegetable oil for deep-fat frying

Melt butter in heavy skillet. Grind onion and garlic and cook in butter until onion is transparent. Grind ham and stir into onion mixture. Heat thoroughly, add beef stock and heat again just to boiling. Stir in flour and immediately reduce heat. Stir constantly, adding more flour if necessary, until mixture is very stiff. Grind sauerkraut and parsley, squeezing dry before stirring into ham mixture in skillet. Blend thoroughly. Cover and refrigerate. Beat egg and milks together in a small bowl. When sauerkraut mixture is cold, roll into small balls. Roll in whole wheat flour, then dip in egg-milk mixture. Roll in wheat germ. Dry for 10 minutes then fry in deep fat heated to 350° to 360° until nicely browned. Sauerkraut balls may be frozen. If frozen, bake without thawing on an ungreased baking sheet at 350° until hot. Yield: approximately 2 dozen.

Parslied Liver Paté

　6　slices bacon
　1　cup chopped onion
　½　pound pork sausage
　1　pound liver, trimmed
⅓　cup milk
　6　fresh sage leaves
　　　Salt
　　　Freshly ground black pepper
⅔　cup minced parsley

Cook bacon in a large skillet until crisp. Drain on paper toweling. Pour off excess fat. Sauté onion in fat until transparent. Add pork sausage, break into bits, and cook until thoroughly browned. Remove onion and sausage. Pour off excess fat. Wash liver in milk and slice, if necessary, to insure quicker cooking. Sauté liver in the same pan pork sausage was cooked in until done. Place all the above ingredients in a food processor fitted with the steel blade or in a meat grinder. Add sage and grind until fine. Taste and correct seasonings. Form into a ball and sprinkle with parsley. Chill until serving time; serve surrounded by crackers or small rounds of bread. Yield: 1½ pounds.

Fresh Fruit Cup

　1　cup watermelon balls
　1　cup canteloupe balls
　1　cup honeydew melon balls
　1　cup sliced banana, sprinkled with lemon juice
　1　cup cubed pineapple
　1　cup hulled strawberries
　1　cup fresh peach slices
　1　cup orange slices
　1　cup seedless green grapes
　1　cup blueberries
　1　cup bing cherries
　　　Sugar, optional
⅓　cup rum, Cointreau, curacao, sherry, or apple juice
　　　Mint leaves

Choose from the above fruits, selecting a total of six cups. Mix fruits, sugar lightly, if desired, and chill, covered. Just before serving, pour liqueur or juice over fruit. Serve in frosted glass bowl, scalloped melon shell, or in individual, stemmed sherbet glasses. Garnish with mint leaves. Yield: 6 servings.

Cornish Pasties

3½ cups sifted, unbleached flour
½ cup ground suet
1 teaspoon salt
¾ cup margarine
½ cup cold water

All ingredients must be *cold*. With a pastry blender, blend flour, suet, salt, and margarine together until mixture resembles crumbs. Add water and mix lightly until dough holds together. Knead on a lightly floured board or cloth for a few moments until dough is smooth. Divide into 2 balls and chill until dough is firm (approximately 20 minutes). Roll out 1 ball of dough at a time on a lightly floured board until it is a little thicker than ⅛-inch. Cut with a 2½-inch round cookie cutter. Cover and refrigerate rounds until ready to fill them. Spread a small amount of the filling on half of each round. Fold the other half over and seal edges well. Place fill pasties on an ungreased baking sheet and bake 15 minutes at 375°; lower heat to 350° and bake 30 minutes or until pasties are golden. Yield: approximately 3 dozen.

Filling

1 cup raw potatoes, pared and sliced
½ pound choice stewing beef, cut in small pieces
4 tablespoons chopped onion
2 tablespoons ground suet
½ cup parsley, chopped fine
½ cup diced turnip
½ cup diced carrots
1 teaspoon salt
Freshly ground black pepper

Mix ingredients together lightly,

Sesame Seed Crackers

1 tablespoon lemon juice
½ cup milk
1⅓ cups unbleached flour
¼ cup rolled oats
¼ cup bulgur (cracked wheat)
3 tablespoons sesame seeds
½ teaspoon salt
½ teaspoon baking soda
3 tablespoons margarine, melted

Stir lemon juice into milk and set aside to clabber. Combine dry ingredients in a bowl. Stir in milk and butter. Knead the dough until ingredients are thoroughly mixed. Form into a ball and chill, wrapped, for about an hour. Preheat oven to 350°. Roll out dough about ⅛-inch thick on a well-floured surface with well-floured rolling pin. Cut with a round biscuit or cookie cutter into 2-inch rounds and place on well-greased baking sheets. Prick a pattern on the crackers with a fork and bake for 10 to 12 minutes or until golden and crisp. Cool on a wire rack. Yield: approximately 3 dozen.

Sardine Paste

1 3¾-ounce can sardines in oil, drained, skinned, and boned
1 tablespoon minced onion
2 tablespoons mayonnaise
1 teaspoon lemon juice
1 teaspoon Worcestershire sauce
½ teaspoon chili powder
1 hard-cooked egg, shelled and chopped
Thin slices bread or toast

Mash sardines with a fork. Stir in all ingredients except bread until thoroughly blended. Trim crusts and flatten bread with a rolling pin. Spread with paste. Roll bread slices, fasten with toothpicks, and place on a lightly greased baking pan. Bake in a 400° oven until bread is toasted and appetizer is heated through. Spread may also be served on buttered toast. Yield: ½ cup.

Wheat Germ Sticks

1 teaspoon baking powder
2 tablespoons soy flour
¾ cup raw wheat germ
½ cup whole wheat pastry flour
1 tablespoon minced chives
⅛ teaspoon salt
¼ cup margarine
2 tablespoons milk
1 egg white
¼ cup raw wheat germ

Mix first six ingredients together; cut in margarine until mixture resembles crumbs. Stir in 1 tablespoon milk and egg white lightly but thoroughly with a fork. Shape into a ball. Preheat oven to 400°. Roll out dough on a well-floured board with a well-floured pin to about ⅛-inch thickness. Cut dough into 36 sticks approximately 3½-inches long. Brush sticks with final tablespoon milk and roll in wheat germ. Place on ungreased baking sheets and bake for about 6 minutes or until golden. Yield: 3 dozen.

Raw vegetables in season or out of the garden are a penny-pincher's dream: no energy is needed to cook them; they are highly nutritious yet inexpensive; and they are low in calories.

Hot Cheese Rounds

¾ cup margarine
⅓ cup blue cheese
½ cup shredded sharp Cheddar cheese
   or similar cheese
1 garlic clove, minced
1 teaspoon minced chives
1 teaspoon minced parsley
1 teaspoon baking powder
1 cup whole wheat flour
1 cup unbleached flour

Cream together margarine and cheeses. Add garlic, chives, parsley, and baking powder. Stir thoroughly. Add flour slowly, mixing thoroughly. Shape into 2 rolls, each about 1½ inches in diameter. Chill well. Preheat oven to 375°. Slice rounds ¼-inch thick and place on well-greased baking sheets. Bake 8 to 10 minutes or until golden. Serve hot. Yield: approximately 5 dozen.

Stuffed Cucumber

½ cup cottage cheese
2 tablespoons parsley
1 tablespoon chives
1 clove garlic
½ teaspoon curry powder (or more, to taste)
   Salt
   Freshly ground black pepper
1 long, European cucumber, unpeeled
   Lettuce, parsley, optional

Place cottage cheese, parsley, chives, and garlic in blender; blend until smooth. Season to taste. Slice cucumber lengthwise and scoop out centers slightly. Spoon cottage cheese mixture into centers and chill thoroughly. To serve, slice each cucumber half into eighths or smaller and serve on a plate garnished with lettuce or parsley, if desired. Yield: approximately 16 servings.

Party Puffs

½ cup margarine
1 cup water
1 cup unbleached flour
4 eggs at room temperature

Preheat oven to 400°. Heat water and margarine to a rolling boil in a heavy saucepan. Quickly stir in flour with a wooden spoon. When mixture looks smooth and forms a ball, stir faster until spoon will leave a smooth imprint on the paste. Remove from heat and add eggs, one at a time, stirring vigorously after each addition. When all eggs are added and mixture is smooth but not slippery, drop dough by slightly rounded teaspoonfuls onto an ungreased baking sheet. Bake 25 to 30 minutes or until puffed and golden. Slice puffs and remove any uncooked bits inside, readying the puffs to be filled. Spoon Filling into puffs. If not served immediately after filling, puffs may be reheated in a 350° oven for about 10 minutes or until heated through. Yield: approximately 50.

Variations: Make herbed puffs by adding 1 teaspoonful of dill seeds, garlic salt, poppy seeds, celery seeds or caraway seeds to the water and margarine combination. Or make cheese puffs by adding ¾ cup grated Swiss, sharp Cheddar, or a combination of Swiss and Parmesan cheese to the warm paste before forming into the puffs.

Filling

2 tablespoons margarine or butter
2 tablespoons unbleached flour
1 cup milk
¼ cup minced onion
1 small bay leaf
1 6½-ounce can tuna fish, drained

Melt margarine in a heavy saucepan; stir in flour and blend for about 5 minutes over very low heat. Add milk gradually, stirring to keep smooth. Finally, add onion and bay leaf and simmer, stirring regularly, until thick. Remove bay leaf. Stir in tuna and heat thoroughly.

Taramasalata

1 2-ounce jar red caviar (lumpfish roe)
3 slices dry bread
¼ cup milk
2 tablespoons lemon juice
½ cup vegetable oil
2 tablespoons minced onion
2 cloves garlic, minced

Soak caviar in water for about 5 minutes to remove salt. Drain. Soak bread in milk; squeeze dry. Place caviar, bread, and remaining ingredients in blender and blend until smooth, light and creamy. Spread on buttered bread rounds or toast or use as a dip for celery sticks, cucumber or green pepper slices, etc. Yield: 1¼ cups.

Soups and Stews

Whether it's a frosty soup on a hot summer's day or a steamy stew on a blustery winter evening, good soups soothe the soul when the pocketbook has little in it.

Potato Soup

- 3 cups water
- 4 cups peeled, sliced potatoes
- 3 cups chopped onion
- 2 bay leaves
  Freshly ground black pepper
- 1½ cups milk
- ½ cup nonfat dried milk powder
- 2 tablespoons margarine or butter
  Salt
  Chopped chives

In a large soup kettle, bring water, potatoes, onion, bay leaves, and pepper to boil; reduce heat and simmer, covered, for about 20 minutes or until potatoes are tender. Stir in milks and margarine. Taste and correct seasonings. Heat but do not boil. Serve garnished with chopped chives. Yield: 6 to 8 servings.

Bean Soup

- 2 cups (16 ounces) dried navy beans
- 2½ quarts water or vegetable cooking liquids or thin broth
- 1 meaty ham bone (approximately 1½ pounds)
- 1 cup chopped onion
- 2 cups chopped carrot
- 2 cloves garlic, minced
- 1 cup chopped celery
- 1 bay leaf
- 2 tablespoons parsley
- ¼ teaspoon ground allspice
- ½ teaspoon freshly ground black pepper
  Salt

Rinse and sort beans. Place in a large soup kettle with water. Bring to boil, reduce heat, and simmer 2 minutes. Remove from heat; let stand, covered, 1 to 2 hours. Add ham bone, vegetables, and seasonings, except salt. Simmer, covered, for 1 hour or until beans are tender. Remove ham bone and slice off meat. Dice meat and add to soup. Reheat until soup is at serving temperature. Taste and correct seasonings before serving. Yield: 8 servings.

Cambrian Stew

- 3 pounds lamb necks or shoulder, cut up (with bones)
- ½ cup whole wheat flour
- ½ teaspoon salt
  Freshly ground black pepper
- 8 to 10 young, small carrots, scrubbed
- 8 to 10 young, small white onions, peeled
- 3 celery stalks, sliced
- 1¼ cups vegetable or other stock
- 1¼ cups beer
- 6 parsley sprigs
- 1 bay leaf
- 1 sprig thyme or ⅛ teaspoon dry
  Parsley

Remove any bone splinters from meat. Mix flour, salt, and pepper in a paper bag. Drop meat pieces in and coat with flour mixture. Place pieces into large saucepan or Dutch oven. Add vegetables, stock, beer, and herbs. Bring mixture to a boil; skim surface and simmer, covered, 1½ to 2 hours or until meat is tender. (If desired, remove bones from the meat and cut meat into bite-size pieces at this point.) Taste and correct seasonings. Serve garnished with chopped parsley. Yield: 6 servings.

Split Pea Soup

- 1 ham hock or meaty ham bone
- 1 pound split peas, rinsed and sorted
- 3 quarts water
- 5 slices lean bacon, chopped
- 1 carrot, chopped
- 1 cup chopped onion
- ¼ cup parsley
- ½ teaspoon thyme
- 2 bay leaves
- ½ cup green part of leeks or green onion
  Salt
  Freshly ground black pepper

Place ham hock, split peas, and water in a large soup kettle and bring to boil. Reduce heat and simmer, covered. Sauté bacon until fat is rendered. Stir in carrot and onion. Sauté until bacon is browned. Add to soup kettle with the rest of the ingredients. Simmer for 3 hours or until meat falls off the bone. Slice meat into serving pieces and discard bone. Add meat to soup; taste and correct seasonings. Yield: 8 to 10 servings.

Pumpkin Soup

 3 pounds diced, peeled pumpkin
   or 4 cups cooked pumpkin puree
 2 tablespoons margarine or butter
 1 cup sliced onion
 8 green onions, chopped
 6 cups well-seasoned chicken broth
 1 bay leaf
 2 tablespoons margarine
 3 tablespoons flour
 1 cup yogurt
   Freshly ground black pepper
   Salt
   Chopped chives
   Garlic croutons

Pumpkin can be chopped fine in food processor fitted with steel knife, if desired. This will speed up cooking but is not necessary. Sauté onions in margarine in a large soup kettle or Dutch oven until golden. Add pumpkin, broth, and bay leaf. Bring to a boil, reduce heat, and simmer, covered, until pumpkin is soft (10 minutes if using puree). Remove bay leaf. Place mixture in blender and blend until smooth (or strain) and return to Dutch oven. Melt margarine in small saucepan and stir in flour. Cook for about 2 minutes, then add a small amount of soup to flour, stirring constantly. Add more soup; then pour flour mixture into the Dutch oven. Bring soup in Dutch oven to boil; stir with a wire whisk until soup thickens. Taste and correct seasonings. Just before serving, stir in yogurt (or use dollops of yogurt as a garnish). When soup is thoroughly heated (do not boil after yogurt is added), garnish with chives and croutons. Yield: 8 servings.

Quick Spinach or Chard Soup

 3 cups well-flavored beef broth
 3 to 4 cups shredded spinach or chard
   Salt
   Freshly ground black pepper
   Parsley

Bring beef broth to the boiling point; add spinach and reduce heat. Simmer, covered, 5 to 10 minutes or until vegetable is tender. Taste and correct seasonings. Serve garnished with parsley. Yield: 3 to 4 servings.

Oxtail Soup

 2 pounds oxtail, cut into 2-inch pieces
 ¼ cup flour
 1 tablespoon bacon drippings or vegetable oil
 2 cups chopped onion
 5 cups well-seasoned beef, vegetable or
   other stock or water
 5 sprigs parsley
 1 bay leaf
 2 whole cloves
 4 peppercorns
 ½ teaspoon thyme
 ½ teaspoon tarragon
 1 cup carrots, sliced
 2 ribs celery, diced
 1 cup turnips, diced
 1 teaspoon lemon juice
   Salt
   Freshly ground black pepper
 ¾ cup minced parsley

Roll oxtail pieces in flour until lightly coated. Heat oil in a Dutch oven or heavy soup kettle and stir in meat to brown thoroughly. Stir in onions and cook until golden. Pour stock over meat, reduce heat, and add parsley sprigs, bay leaf, cloves, peppercorns, thyme, and tarragon. Cover and simmer about 3 hours. Add vegetables and continue simmering until meat falls from the bones, (1 hour or more). Discard bones, skim fat from the surface, and stir in lemon juice. Taste and correct seasonings; sprinkle on parsley and serve. Yield: 6 to 8 servings.

Note: In a slow cooker, this dish would take about 8 hours on high.

Make broths and stock from the inexpensive bones the butcher has to offer, as well as from the leftover bones from meats and poultry.

Save steaming and cooking liquids from all cooking; freeze if necessary until needed for a highly flavored, nutritious soup.

Save all cooking liquids for later use in flavorful, highly nutritious soups; freeze any liquid which will not be used within a short time.

Cream of Tomato Soup

    2 cups canned tomatoes with juice
    ½ cup chopped onion
    2 ribs celery, chopped
    ¼ cup chopped parsley
      Freshly ground black pepper
    2 tablespoons margarine
    2 tablespoons flour
    3 cups milk
      Salt
      Freshly ground black pepper
      Croutons, parsley, chives, or dollops of yogurt
      to garnish

Cook tomatoes, onion, celery, and parsley together until vegetables are tender. Place in blender and blend until smooth. Meanwhile, stir flour into melted margarine in a heavy saucepan. Cook, stirring regularly, for about 5 minutes over very low heat. Stir in milk gradually, keeping mixture smooth. Stir blended tomato mixture into cream sauce. Taste and correct seasonings. Serve, garnished as desired. Yield: 4 to 6 servings.

The Meiners' Cauliflower Soup

    5 cups cauliflowerets
 2½ cups chicken, onion, or
      vegetable stock
    1 teaspoon soy sauce
    ½ teaspoon paprika
    ½ teaspoon savory
    ½ teaspoon garlic powder
    ¼ teaspoon freshly ground black pepper
    2 teaspoons butter or margarine
    2 teaspoons flour
 1½ cups milk
    ¾ cup nonfat dried milk powder
    ¼ cup freshly grated Parmesan
      or Romano cheese
    ¼ cup grated Swiss cheese
    2 egg yolks, beaten
    3 tablespoons lemon juice

Reserve ½ cup flowerets for garnish. Cook remainder in desired stock with soy sauce, paprika, savory, garlic powder, and black pepper until cauliflower is soft. Puree in blender. Melt butter in a small saucepan; add flour and stir until flour is cooked through. Gradually add milk; cook and stir until thick. Add puree, dried milk, and cheeses. Reheat to melt cheese but do not boil. Beat egg yolks with lemon juice; whisk into ½ cup hot soup and return to remaining soup. Reheat; do not boil. Taste and correct seasonings. Garnish with reserved flowerets and extra cheese, if desired. Yield: 4 to 6 servings.

Winter Garbure (Thick French Stew)

    2 cups Great Northern beans
    8 cups water
 1½ pounds smoked pork rump
      or meaty ham bone
    5 large cloves garlic
    ½ teaspoon thyme
    ½ cup parsley
    ½ teaspoon marjoram
    5 potatoes, peeled and sliced
    2 cups fresh or frozen green beans or peas
    ½ medium-sized green cabbage,
      washed and shredded
      Salt
      Freshly ground black pepper
    8 to 10 slices dry whole wheat bread
    1 cup grated Swiss cheese

Soak beans in water overnight. Bring beans and liquid, pork rump, garlic, and herbs to a boil in a large heavy soup kettle or Dutch oven. Reduce heat and simmer, covered, for 1½ hours. Add potatoes and cook another 30 minutes. Finally, add cabbage and green beans and additional liquid, if needed. Simmer until vegetables are tender. Remove meat to serve separately. Taste and correct seasonings. Ladle soup into oven-proof bowls, placing bread slices on top. Sprinkle Swiss cheese on top and place under broiler until cheese is melted and browned. Serve immediately. Yield: 8 to 10 servings.

Lynn's Budget Chili

    2 cups pinto beans
    6 cups water
    ½ cup chopped onion
    ¼ cup bacon or chicken fat or margarine
    2 cloves garlic, minced
      Cumin to taste
      Chili powder to taste
      Salt to taste
      Freshly ground black pepper to taste
    ½ cup grated sharp Cheddar or Monterey Jack cheese

Soak beans in water overnight. Bring beans, liquid, and onion to a boil. Reduce heat and simmer, covered, for 1 hour. Add more water if necessary. Stir in fat, garlic, cumin, and chili powder. Simmer for 30 minutes. Taste and add salt and pepper. Stir in cheese until it melts. Serve immediately. Yield: 4 to 6 servings.

Soups and Stews

Danish Apple Soup

   4 cups quartered apples (unpeeled), cores removed
   4 cups water
   1 teaspoon grated lemon rind
   1 stick cinnamon
   2 tablespoons cornstarch
   ¼ cup water
   ½ cup dry white wine
   ¼ cup sugar

Place apples, water, lemon rind, and cinnamon in a large, heavy-bottomed saucepan over low heat. Simmer until apples are tender. Remove cinnamon stick and puree mixture in blender (or through sieve) until smooth. For a thinner soup, add more water. Bring mixture to simmer again. Blend cornstarch and water together until smooth. Stir into soup and cook over low heat until soup is thick and smooth. Stir in wine and sugar. Taste and correct seasonings. Serve hot. Yield: 6 servings.

Barley-Vegetable Soup

   2 tablespoons margarine
   1 cup chopped onion
   2 cloves garlic, minced
 2½ cups well-flavored beef broth or stock
   6 cups water
   3 tablespoons tomato paste
     Freshly ground black pepper
   1 bay leaf
   ½ cup barley
   2 cups chopped celery and leaves
   2 cups sliced carrots
   ½ cup chopped parsley
     Salt
     Yogurt

Sauté onions and garlic in margarine until onions are translucent. Add broth, water, tomato paste, pepper, and bay leaf. Heat to boiling. Stir in barley, reduce heat and simmer, covered, 1 hour. Stir in vegetables and simmer, covered, about 30 minutes longer or until vegetables and barley are tender. Taste and correct seasonings. Serve hot, garnished with a dollop of yogurt. Yield: 8 servings.

Add high-protein, low-cost legumes and garden produce to a well-flavored broth for a meal fit for a prince at a price a pauper could afford.

Ham Hock and Bean Soup

   1 pound Great Northern or navy beans, rinsed and sorted
   8 cups water
   4 cups vegetable cooking liquid, broth, or other flavorful liquid on hand
   1 1-pound smoked ham hock
   1 cup chopped onion
   1 cup chopped celery
     Salt
     Freshly ground black pepper

Soak beans overnight in water. Combine soaked beans and liquid with well-flavored broth and ham hock in a large soup kettle or Dutch oven. Bring to boil, reduce heat and simmer, covered, for 2 hours. Add onion and celery and continue to simmer 1 hour. Remove ham hock and slice off meat into bite-sized pieces. Discard bone. Return meat to soup. If desired, mash beans slightly. Taste and correct seasonings. Serve hot. Yield: 6 to 8 servings.

End-of-the-Month Lentil Soup

   2 slices bacon, chopped
   1 cup lentils, washed and sorted
   1 cup carrots, sliced
   1 cup chopped onion
   2 ribs celery, chopped
   3 cloves garlic, minced
  10 cups stock, vegetable cooking liquid, broth, and/or water
   1 bay leaf
   ½ cup chopped parsley
   ¼ teaspoon thyme
     Salt
     Freshly ground black pepper

Sauté bacon in a Dutch oven or heavy soup kettle until fat is rendered. Stir in lentils, carrots, onions, celery, and garlic. Sauté for about 5 minutes, stirring regularly. Add remaining ingredients, except salt and pepper, and bring to a boil. Reduce heat and simmer, covered for 1 hour or until lentils and vegetables are tender. Taste and correct seasonings. If desired, put soup through blender. Serve hot. Yield: 8 servings.

Lou Snow's Spanish Lentil Soup

- 2 tablespoons olive oil
- 1 green pepper, chopped
- ¾ cup chopped onion
- 1 clove garlic, minced
- 1 heaping tablespoon flour
- 2 cups stewed or canned tomatoes
- 1 cup thinly sliced carrots
- 1 cup dry lentils
- 1 teaspoon salt
- 1 quart water
  Freshly ground black pepper

Heat oil in a very large frying pan or Dutch oven. Stir in green pepper, onion, and garlic. Cook until soft. Sprinkle with flour, and stir. Add remaining ingredients. Bring to boil; reduce heat and simmer, covered, 2 hours. Taste and correct seasonings. Serve immediately. Yield: 4 to 6 servings.

Soybean and Sausage Stew

- 2 strips bacon, chopped
- 1 cup sliced onion
- 6 carrots, peeled and sliced
- 3 to 4 cups shredded cabbage
- 2 cups cooked soybeans
- 1 tablespoon minced parsley
- 1 bay leaf
- 3 to 4 cups water, vegetable stock, or broth
- ½ pound smoked sausage, cut into serving pieces
  Salt
  Freshly ground black pepper

Fry bacon in a very large frying pan or Dutch oven until it renders its fat. Stir in onion and sauté until golden. Add carrots, cabbage, soybeans, parsley, bay leaf, and water and simmer, covered, 30 minutes or until vegetables are tender. Stir in sausage and simmer, covered, 15 more minutes. Taste and correct seasonings with salt and pepper. Serve very hot. Yield: 4 to 6 servings.

Corn Chowder

- 2 tablespoons margarine or butter
- 1 cup chopped onion
- 1½ cups peeled and chopped potatoes
- 4 cups milk
- ¼ cup non-instant powdered milk
- 2 cups fresh corn
- ¼ teaspoon paprika
  Freshly ground black pepper
  Salt
  Parsley, minced

Melt margarine in a Dutch oven or heavy soup kettle. Sauté onion and potatoes in the margarine for about 5 minutes. Add milk which has been mixed with powdered milk, corn, and paprika. Cover and simmer until vegetables are tender. In the last minute of cooking, add salt and pepper to taste. Serve hot, garnished with parsley. Yield: 6 servings.

Zucchini Soup

- 1 tablespoon margarine
- 1 cup chopped onion
- 4 cups well-flavored chicken broth
- 4 to 6 cups zucchini slices
- 1 tablespoon fresh dill
  Chopped parsley
  Unflavored yogurt or sour cream

Melt margarine in a large frying pan or soup kettle. Sauté onion until transparent. Add chicken broth, zucchini, and dill. Simmer 10 to 15 minutes until zucchini is tender. Taste and correct seasonings. Soup can be served as is or placed in a blender until smooth. Garnish with chopped parsley and dollops of yogurt or sour cream, as desired. Yield: 4 to 6 servings.

Julia's Sausage-Vegetable Soup

- 8 cups water, vegetable cooking liquid, stock, or broth
- ½ pound sliced Polish, smoked, or other sausage
- 1 cup sliced carrots
- ½ cup chopped onion
- 2 cloves garlic, minced
- 1 teaspoon marjoram
- ½ teaspoon thyme
- ¼ teaspoon freshly ground black pepper
- 1 bay leaf
- 1 cup diced potatoes
- 3 cups thinly sliced cabbage
  Salt

In a large soup kettle or Dutch oven, bring water, sausage, carrots, onion, garlic, marjoram, thyme, pepper, and bay leaf to the boiling point. Reduce heat and simmer, covered, 30 minutes. Add potatoes and cabbage and simmer, covered, until vegetables are tender, about 30 minutes. Taste and correct seasonings. Yield: 8 servings.

Fish, Poultry, and Meat

The part of the family food budget that seems to receive more attention than any other is that devoted to fish, poultry, and meat. The important thing to remember is to be flexible—to know that one year you may not be able to afford much bacon, for instance, and another year, not much beef. Try new dishes, including meatless meals, to provide protein without spending a fortune.

Haddock Newburg

- 1 pound haddock fillets (fresh or frozen)
- 1½ cups milk
- 5 tablespoons margarine
- ¾ cup mushrooms
- 4 tablespoons unbleached flour
- 1 egg yolk, lightly beaten
- 1 teaspoon Worcestershire sauce
- 1 teaspoon lemon juice
- 2 tablespoons dry sherry
- Salt
- Freshly ground black pepper
- Chopped parsley

If haddock is frozen, thaw according to package directions. Poach haddock in milk in a large frying pan until fish just begins to flake. Meanwhile, sauté mushrooms in 1 tablespoon margarine until they are lightly browned (8 to 10 minutes). In a small pan, melt remaining margarine. With a wire whisk stir in flour and cook gently for about 2 minutes. When fish is poached, remove from heat and pour the hot milk into the flour mixture. Beat with wire whisk until sauce is thickened. Mix a small amount of the flour-milk mixture with the egg yolk. Gently stir mixture into the cream sauce. Add the seasonings; taste and correct. Finally, stir in the mushrooms and pour the sauce over the fish (break up the fish, if desired). Simmer, stirring constantly, until the dish is heated through, about 2 minutes. Serve over rice, garnished with parsley, if desired. Yield: 3 to 4 servings.

Chinese Beef with Peas and Peanuts

- 1 10-ounce package frozen peas
  or 1 cup fresh
- 1 cup vegetable oil
- ½ cup raw, fresh, unsalted peanuts
- 1 cup chopped onion
- 1 small clove garlic, minced
- 1 cup chopped celery
- ¾ pound ground beef
- 1 cup sliced fresh mushrooms, (optional)
- 1 cup well-flavored beef broth
- 2 tablespoons cornstarch
- 2 tablespoons soy sauce
- 2 tablespoons sherry

Thaw peas slightly. Pour peanuts into hot oil in a wok or large frying pan. Turn off heat and let peanuts stand about 1½ minutes until golden. Drain, leaving 1 tablespoon oil. Stir-fry onion, garlic, and celery and then add ground beef. Cook briskly until just browned. Remove meat and vegetables. Add peas and mushrooms to skillet; pour in broth and cook until peas are crisp-cooked. Mix cornstarch, soy sauce, and sherry; stir into mixture in skillet. Add beef and vegetables and cook, stirring constantly, until sauce thickens. Transfer to serving dish and sprinkle with peanuts. Serve with rice. Yield: 4 to 6 servings.

Roast Stuffed Chicken

- 1 3- to 4-pound fryer
- 3 cups slightly dry, cubed bread
- 1 rib celery, diced
- 3 tablespoons minced onion
- ½ teaspoon salt
- ½ teaspoon crumbled sage
- ⅛ teaspoon freshly ground black pepper
- 1 small apple, chopped
- ¼ cup raisins
- 2 cloves garlic, minced
- 2 tablespoons butter or margarine
  at room temperature

Preheat oven to 400°. Wash chicken and pat dry. Mix together remaining ingredients except butter, and stuff chicken. (Any excess can be baked in aluminum foil alongside the bird.) Truss bird as desired and rub skin with butter. Place, breast up, on rack in roasting pan. Roast uncovered 1¾ to 2 hours or until done (drumstick will move up and down easily). Baste occasionally with drippings. Yield: 4 servings.

Hamburger Stroganoff

 2 slices bacon, chopped
 1 pound ground beef
 1 cup chopped onion
 2 tablespoons whole wheat flour
 2 cups beef broth
 ¼ pound sliced mushrooms
 1 teaspoon Worcestershire sauce
   Salt
   Freshly ground black pepper
 1 cup sour cream

Heat bacon in a large frying pan until it begins to render its fat. Stir in ground beef and onion and brown meat thoroughly. Stir in flour and pour in beef broth. Bring to boil, then reduce heat and simmer for about 30 minutes. Stir in mushrooms and Worcestershire sauce and simmer until mushrooms are cooked. Taste and add salt and pepper to taste. Finally, stir in sour cream and heat thoroughly; do not boil. Serve over boiled noodles or rice. Yield: 8 to 10 servings.

Mock Chop Suey

 1 tablespoon vegetable oil
 1 cup chopped onion
 1 cup chopped celery
 1 pound ground beef
 1 cup uncooked brown rice
 1 can cream of mushroom soup
 1 can cream of chicken soup
 2 tablespoons soy sauce
 2 cups bean sprouts (canned sprouts can be used)
 1 8-ounce can water chestnuts,
   drained and sliced (optional)
 1 3-ounce can chow mein noodles
 1 10-ounce package frozen peas

Preheat oven to 350°. In vegetable oil in a large frying pan, sauté onion and celery for 5 minutes. Add ground beef and brown well. Stir in rice and cook until transparent. Finally, stir in soups, soy sauce, bean sprouts, and water chestnuts. Bake in a large casserole, uncovered for 30 minutes. Stir in ⅓ can chow mein noodles and frozen peas. (Add water if mixture is too dry.) Bake 30 more minutes or until rice is just tender; sprinkle remaining noodles on top and bake 10 minutes more. Serve immediately. Can be frozen before baking. Thaw and bake, following directions for adding noodles and peas. Yield: 10 servings.

The Benvenutos' Pizza

 ½ package active dry yeast
 ¾ cup lukewarm water
 1 cup whole wheat flour
 1 cup unbleached flour
   Olive oil

Sprinkle yeast into water; stir until dissolved. Add 1 cup of whole wheat flour and stir thoroughly. Add 1 cup unbleached flour; continue to stir until dough can be turned out onto a lightly floured board. Knead 10 minutes or until dough is pliable. Oil a bowl with olive oil, place dough into the bowl and turn to grease all surfaces. Cover and put in a warm place (85°); let rise until doubled in bulk (about 1½ hours). Oil an 11 x 17 x 1-inch baking sheet with olive oil; with greased hands, spread dough in pan. Brush olive oil evenly on top of crust to keep topping from sinking in. Spread on the topping and bake in a 425° oven for 25 to 30 minutes or until done. Yield: 12 slices pizza.

Topping

 2 cups Grandma Ben's Tomato Sauce (page 47)
 1 pound mozzarella cheese, sliced thin
 1 green pepper, diced
   Thin slices pepperoni, chopped, shaved ham,
   or 1 2-ounce can anchovies
 2 tablespoons oregano

Spread tomato sauce on pizza crust; cover with cheese; add green pepper and other desired topping. Finally, sprinkle oregano over all.

Scalloped Potatoes and Ham

 2 tablespoons margarine
 2 tablespoons whole wheat flour
 2 cups milk
 1½ pounds potatoes, sliced thin (4 medium-sized)
 ¾ pound ham, sliced into bite-sized pieces

Preheat oven to 350°. Melt margarine in a small, heavy-bottomed saucepan. Stir in flour and cook for a few minutes until golden. Add milk and stir with wire whisk until sauce is thickened. Remove from heat. Pour a small amount of the sauce into the bottom of a greased, 2-quart casserole. Layer potatoes, ham, and white sauce into casserole, finishing with white sauce. Cover and bake for about 1¼ hours. Remove cover and bake 15 more minutes or until potatoes are tender. Yield: 4 servings.

Easy, Cheesy Fish Fillets

    2 pounds cod, halibut, flounder or
      other white fish fillets
    1 tablespoon lemon juice
  1/8 teaspoon thyme
      Salt
      Freshly ground black pepper
  1/3 cup finely grated bread crumbs
  1¼ cups grated Swiss cheese
    2 tablespoons margarine or butter

If fish is frozen, thaw at room temperature until fillets will separate. Rinse lightly and pat dry with paper towels. Preheat oven to 350° and lightly grease a baking dish that will hold all the fillets in one layer. Arrange fillets in dish, sprinkle with lemon juice, thyme, and salt and pepper to taste. Bake for 25 minutes or until fish begins to look opaque. Mix together the crumbs and cheese; remove dish from oven and sprinkle cheese mixture over the top evenly. Dot with margarine and return to oven for another 10 minutes or until fish flakes easily with a fork. Yield: 4 to 6 servings.

For high-quality, no-waste meals which can be relatively inexpensive, watch for fish specials. Sniff the package of frozen fish; if it smells "fishy," don't buy it.

Stuffed Cabbage

    1 medium-size Savoy cabbage, chilled
  ½ pound pork sausage
    1 cup chopped onion
    3 cups meaty broth
      Freshly ground black pepper
      Salt

Steam cabbage until just pliable. Brown pork sausage with chopped onion until pork is well cooked. When cabbage is steamed, chop the core into small pieces and stir into pork mixture. Cook a few minutes to blend well. Taste and correct seasonings. Place cabbage stem down, on a piece of cheesecloth large enough to tie around the cabbage. Place pork mixture among the leaves and reshape cabbage. Bring cheesecloth up around cabbage and tie on top so that cabbage holds its shape. Place in a pot over meaty broth and simmer, covered, for about 1 hour or until cabbage is tender. Remove cheesecloth before serving. You can reserve broth for another purpose or serve as a soup for the first course. Taste and correct seasonings before serving. Yield: 4 servings.

Lemon Chicken

    4 large chicken breasts, split in half
  ¼ cup margarine or butter, melted
  ½ cup whole wheat flour
    2 tablespoons olive or vegetable oil
  1½ cups sliced onion
    3 cloves garlic, minced
    1 tablespoon crumbled, dried oregano
      Juice of 1 lemon
      Freshly ground black pepper
  ½ teaspoon salt

Wash chicken breasts and pat dry with towels. Spread butter on all sides of the chicken; then roll breasts in flour. Over medium heat in a large skillet or Dutch oven, heat the oil. Stir in onion and garlic and cook until golden. Add chicken and cook, turning occasionally, for 20 minutes. Add remaining ingredients and cook, covered, for 15 to 20 minutes, or until chicken is tender. Taste and correct seasonings before serving. Serve with buttered pasta, Fettucine Alfredo, or Risotto. Yield: 8 servings.

Risotto

    1 tablespoon margarine
    1 cup chopped onion
    1 cup rice
  2½ cups chicken broth
      Salt
      Freshly ground black pepper

Heat margarine over medium heat until melted; stir in onion and cook until translucent. Add rice and cook until the rice is coated with butter. Stir in broth and simmer, covered, until the liquid is absorbed and the rice is tender. If additional liquid is needed, add more broth or a small amount of white wine. Taste and correct seasonings before serving. Yield: 4 servings.

Rather than buy sliced ham for sandwiches, check the regular hams or picnics and after cooking, slice them. Freeze what won't be used immediately for casseroles, soups, and other uses. To eliminate the saltiness of ham, boil the meat in several changes of water; much of the saltiness will boil out.

Fish, Poultry and Meat

Creole Stuffed Peppers

3 very large (or 6 small) green stuffing peppers
½ pound ground beef
¼ cup chopped onion
2 cups cooked rice
½ teaspoon salt
　Freshly ground black pepper
1 tablespoon vegetable oil
⅓ cup diced celery
2 cloves garlic, minced
2 cups seasoned tomato sauce plus 1 cup water
　or 3 cups tomatoes in juice
1 teaspoon Worcestershire sauce
⅛ teaspoon ground cloves
2 tablespoons minced parsley
　Salt
　Freshly ground black pepper
1 to 2 cups whole kernel corn

Remove core, membrane, and seeds from peppers. Sauté ground beef and ¼ cup onion (adding oil only if necessary) until meat is browned. Remove from heat and stir in rice, salt, and pepper. In a medium-sized skillet, sauté remaining onion, celery, and garlic in oil until onion is translucent. Stir in tomato sauce and remaining seasonings. Taste and correct. Stir ¼ cup sauce into rice mixture. Stuff peppers with rice mixture. Place peppers in slow-cooker, pour remainder of sauce around them, and cook 6 to 8 hours on low or 3 hours on high. Add corn, if desired, in the last 1 to 2 hours of cooking. Yield: 3 to 6 servings.

Note: To decrease cooking time, steam pepper cases and continue with the recipe from that point, baking peppers in sauce at 350° for 30 minutes or until tender.

Perfect Scrod

1 pound scrod fillets (thawed, if frozen) or
　other similar fish
½ cup milk
½ cup bread crumbs
1 tablespoon margarine or butter
　Lemon wedges

Preheat oven to 350°. Place fillets in a 2-quart casserole. Pour milk over and bake for 10 to 12 minutes or until fillets are white. Pour off milk. Sprinkle bread crumbs on top of fish, dot with butter, and broil 3 to 4 minutes until crumbs become crisp. Serve immediately. Yield: 2 to 3 servings.

Easy Curried Cod Fillets

1 pound frozen cod fillets, thawed
¼ teaspoon salt
2 tablespoons margarine
1½ teaspoons curry powder
1 cup chopped onion
1 cup chopped apples

Preheat oven to 350°. Place fillets in a well-greased baking dish. Sprinkle with salt. Melt margarine in frying pan; stir in curry powder, onion, and apples. Cook for about 5 minutes. Pour onion mixture onto fillets. Cover baking dish with foil, and bake for 30 minutes or until fish flakes easily with fork. Remove foil near the end of baking time to allow fish to brown slightly. Yield: 4 servings.

Meatball Stew

1 pound ground beef
½ cup bread crumbs
¼ cup minced onion
4 tablespoons minced parsley
1 teaspoon salt
¼ teaspoon freshly ground black pepper
½ teaspoon crushed oregano
¼ teaspoon crushed sweet basil
1 egg
¼ cup milk
2 tablespoons vegetable oil
1 green pepper, cut into strips
4 cups cooked or canned red kidney beans
3 to 4 cups canned tomatoes
2 cups tomato sauce (16 ounces)
1 bay leaf
½ teaspoon crushed oregano
⅓ teaspoon crushed basil
1 teaspoon fennel seed, optional
　Shredded cheese

Combine first 10 ingredients in a bowl. Mix lightly, but thoroughly. Shape into 30 meatballs. Heat vegetable oil in a large frying pan or Dutch oven; brown half the meatballs. Remove and drain. Pour off all but 2 tablespoons of pan drippings and sauté green pepper strips until tender. Stir in remaining ingredients, mixing well. Add meatballs. Bring mixture to the boil; reduce heat, cover, and simmer 30 minutes, stirring occasionally. Taste and correct seasonings. Serve in soup bowls, garnished with shredded cheese. Yield: 10 servings.

Fish, Poultry and Meat

Alpine Casserole

- 2 pounds (or more) boneless pork shoulder butt (smoked)—also called a cottage ham
- 2 cups sliced onion
- 4 large cloves garlic, minced
- 3 tablespoons whole wheat flour
  Freshly ground black pepper
- ¾ teaspoon dried sweet basil
- 2 tablespoons chopped parsley
- ⅛ teaspoon nutmeg
- 6 large potatoes, peeled and sliced
- 1½ pounds fresh or frozen green beans, trimmed and halved

Trim excess surface fat from shoulder butt. Cover with water in a saucepan. Simmer, covered, 1½ to 2 hours, until meat is tender. Reserve broth. In a very large kettle or Dutch oven, heat oil over medium heat and cook onion and garlic until they are golden. Stir in flour thoroughly and cook a few minutes, stirring constantly. Gradually pour 3 cups of the pork broth into the onion mixture, stirring constantly until sauce is smooth. Add seasonings; put the meat in the center of the Dutch oven and surround with potato slices and green beans. Simmer over low heat, covered, for about 1 hour or until the vegetables are tender. (Occasionally stir vegetables and turn meat during cooking.) Taste and correct seasonings before serving. Yield: 8 servings.

Carolyn's Sicilian Pasta

- 6 quarts water
- 1 cup chopped onion
- 1 tablespoon olive oil
- 2 cloves garlic, minced
- 3 3¾-ounce cans sardines in oil, drained and mashed
- 1 2-ounce can anchovies, drained and mashed, optional
- 1 tablespoon fennel seed
- ¼ cup raisins
- 1 tablespoon chopped parsley
  Freshly ground black pepper
- 1½ pounds spaghetti, fettuccini, or other pasta

In a large kettle, bring water to a boil. In a skillet sauté onion in oil until tender. Stir in remaining ingredients, except spaghetti, in order and cook over low heat until heated through. When water boils, stir in spaghetti. Cook until "al dente." Serve immediately with sauce. Yield: 6 servings.

Note: This recipe is ideal for the cook in a hurry. The pasta should be cooked by the time the sauce is ready.

Beefy Yorkshire Pudding

- 1 pound ground beef
- ½ cup chopped onion
- ¾ teaspoon salt
  Freshly ground black pepper
- 2 sprigs parsley, minced
- 3 eggs
- 1½ cups milk
- 1½ cups unbleached flour
- ¼ teaspoon salt
- ½ teaspoon Worcestershire sauce

Preheat oven to 400°. Brown ground beef and onion in a skillet until onion is tender. Drain off fat; pour ⅓ cup of the drippings into the bottom of a 10 x 13-inch baking pan. Add salt, pepper, and parsley to ground beef mixture. Beat eggs until foamy; add remaining ingredients and beat until smooth. Pour half the egg batter into the bottom of the baking pan. Spoon meat mixture evenly over batter. Pour remaining batter on top. Bake 30 to 35 minutes or until golden. Yield: 6 servings.

Diana Johnson's Chicken Enchiladas

- 1 chicken, cooked, deboned and diced
- 1 tablespoon vegetable oil
- ½ cup chopped onion
- 1 clove garlic, minced
- 5 small whole green chilies, canned or fresh, chopped (more or less to taste)
- 1 cup tomato sauce (8 ounces)
- 3 cups (24 ounces) canned tomatoes
  Salt
  Freshly ground black pepper
- 12 to 15 corn tortillas
- 2 tablespoons vegetable oil, heated
- 1 pound Monterey Jack cheese, grated
- 1 to 2 cups sour cream, optional

Heat vegetable oil in a large frying pan. Sauté onion and garlic in oil until onion begins to soften. Stir in chilies, tomato sauce, and canned tomatoes. Simmer 5 minutes. Add diced chicken, salt and pepper to taste. Simmer 20 minutes. Preheat oven to 350°. Dip tortillas into hot vegetable oil quickly, just to soften tortilla. Divide chicken mixture among tortillas and roll. Place in a large, lightly greased flat baking dish and top with cheese. Bake until cheese melts and enchiladas are hot, 15 to 20 minutes. Top with sour cream, if desired. Yield: 12 to 15 servings.

Meatless Main Dishes

While much of the protein in our diet comes from meat, it is possible to obtain sufficient protein even from meatless meals using protein "complements." Since not all grains and legumes have complete proteins within themselves, eating foods from the following complementary groups will ensure more than adequate protein intake: whole grains and milk products; legumes and seeds; rice and beans; whole grains and legumes.

Split Pea Croquettes

    1 cup split peas
 2½ cups boiling water
    2 tablespoons butter or margarine
      Freshly grated nutmeg
    2 tablespoons minced onion
    1 egg, beaten
    1 slice whole wheat bread broken
      into soft crumbs
  ½ cup raw wheat germ

Gradually drop split peas into boiling water, making certain water continues to boil. Reduce heat, cover, and simmer 25 minutes or until peas are tender. Preheat oven to 350°. Drain (reserving liquid) and place peas in blender or a sieve. Puree and add butter, nutmeg, onion, egg, and bread crumbs. If the mixture won't hold together, add a little of the reserved cooking liquid. Form into oblong patties and roll in wheat germ. Chill if necessary. Place on well greased baking sheet and bake for about 5 minutes; turn and bake another 5 minutes or until lightly-browned. Croquettes may also be fried until browned. Yield: 6 servings.

Banana-Tofu-Peanut Butter Sandwiches

    8 slices whole wheat bread
    1 banana
    1 teaspoon lemon juice
    1 cup tofu
  ½ cup peanut butter

Mash banana thoroughly; mix in lemon juice. Mash tofu; blend in tofu and peanut butter until thoroughly mixed. Spread on bread and garnish as desired. Yield: approximately 8 open-faced sandwiches.

If desired, garnish with strawberry halves, pineapple slices, orange slices, mandarin orange segments, chopped nuts, raisins, cinnamon, etc.

Julia's Black Beans and Rice with Tomato Sauce

 2½ cups dried black beans
    7 cups water, broth, or vegetable cooking liquid
  ¼ teaspoon freshly ground black pepper
    3 garlic cloves, minced
    1 large onion, peeled, studded with 4 whole cloves
    2 tablespoons vegetable oil
    1 large green pepper, seeded and chopped
    1 cup chopped onion
      Salt

Bring beans and water to a boil in a large, heavy saucepan or Dutch oven. Boil for 2 minutes, remove from heat, cover, and let stand for at least 1 hour. Add black pepper to beans and reheat; cover and simmer for 1 hour. Stir garlic and whole onion into beans; simmer, covered, 30 minutes longer or until beans are tender. Heat oil in a medium-size frying pan; stir in pepper and onion. Sauté until onions are golden. Remove whole onion from beans, and, if desired, chop onion and return to beans along with sautéed pepper and onion mixture. Add salt to taste; correct seasonings. Serve over rice with Tomato Sauce. Yield: 8 servings.

Tomato Sauce

    2 cups canned tomatoes, drained
  ¾ cup chopped sweet onion
    2 cloves garlic, minced
    1 teaspoon vegetable oil
    1 tablespoon wine vinegar
    1 tablespoon parsley, minced
      Dash bottled hot pepper sauce

Place ingredients into blender container and blend until smooth. Refrigerate sauce overnight to allow flavors to combine. Serve with Julia's Black Beans and Rice.

Meatless foods which have complete proteins are soybeans and soy products, cottonseed flour, eggs, nutritional (brewers') yeast, wheat germ, and milk and milk products such as nonfat milk and cheese. Several of these offer very inexpensive sources of protein.

Spinach-Onion Stuffed Crepes

  3 pounds spinach and/or Swiss chard
  2 cups minced onion
  4 tablespoons margarine
2½ tablespoons flour
  ¾ cup milk
  1 cup grated Swiss cheese
     Salt
     Freshly ground black pepper
 20 crepes

Wash spinach thoroughly and steam until tender (about 10 minutes). Press excess liquid out and place spinach in a grinder fitted with a fine blade. Meanwhile, sauté onion in margarine until tender. Stir in cooked and minced spinach until well blended. Add flour and cook again. Stir in milk and cook until sauce is thickened. Finally add cheese and season to taste. Divide spinach among crepes; roll up and place in a well-greased baking dish. Cover with foil. Bake immediately at 350° for 30 minutes or refrigerate and bake as needed for 40 minutes.

Batter for Crepes

  1 cup whole wheat flour
  1 cup unbleached flour
  ½ teaspoon salt
  4 eggs, lightly beaten
  2 cups milk
  7 tablespoons vegetable oil

Mix flour and salt together in a medium-sized bowl. Make a well in the middle and pour in eggs. Beat until smooth. Add milk slowly, keeping batter smooth. Finally, add oil. Let rest several hours. Stir well just before using and pour by the ladleful into a lightly greased, 9-inch crepe pan. Turn when first side is golden and cook other side. Repeat until all batter is used. Set crepes aside on paper towels until ready for filling, or keep hot if using immediately.

Chris's Cottage Cheese Pancakes

  1 cup cottage cheese
  3 eggs
  ¼ cup raw wheat germ
  ¼ cup unbleached or whole wheat flour
  1 teaspoon vanilla

Beat cottage cheese and eggs together thoroughly. Stir in wheat germ, flour, and vanilla lightly. Cook on very hot griddle; when well browned on one side, flip and brown the other. Yield: 1 dozen pancakes.

Stuffed Eggplant

  2 tablespoons vegetable or olive oil
  2 cups chopped onion
  2 cloves garlic, minced
  ½ cup chopped carrot
  1 cup chopped celery
  ½ cup chopped parsley
  4 fresh mint leaves (or 1 teaspoon dried)
  1 cup canned tomatoes, with juice
  1 teaspoon salt
  ¼ teaspoon freshly ground black pepper
  1 eggplant (weighing about 2 pounds)
  ½ cup cooked brown rice

In a large frying pan, cook onion in oil until translucent. Stir in all ingredients except eggplant and rice. Simmer for about 30 minutes. Cut eggplant lengthwise, scoop out pulp, leaving a ⅜-inch shell. Chop pulp and cook with vegetables until tender. Add a teaspoon of tomato juice, if necessary. Preheat oven to 350°. Stir in rice and stuff mixture into eggplant. Place eggplant halves in a well-greased casserole. Cover tightly and bake about 1½ hours or until tender. Yield: 6 servings.

Vic's Kidney Bean Casserole

  ¼ cup butter or margarine
1½ cups sliced onion
  2 large cloves garlic, minced
  1 medium green pepper, seeded and chopped
  4 cups cooked, red kidney beans (drained)
⅓ teaspoon ground cloves
  3 tablespoons tomato puree or paste
  1 cup dry red wine
     Salt
     Freshly ground black pepper

Melt butter in a large frying pan; stir in onion, garlic, and green pepper. Cook until onion is transparent. Preheat oven to 375°. Mix beans, onion mixture, cloves, puree, and wine in a large casserole dish. Taste and season with salt and pepper, as desired. Bake for about 45 minutes or until mixture is hot and bubbly. Yield: 6 servings.

Mom's Zucchini Pancakes

4 medium zucchini, grated
½ cup grated onion
3 eggs, beaten
1 teaspoon salt
½ cup raw wheat germ

Mix ingredients together thoroughly. Drop by tablespoonsful onto a lightly greased griddle. Brown on both sides. Serve with yogurt or apple-sauce. Yield: 4 servings.

Irene's Cheese and Spinach Pie

1 tablespoon margarine or vegetable oil
¼ pound sliced mushrooms
1 small zucchini, thinly sliced
1 green pepper, diced
1 cup diced ham
1 pound drained ricotta or cottage cheese
1 cup grated mozzarella
3 eggs, lightly beaten
½ cup cooked, drained, and chopped spinach
1 tablespoon diced dill
Salt
Freshly ground black pepper
1 tablespoon melted butter or margarine

Sauté mushrooms, zucchini, and green pepper in margarine for 5 minutes or until vegetables are soft. Add ham and sauté 2 minutes more or until all moisture is evaporated. Cool. Preheat oven to 350°. Combine cottage cheese with mozzarella, eggs, and spinach. Finally, beat in ham mixture and dill. Season to taste. Pour mixture into an oiled pie plate or casserole dish which will hold about 1½ quarts. Sprinkle with melted butter and bake 45 minutes or until set. Yield: 6 to 8 servings.

Eggplant Creole

1 tablespoon vegetable oil
1 cup chopped onion
½ cup chopped celery
2 cups eggplant, cut into 1-inch cubes
½ cup chopped green pepper
1 cup tomato sauce
1 bay leaf
Salt
Cayenne pepper

Sauté onion in oil until onion is translucent; stir in remaining ingredients, except salt and pepper, in order. Cover and simmer until eggplant is tender. Taste and add salt and cayenne to taste. Yield: 4 servings.

Soybean Loaf

1 cup dry, cooking soybeans, washed and sorted
2 cups water
½ cup well-flavored broth or vegetable cooking liquid
1 tablespoon vegetable oil
½ cup chopped onion
1 clove garlic, minced
⅛ teaspoon sage
1 cup bread crumbs
1 cup canned tomatoes, well chopped
Salt
Freshly ground black pepper
2 eggs, beaten

Soak beans for about 2 hours in the 2 cups water. Place container in freezer and freeze until solid. Bring vegetable cooking liquid to a boil and drop the frozen soybeans into it. Cover and simmer 2 to 4 hours or until soybeans are tender. Grind soybeans very fine in a food grinder. Pre-heat oven to 350°. Sauté onion in oil until golden. Stir in garlic, sage, bread crumbs, toma-toes, and cooked soybeans. Taste and correct seasonings. Finally, add beaten eggs. Pour into a well-greased 8½ x 4½ x 1-inch loaf pan. Bake 45 minutes or until done. Serve as is or with a tomato sauce. Yield: 6 servings.

Fettuccine Alfredo

1 pound noodles
3 quarts rapidly boiling, salted water
1 cup margarine, melted
2 cups freshly grated Romano or Parmesan cheese
⅓ cup milk
¼ cup powdered milk
Freshly ground black pepper
Minced parsley (optional)

Cook noodles in water until tender. Drain and place in a large serving dish that can be heated on low burner. Then slowly add cheese. Mix milk and powdered milk together and stir into noodles gently. When well blended, stir in pepper, to taste, and minced parsley, if desired. Yield: 6 servings.

Chinese Walnut Tofu Dinner

- 1 cup broken walnuts
- 3 tablespoons vegetable oil
- 1 cup sliced onion
- 1½ cups celery, sliced lengthwise
- 1 cup sliced mushrooms
- 1¼ cups vegetable broth
- 1 tablespoon cornstarch
- 2 tablespoons soy sauce
- 2 tablespoons dry sherry
- 1 cup tofu, cut into small cubes
- 1 10-ounce package tiny green peas (fresh or frozen)
- 1 5-ounce can bamboo shoots, drained
- 1 5-ounce can water chestnuts, drained and sliced

Toast walnuts in hot vegetable oil in a large frying pan or wok. Remove walnuts and drain on paper towels. Stir in onion, celery, and mushrooms. Stir-fry until onion is tender. Mix together the vegetable broth, cornstarch, soy sauce, and sherry. Pour into wok. Stir until sauce thickens. Stir in tofu, green peas, bamboo shoots, and water chestnuts. Heat thoroughly. When peas are just tender, sprinkle walnuts on top and serve immediately with Brown Rice. Yield: 4 to 6 servings.

Brown Rice

- 3½ cups water
- 1½ cups brown rice
- 1 tablespoon margarine
- 1 teaspoon salt
- 1 bay leaf
- 1 tablespoon parsley, optional
- ¼ teaspoon thyme
  Freshly ground black pepper

Bring water to boil, stir in rest of ingredients, reduce heat and simmer, covered, until all water is absorbed. Fluff rice with fork before serving. Yield: 8 servings.

Even a child's peanut butter sandwich made with whole grain bread and non-hydrogenated peanut butter contains the complementary proteins of whole grains and legumes. Add a glass of milk, carrot sticks and an apple to create an inexpensive, nutritious lunch that children will actually eat.

Olive-Nut Sandwiches with Alfalfa Sprouts

- 8 thin slices whole wheat bread
- 1 3-ounce package cream cheese, softened
- 2 tablespoons toasted wheat germ
- ¼ cup chopped walnuts
- 8 to 10 pimiento-stuffed olives, chopped
- 1 cup alfalfa sprouts, firmly packed

Cream together cheese, wheat germ, and nuts until well blended. Stir in olives. Spread mixture on all the bread slices. Divide alfalfa sprouts among four slices. Assemble sandwiches. Yield: 4 sandwiches.

Note: Can also be used on open-faced sandwiches or on small rounds as hors d'oeuvres; or form into a cheese ball, roll in wheat germ, and served as a cracker spread.

Chris's Bhanoo Rice

- 2½ tablespoons butter
- 5 cups rice
- 1 teaspoon turmeric
- ¼ teaspoon cardamom
- 10 cups water
  Stir-fried vegetables and nuts, (cauliflower, peas, carrots, peanuts, etc.)
  Salt
  Freshly ground black pepper

Melt butter in a large skillet or Dutch oven. Stir in rice and seasonings and cook, stirring constantly, for 5 to 8 minutes or until rice is golden. Add water and cover. Reduce heat to low and cook until all water is absorbed (10 to 20 minutes). Mix in choice of stir-fried vegetables and nuts. Re-fry for several minutes at low heat. Add salt and pepper to taste and serve. Yield: 10 servings.

Parslied Rice

- 2½ cups uncooked rice
- 2 tablespoons margarine
- 5 cups vegetable broth
  Salt
  Freshly ground black pepper
- ½ cup finely chopped parsley

Combine rice, margarine, and broth in a large, heavy saucepan. Heat to boiling, stir well, and cover. Reduce heat and simmer 30 minutes or until rice is tender. (Add more broth if necessary.) Taste and add salt and pepper, if necessary. Fold in parsley and serve immediately. Yield: 8 servings.

Salads and Vegetables

For some reason, Americans are paying less attention to vegetables than ever before. Yet vegetables are an important part of our diet. Often, adding a second or third vegetable to a meal supplies high nutrition at a modest cost. Put a garden plot (rent or borrow one, if necessary) to work. Even in a northern climate, it's possible to have huge, green, nourishing salads in mid to late May—just about the time that many people are just beginning to think about planting a garden.

Navy Bean Salad

    2 cups dry navy beans
    2 to 3 tablespoons chopped chives
    5 green onions, with tops, chopped
    5 tablespoons finely chopped parsley
    3 tablespoons olive or vegetable oil
    2 tablespoons lemon juice
    1 tablespoon wine vinegar
    1 tablespoon soy sauce, optional
       Salt
       Freshly ground black pepper
    1 cup sliced radishes, garnish

Wash and sort navy beans. Soak in enough water to cover overnight. Heat to boiling, then reduce heat; simmer until tender (about 1½ hours). Cool. Drain. Mix vegetables with cooled beans. Combine the liquid ingredients in a covered jar or blender and blend well. Pour dressing over salad and marinate overnight. Taste and add salt and pepper; correct other seasonings, if necessary. Garnish with radishes. Yield: 8 servings.

Mom's Sauerkraut Salad

    2 cups packed down sauerkraut,
       drained and chopped (if desired)
    1 cup chopped celery
    ½ cup chopped onion
    1 small green pepper, chopped
    1 teaspoon caraway seeds (or more, to taste)
    ¼ teaspoon fresh horseradish, optional
       Pimiento, optional

Mix ingredients well and let stand 24 hours. (Add a little of the drained juice for a less dry salad.) Serve cold with chopped pimiento for color. Yield: 4 to 6 servings.

Remember that the darker green, leafy vegetables are generally highest in nutrition, yet often lowest in cost.

Marinated Green Beans

    2 pounds green beans
    ½ cup vegetable oil
    3 tablespoons wine vinegar
    ¾ teaspoon salt
       Freshly ground black pepper
    1 teaspoon French mustard
    1 to 2 cloves garlic, minced
       Parsley, minced

Cut the tips and tails off well-washed green beans. Steam until just tender. Reserve steaming liquid for soup or other purpose. Set beans aside to cool quickly. Meanwhile, mix the rest of the ingredients together in a blender or shake vigorously in a covered jar. Pour over cooled beans and toss gently. Cover and refrigerate for at least 2 hours before serving, tossing gently from time to time. Garnish with minced parsley. Yield: 10 servings.

Steamed Celery

    3 cups celery, sliced
       Celery seed
       Salt
       Freshly ground black pepper
       Toasted sunflower seeds

In a vegetable steamer, steam celery until just tender. Season to taste with seeds, salt, and pepper. Sprinkle sunflower seeds over all and serve hot. Yield: 4 servings.

Main Dish Salad

    6 cups shredded greens
       Salt
       Freshly ground black pepper
    5 hard-cooked eggs, shelled and sliced thin
    1 10-ounce package frozen peas
    2 cups shredded Swiss cheese
    ½ cup bacon bits, crisp-cooked, drained, and crumbled
    1 cup salad dressing or mayonnaise
    ¼ cup sliced green onion with tops
       Paprika

Place half the greens into a large salad bowl. Sprinkle with salt and pepper. Layer eggs on top of greens and sprinkle again with salt and pepper. Place remaining greens on top, then add peas, cheese, and bacon bits in order. Spread mayonnaise evenly over top. Cover well and chill about 24 hours. Toss well before serving. Garnish with green onion and paprika. Yield: 12 servings.

Salads and Vegetables

Bavarian Cabbage

  4 strips bacon, diced
  1 tablespoon brown sugar
  ½ cup chopped onion
  ½ cup chopped apple
  2 pounds green cabbage, chopped or shredded
     Caraway seed, to taste
  1 cup beef or other stock
  3 tablespoons dry white wine
  2 tablespoons cider or wine vinegar, to taste
     Salt
     Freshly ground black pepper

In a very large frying pan over medium heat, brown bacon. Add sugar and stir until melted. Add onion and apple and simmer a few minutes. Stir in cabbage and caraway seeds thoroughly; pour in stock. Cover and simmer 1 to 1½ hours. Just before serving, stir in wine and vinegar to taste. Add salt and pepper as desired. Yield: 6 to 8 servings.

Note: Can be simmered in casserole in oven if something else is baking.

Marinated Carrot Salad

  2 pounds carrots, scrubbed and sliced
     into 1-inch lengths
  ¾ teaspoon salt
     Freshly ground black pepper
  1 teaspoon prepared French mustard
  ½ cup vegetable oil
  ½ cup cider vinegar
  1 cup tomato sauce
  1 cup onion, minced
  1 cup green pepper, minced
     Parsley

Steam carrots until just tender (about 10 minutes); cool. Place salt, pepper, and mustard into a medium-size bowl. Beat in a small amount of oil to blend with seasonings. Add remaining oil, beating continuously; finally add vinegar and tomato sauce. Stir in onion and green pepper and taste; correct seasonings. Lightly fold carrots into vinegar and oil mixture, cover tightly, and chill for at least 8 hours or overnight. Serve alone or on salad greens, garnished with parsley. Yield: 10 to 12 servings.

Continue an herb garden through the winter by planting or transplanting herbs into pots. Basil, mint, parsley, coriander, chives, oregano, and others do well indoors but need plenty of light.

Stir-fried Cauliflower

  1   tablespoon vegetable oil
  ⅓ cup sliced or slivered almonds
  1   tablespoon butter or margarine
  1   medium-large cauliflower, broken into flowerets
  ½ cup water
      Freshly ground black pepper
  1   tablespoon cornstarch
  1   tablespoon water
      Salt

Heat oil in a wok or large frying pan. Stir in almonds until they are golden. Remove to absorbent paper. Add butter and flowerets and stir over medium heat for about 3 minutes. Add ½ cup water and pepper to taste; cover and simmer 5 minutes. Mix cornstarch with remaining water; pour into wok and stir gently until sauce thickens. Cauliflower should be tender-crisp. Serve immediately, sprinkled with toasted almonds. Yield: 4 to 6 servings.

Diana's Winter Salad

  2 to 3 cups chopped cabbage
  2 carrots, chopped
  ½ tomato, chopped
  ½ green pepper, chopped
     Creamy dressing, such as Thousand Island,
     French, blue cheese
     Mayonnaise
     Prepared mustard, optional

Mix vegetables in a serving bowl. Combine creamy dressing and mayonnaise, to taste and in quantity desired. Add mustard to taste. Pour over salad and toss gently but thoroughly. Chill, if desired, before serving. Yield: 4 to 6 servings.

Hot Pepper and Celery Sambal

  3 to 4 short or long green chilies (shorter ones are
     usually hotter)
  1 sweet or hot red pepper, chopped fine
  1 cup finely chopped celery
  1 tablespoon lemon or lime juice
  ¼ teaspoon shrimp paste (trassi)
     or anchovy paste, optional

Wash chilies and cut off stems. Cut open and remove seeds, taking care that chilies or juice do not touch face or eyes (or they will burn). Chop chilies fine and wash hands thoroughly after handling. Combine chopped chilies, pepper, celery, and lemon juice together and refrigerate until needed. Serve with curried dishes. Guests can help themselves to make their curries as hot as desired. Yield: approximately 2 cups.

Indonesian Fruit Salad

- 1 15-ounce can pineapple chunks, drained
- 2 tablespoons brown sugar
- 2 tablespoons lemon juice
- 2 cups apples, quartered and sliced
- 2 tablespoons lemon juice
- 1 large pear, quartered and sliced
- 1 orange, segmented
- 1 cup raw sweet potato, pared and sliced
- 2 cups quartered and sliced cucumber
- 1 ripe avocado, peeled and cut into strips

Pour drained pineapple juice into a small pan; add sugar and lemon juice. Heat until sugar is dissolved. Cool. Sprinkle lemon juice over apples and avocados to keep slices from turning brown. Place fruits and vegetables in a large salad bowl. Pour cooled pineapple sauce over salad ingredients and toss carefully. Cover the salad bowl with plastic wrap and chill salad until serving time. Yield: 8 servings.

Indonesian Vegetable Salad

- 2 cups sliced red onion
- 2 cups thinly sliced cucumber
- 2 cups shredded carrot
- 6 cups thinly sliced cabbage
- ½ cup white vinegar
- ¼ cup vegetable oil
- ½ cup cold water
- 1 tablespoon grated fresh ginger
- 1 to 2 tablespoons brown sugar
- 1½ teaspoons salt

Place vegetables in a large salad bowl. Mix together vinegar, oil, water, ginger, sugar, and salt. Pour over cabbage mixture and stir lightly. Refrigerate at least 3 to 4 hours before serving, stirring every hour or so. Yield: 8 to 10 servings.

Classic Vinegar and Oil Dressing

- ⅔ cup vegetable or olive oil
- ⅓ cup red wine vinegar (or part lemon juice)
- ¼ teaspoon salt
  Freshly ground black pepper
- 1 tablespoon minced chives
- 1 tablespoon minced parsley
- ½ teaspoon dry mustard
- 1 clove garlic, minced, optional
  Any other fresh herbs desired, minced

Place all the above ingredients in a jar, cover tightly, and shake. Taste and correct seasonings. Chill until needed, shaking just before using. Yield: 1 cup.

Moroccan Carrot Salad

- 1 pound carrots, scraped
- ¼ cup vegetable or olive oil
- 3 tablespoons lemon juice
- 1 large clove garlic, minced
- ½ teaspoon cumin
- ½ teaspoon dried mint leaves
  Salt
  Freshly ground black pepper
- ¼ teaspoon cayenne pepper

Shred carrots with a grater or in a food processor using the julienne cutter. Blend together the remaining ingredients. Taste and correct seasonings. Pour over carrots and chill before serving. Yield: 8 to 10 servings.

Famous Recipe Salad Dressing Mix

- 2 teaspoons salt
- 2 to 3 teaspoons parsley flakes
- 1 teaspoon garlic salt
- ½ teaspoon freshly ground black pepper
- ½ teaspoon onion powder
- 1½ cups mayonnaise
- 1¼ cups buttermilk

Mix together first five ingredients and store in a small, tightly covered container until needed. Combine 2 teaspoons of above mixture with remaining ingredients; taste and correct seasonings. For a thicker salad dressing, add more mayonnaise. Add more buttermilk for a thinner dressing. Yield: dressing for 3 salads.

Blender Mayonnaise

- 2 egg yolks
- ¾ teaspoon salt
- ¼ teaspoon ground white or black pepper
- ½ teaspoon dry mustard
- ½ teaspoon paprika
- 2 tablespoons lemon juice or wine vinegar
- 1 cup vegetable oil

All ingredients must be at room temperature. Place all ingredients except juice and oil in blender. Cover and blend on low. When mixture is thick and foamy, add 1 tablespoon juice. Add half of the oil, drop by drop. Blend until thick; then run at high speed. Stop occasionally to scrape sides. Add remaining juice and with blender on high, slowly pour in remaining oil. Cover tightly and refrigerate; use within 1 week. Yield: 1 cup.

When lettuce is at its high winter price, the budget-conscious shopper should use more cabbage and canned vegetables in salads.

Salads and Vegetables

Welsh Onion-Potato Dish

2 pounds potatoes, pared and sliced thin
1½ cups chopped onion
4 tablespoons margarine
1 teaspoon salt
  Freshly ground black pepper
  Pimiento, optional

Preheat oven to 350°. Layer about one-third of the potato slices into a well-greased 9 x 1½-inch pie plate and sprinkle with half the onion. Dot with butter and season lightly. Repeat, ending with a layer of potatoes, butter, and seasonings. Cover with foil and bake 1 hour. Remove foil, test for doneness. Bake up to 30 minutes longer or until lightly browned and tender. Yield: 6 servings.

Oriental Salad

10 ounces fresh spinach, washed and patted dry
1 cup bean sprouts
4 slices bacon, cooked and crumbled
1 8-ounce can water chestnuts, drained and sliced

Toss above ingredients together lightly but thoroughly with Dressing in a large salad bowl. Serve immediately. Yield: 12 servings.

Dressing

½ cup vegetable oil
⅓ cup catsup
½ cup minced onion
½ teaspoon salt
¼ cup vinegar
1 teaspoon Worcestershire sauce
  Freshly ground black pepper

Place dressing ingredients together in a jar with a lid. Close tightly and shake well. Pour on salad.

Quick Curried Vegetables

2 tablespoons vegetable oil
1 cup chopped onion
2 large garlic cloves, minced
1 green pepper, seeded and chopped
1 cup sliced yellow summer squash
2 cups sliced zucchini
1 tablespoon water
1 teaspoon curry powder
  Freshly ground black pepper
  Salt

Heat oil in a large frying pan. Add onion and garlic and sauté until onion begins to soften. Stir in remaining vegetables and water. Add seasonings to taste, cover and cook 5 to 10 minutes or until tender. Serve immediately with cooked brown rice. Yield: 4 servings.

Twice-Baked Potatoes

5 baking potatoes
  Butter or margarine
2 to 3 tablespoons hot milk or cream
2 tablespoons raw wheat germ
½ cup grated sharp Cheddar cheese
  Paprika

Preheat oven to 400°. Butter skins of potatoes and puncture each a few times with a fork; bake 45 minutes to 1 hour or until tender. Slice each potato lengthwise; scoop out pulp into a medium-size bowl; mash. Stir in 3 to 4 tablespoons butter, hot milk, and wheat germ. Taste and season if needed. Beat until mixture is smooth; spoon back into potato cases. Top with the grated cheese, sprinkle with paprika. Cover with foil and bake for about 10 minutes or until piping hot and cheese is thoroughly melted. Yield: 10 servings.

Louise Lindsey's Cabbage Salad

8 cups shredded cabbage
2 carrots, shredded
1 green pepper, minced
½ cup chopped onion
¾ cup cold water
1 envelope unflavored gelatin
⅔ cup sugar
⅔ cup vinegar
2 teaspoons celery seed
1½ teaspoons salt
¼ teaspoon freshly ground black pepper
⅔ cup vegetable oil

Mix cabbage, carrots, green pepper, and onion. Sprinkle with ½ cup cold water and chill. Soften gelatin in remaining water. Mix sugar, vinegar, celery seed, salt, and pepper in a saucepan. Bring to the boil. Stir in gelatin mixture; cool slightly until thickened. Beat in vegetable oil gradually. Drain cabbage mixture, place in serving bowl, and pour dressing over. Toss until cabbage mixture is well coated. Serve immediately or store in refrigerator until needed. Stir just before serving. Yield: 12 servings.

The handiest place to have an herb garden is right by the back door. Garlic, chives, sage, thyme, and mint will continue to grow year after year. Add parsley, fennel, dill, oregano, sweet basil, coriander, or whatever herbs you use most in cooking.

Desserts

Desserts need not be expensive, and sometimes they are the special treat that takes away the "sting" of a tight budget. Fresh fruit in season is always a smart dessert, but there are plenty of penny-wise desserts in this chapter to help meet your family's nutritional needs.

Irene's Superbars

½ cup margarine or butter
½ cup firmly packed brown sugar
½ cup rolled oats
½ cup whole wheat flour
½ cup unbleached flour
¼ cup raw wheat germ
1 teaspoon grated orange or lemon rind
1 teaspoon cinnamon
2 eggs
2 cups mixed dried fruits, nuts, and seeds and/or granola (such as raisins, cut dates, raw sunflower seeds, flaked coconut, walnuts, etc.)
2 tablespoons brown sugar

Preheat oven to 350°. Cream margarine and sugar together. Beat in oats, flours, rind, and wheat germ and cinnamon. Pat into 8 x 8 x 2-inch baking pan. Mix eggs, mixed fruits and nuts, and brown sugar together. Pour over base and spread evenly. Bake 30 to 35 minutes. Cool, then cut into 12 bars. Yield: 12 bars.

Aunt Ruby's Pinch Cookies

2 cups brown sugar, firmly packed
1 cup shortening
2 eggs
½ teaspoon salt
1 teaspoon baking soda
1 teaspoon vanilla
3 cups unbleached flour

Preheat oven to 350°. Cream sugar and shortening together thoroughly. Beat in eggs until light. Stir in the rest of the ingredients until well-blended. Pinch off pieces of dough the size of walnuts; roll and flatten with fingers and place on well-greased baking sheets. Bake 8 to 10 minutes or until done. Cool on wire racks. Yield: 4 dozen.

Mom's Prize-Winning Gingerbread

2 teaspoons vinegar stirred into ½ cup milk
½ cup margarine
½ cup brown sugar, firmly-packed
½ teaspoon ginger
1 egg
½ teaspoon cinnamon
¼ teaspoon salt
½ cup molasses
1¼ cups flour
1 teaspoon baking soda

Preheat oven to 350°. Allow vinegar and milk to clabber while mixing remaining ingredients, (except soda) in order. When ingredients are well-blended, dissolve soda in the clabbered milk and stir into flour mixture. Spread in greased 8 x 8 x 2-inch baking pan. Bake 20 to 25 minutes or until top springs back when touched lightly. Cool in pan on wire rack before cutting into squares. Yield: 16 squares.

Low-Cost Whipped Topping

¾ cup nonfat dried milk
¾ cup very cold water
½ teaspoon vanilla
Sugar

Chill beaters and bowl thoroughly; pour ingredients into bowl and whip until thick. Add vanilla and sugar, to taste. Yield: approximately 1 cup.

Cherry Pie

¾ cups granulated sugar
4 tablespoons whole wheat or unbleached flour
⅛ teaspoon salt
4 cups fresh, pitted cherries
  or 2½ cups drained, canned cherries
¼ cup cherry juice
1 8-inch pastry crust plus extra pastry for strips or top crust

Preheat oven to 425°. Mix together sugar, flour, and salt. Stir in cherries and juice. Pour into pastry crust and cover with latticed strips or top crust. Seal edges. If top crust is used, slit to allow steam to escape. Bake for 10 minutes; then lower heat to 350° for 30 minutes or until done. Yield: 6 servings.

Banana Cream Cake

- ½ cup shortening
- 2 cups whole wheat pastry flour
- 1 cup firmly packed brown sugar
- 1½ teaspoons baking powder
- 1 teaspoon baking soda
- 1 teaspoon salt
- ½ teaspoon nutmeg
- 1 cup mashed, ripe banana
- ¼ cup milk
- 1 teaspoon vanilla
- 2 eggs
- ¼ cup chopped nuts, optional

Preheat oven to 350°. Cream shortening to soften. Stir in dry ingredients. Add banana, milk, and vanilla. Mix until dry ingredients are all moistened. Then beat vigorously for 2 minutes. Add eggs and beat 2 more minutes. Finally, add nuts and pour batter into a well-greased and lightly-floured 9 x 9 x 2-inch cake pan. Bake 35 to 40 minutes or until done. Yield: 9 to 12 servings.

Diana's Pie Crusts

- 3 cups flour
- ¾ teaspoon salt
- 1½ cups shortening
- 1 egg
- 1 tablespoon lemon juice
- Water

Mix together flour and salt. Cut in shortening with a pastry blender until mixture resembles crumbs. Make a well in the center of the dry ingredients. In a measuring cup mix together the egg and lemon juice. Add enough water to make three-fourths cup liquid. Pour the egg mixture into the well in the dry ingredients. Mix with a fork until all the dry ingredients are moistened. Form the dough into a ball and chill until needed. Or divide the ball into thirds and roll out on a well-floured surface with a well-floured rolling pin. Both baked and unbaked crusts can be frozen, well-wrapped. Add fillings as desired and bake according to specific recipe directions. Yield: 3 9-inch crusts.

Vanilla Ice Cream

- 2 cups whole milk
- ½ cup non-instant powdered milk
- ¼ cup honey (or less, to taste)
- 1 teaspoon vanilla
- 1 rennet tablet
- 1 tablespoon cold water

Blend powdered milk with whole milk in a blender or with an electric beater or hand mixer. Pour into a heavy pan along with honey and vanilla and heat over medium heat until lukewarm (110°). While mixture is heating, dissolve rennet in cold water. When milk mixture is at lukewarm, add the rennet mixture and mix well. Pour quickly into ice cube tray or any other container that holds 2½ cups of liquid. Let stand at room temperature without disturbing for 10 minutes. Place tray in freezer compartment and freeze until almost totally firm. Break up mixture in a large mixing bowl and quickly beat until smooth. Pour immediately back into tray and finish freezing. Serve plain or with crushed fruit, nuts, sesame seeds, sunflower seeds, or with Peanut Butter Sauce. Yield: 1 pint.

Peanut Butter Sauce

- ¾ cup non-hydrogenated peanut butter
- 1 tablespoon honey
- ¼ cup whole, salted peanuts
- 2 tablespoons sunflower seeds
- 2 tablespoons sesame seeds
- ½ teaspoon vanilla

Gently mix together ingredients. Spoon into small, heavy pan and place over extremely low heat. Stir continuously. When warmed and well-blended, serve on ice cream. Yield: about 1 cup.

Rhubarb Cream Pie

- 1¼ cups brown sugar, firmly packed
- 3 tablespoons whole wheat or unbleached flour
- ½ teaspoon nutmeg
- 1 tablespoon butter
- 2 well-beaten eggs
- 3 cups cut up rhubarb
- 1 9-inch pastry crust

Preheat oven to 425°. Blend first 4 ingredients together thoroughly. Add eggs. Finally, stir in rhubarb. Sprinkle more nutmeg on top, if desired. Bake for 10 minutes; then lower heat to 350° and bake for 30 more minutes or until done. Yield: 6 to 8 servings.

Desserts

Whole Wheat Fruitcake

2¼ cups whole wheat flour
¼ cup soy flour
¼ cup raw wheat germ
1 teaspoon baking soda
2 eggs, lightly beaten
3½ cups mincemeat
1 14-ounce can sweetened condensed milk
¾ cup walnuts, hickory nuts, or mixed nuts
¼ cup sunflower seeds
2 cups candied peel

Preheat oven to 300°. Mix together flours, wheat germ, and soda. Combine eggs, mincemeat, milk, nuts, and fruit. Fold dry ingredients into wet. Pour into well-greased 9-inch tube pan or spring-form. Bake for 2 hours or until center springs back when touched lightly and top is golden. Cool before turning out. Yield: 1 large fruitcake.

Note: This recipe can be baked in several smaller cake pans or baking molds. Reduce baking time, checking frequently for doneness.

Candied Fruit Peel

2 cups mixed grapefruit, orange, lime, and lemon peel
1½ cups cold water
1 cup sugar
½ cup water

Cut peel into very thin strips and place in a heavy pan. Cover with cold water and bring slowly to a boil. Reduce heat and simmer 10 to 12 minutes, drain and repeat process about 4 times or until peel has lost its bitter taste. Combine sugar and ½ cup water, making a syrup, and add peel. Boil gently until all syrup is absorbed and peel is transparent. Watch carefully to keep from burning. Spread on racks to dry. Yield: about 2 cups.

On cold winter days when the wind is howling, why not turn down the heat in the rest of the house, close the doors to the kitchen, and bake? Keeping the oven filled with various dishes that need to be cooked at the same temperature will use energy well—and keep the cook warm!

Because moisture content in flour varies, always test-bake one cookie to make certain there is enough flour in the dough before baking the whole batch.

Aunt Ruth's Icebox Cookies

1¾ cups brown sugar, firmly packed
1 cup shortening or margarine
2 eggs
1 teaspoon baking soda, dissolved in
2 tablespoons water
1 teaspoon cinnamon
2 teaspoons vanilla
4 cups unbleached flour
½ teaspoon salt
¾ cup chopped nuts or raisins
1 cup Flaked Coconut, optional (page 60)

Cream sugar and shortening together thoroughly. Beat in eggs until light. Add soda-water mixture, cinnamon, and vanilla. Stir flour and salt together and mix in thoroughly. Finally, add nuts or raisins. Roll dough into 2 12-inch long rolls; wrap and chill until ready to bake. Preheat oven to 350°; slice rolls into ¼-inch slices and place on greased baking sheets. Bake 8 to 10 minutes or until done. Cool on wire racks. Yield: approximately 8 dozen.

Mom's Apple-Bran Cake

1 cup brown sugar, firmly packed
½ cup (1 stick) margarine
2 eggs
1½ cups unbleached flour
2 teaspoons baking soda
½ teaspoon salt
1 teaspoon cinnamon
1 teaspoon grated nutmeg
1 cup bran flakes
4 cups chopped apples
Cream Cheese Icing

Preheat oven to 350°. Cream sugar and margarine together thoroughly. Add eggs and beat until light and fluffy. Mix together dry ingredients and stir into egg mixture, beating well. Finally, fold in chopped apples well. Pour into a well-greased 9 x 9-inch cake pan and bake for 45 minutes or until top springs back when touched lightly. Cool on wire rack. Spread with Cream Cheese Icing.

Cream Cheese Icing

1 3-ounce package cream cheese, softened
1 tablespoon margarine
1 teaspoon vanilla
1½ cups confectioners' sugar

Blend ingredients together thoroughly and spread onto cake.

Desserts

Applesauce Cake

- 1 cup firmly packed brown sugar
- ½ cup (1 stick) margarine
- 2 eggs (at room temperature)
- 2 cups whole wheat pastry flour or unbleached flour
- 2 teaspoons baking soda
- ¼ teaspoon salt
- ¼ cup raw wheat germ
- 2 cups thick applesauce
- ½ cup apple cider
- ½ cup chopped nuts, optional
  Confectioners' sugar

All ingredients should be at room temperature. Preheat oven to 325°. Cream sugar and margarine together until light; beat in eggs thoroughly. Stir in remaining ingredients except ¼ cup cider and nuts and beat at medium speed for 3 minutes, scraping the sides of the bowl regularly. Stir in nuts. Pour batter into 9 x 5 x 3-inch loaf pan. Bake for 1½ hours or until center springs back when lightly touched. Cool in pan for 10 minutes on a wire rack; remove. If desired, spoon remaining cider onto cake. Cool cake completely and sprinkle with confectioners' sugar. Yield: 1 loaf cake.

Mincemeat Cookies

- ¾ cup shortening
- 1 cup granulated sugar
- 3 eggs
- 3 cups unbleached flour
- ¾ teaspoon salt
- 1 teaspoon baking soda
- 1 teaspoon cinnamon
- 1 teaspoon allspice
- 1 cup mincemeat
  Rind of 1 lemon, grated
- ¾ cup chopped nuts
- ½ cup raisins

Preheat oven to 350°. Cream together shortening and sugar. Beat in eggs until light and fluffy. Mix dry ingredients. Add half the dry ingredients to the egg mixture. Stir in mincemeat and lemon rind. Add remaining dry ingredients and mix thoroughly. Stir in nuts and raisins. Drop by teaspoonfuls on greased baking sheets. Bake for 10 minutes or until done. Yield: 4 dozen cookies.

Look for more excellent dessert recipes in the "Timesaving Basic Mixes" chapter.

Fudge Sheet Cake

- 2 cups unbleached flour or whole wheat pastry flour
- 1½ cups granulated sugar
- 1 cup (2 sticks) margarine
- 7 tablespoons cocoa
- 1 cup water
- ½ cup milk soured with 1½ teaspoons vinegar
- 1 teaspoon baking soda
- 2 eggs, lightly beaten
- 1 teaspoon vanilla

Preheat oven to 375°. Combine flour and sugar in a large mixing bowl. Place margarine, cocoa, and water into a small, heavy saucepan and heat to boiling, stirring regularly. Blend with flour mixture thoroughly. Mix soda with soured milk and combine with eggs and vanilla. Stir the milk mixture into the flour mixture until thoroughly blended. Pour mixture into a jelly-roll pan (10 x 15 x 1-inch) that has been lightly greased and floured. Bake about 20 minutes. Prepare icing during last few minutes of baking time. Cake is done when pick inserted in center comes out clean. Remove cake from oven, and immediately pour hot icing on top, spreading evenly. Cool before serving. Yield: 2 dozen servings.

Icing

- ½ cup (1 stick) margarine
- 4 tablespoons cocoa
- 6 tablespoons milk
- 1 pound confectioners' sugar, sifted
- 1 cup chopped nuts, optional

Place margarine, cocoa, and milk in a medium-size, heavy saucepan and heat to boiling, stirring, regularly. Stir in sugar, nuts and mix well.

Charlotte's Quick Fruit Dessert

- ¼ cup margarine
- ¾ cup milk
- ½ cup brown sugar, firmly packed
- 1 cup whole wheat pastry flour or unbleached flour
- 1½ teaspoons baking powder
- 2 cups freshly sliced apples, berries, etc.
- 1 teaspoon cinnamon or nutmeg, optional

Preheat oven to 350°. Melt margarine in bottom of 8 x 8-inch pan placed in oven. Combine milk, sugar, flour, and baking powder. Stir slightly, just moistening ingredients. Pour mixture evenly onto melted margarine. Don't stir. Pour fruit evenly over batter; push apple slices into batter slightly. Sprinkle on cinnamon or nutmeg, if desired. Bake about 1 hour or until done. Serve hot or cold. Yield: 12 servings.

Zucchini Bars

- ¾ cup soft margarine or butter
- ½ cup brown sugar, firmly packed
- 2 eggs
- 1 teaspoon vanilla
- 1¾ cups whole wheat flour
- ½ teaspoon salt
- 1½ teaspoons baking powder
- ¾ cup dates, finely chopped
- ¾ cup raisins, optional
- 2 cups raw, unpeeled, grated zucchini
  Chopped nuts, optional

Preheat oven to 350°. Cream together margarine and sugar. Add egg and vanilla and beat until light. Stir together flour, salt, and baking powder and add to creamed ingredients. Finally, add dried fruit and zucchini. Spoon into a greased 10 x 13-inch cake pan and bake for 35 to 40 minutes or until top springs back. While still warm, spread glaze evenly over bars. Sprinkle with chopped nuts if desired. Bars can be frozen. Yield: 15 to 18 bars.

Glaze

- 1 tablespoon margarine, softened
- 1 cup confectioners' sugar
- ¼ teaspoon cinnamon
- 1 teaspoon vanilla
- 1 to 2 tablespoons milk
- ½ cup chopped nuts, optional

Mix to desired consistency.

Mom's Miracle Brownies

- ¾ cup unbleached flour
- ¾ cup granulated sugar
- ½ teaspoon baking powder
- 7 tablespoons cocoa
- ¾ teaspoon salt
- ⅔ cup shortening
- 2 eggs
- 1 teaspoon vanilla
- 1 tablespoon honey
- 1 cup chopped nuts

Preheat oven to 350°. Sift flour, sugar, baking powder, cocoa, and salt together into a medium-size mixing bowl. Beat in remaining ingredients, in order, mixing well after each addition. Finally, stir in nuts. Spread into a greased 8 x 8 x 2-inch baking pan and bake for 30 to 40 minutes, or until done. Cool in pan before slicing into squares. Yield: 16 squares.

Apple-Candied Peel Bars

- 2 cups unbleached flour
- 1 teaspoon baking powder
- ¼ teaspoon ground cloves
- 2 teaspoons cinnamon
- 2 eggs
- ¾ cup firmly packed brown sugar
- 2 tablespoons water
- 1 teaspoon rum flavoring
- ¼ cup Candied Peel, (page 38)
- ⅔ cup chopped almonds
- 1 apple, chopped

Preheat oven to 350°. Mix first 4 ingredients together. In a separate bowl, beat eggs well; stir in brown sugar, water, and rum flavoring. When thoroughly blended, mix dry ingredients with egg mixture. Finally, stir in peel, almonds, and apple. Spread in a well-greased 9 x 13-inch baking pan or in miniature muffin tins to make small "fruit cakes." Bake for 20 minutes or until done. Glaze, if desired. Yield: 20 bars.

Glaze:

- 1 cup confectioners' sugar
- ¾ teaspoon rum flavoring
- 1½ tablespoons water

Blend glaze ingredients together until smooth. Glaze bars while still warm. Cool thoroughly before cutting into squares.

Kate's Self-Frosting Cake

- ½ cup margarine
- 1 cup brown sugar, firmly packed
- 1 cup unbleached flour
- ½ cup whole wheat flour
- 1 teaspoon baking powder
- 1 egg
- 1 8½-ounce can crushed pineapple
- ½ cup granulated sugar
- ½ cup Flaked Coconut (page 60)
  Chopped nuts, optional

Preheat oven to 350°. Cream margarine and brown sugar together thoroughly. Add flours, baking powder, egg, and pineapple. Stir well. Spread into a greased 8 x 8 x 2-inch baking pan. Mix sugar, coconut, and nuts, and sprinkle evenly on top of cake. Bake for 30 to 35 minutes or until done. Yield: 16 squares.

Karl's Pumpkin Cookies

- 1 cup margarine, softened
- ¾ cup brown sugar, firmly-packed
- 2¼ cups whole wheat pastry flour or unbleached flour
- ¼ cup raw wheat germ
- 1 tablespoon baking powder
- 1½ teaspoons salt (if pumpkin is salted, use less)
- 2 teaspoons allspice
- 1 teaspoon cinnamon
- 2 eggs
- 1 cup canned or cooked pumpkin
- 2 cups old-fashioned rolled oats
- 1 teaspoon vanilla
- ½ cup (or more) raisins or currants
- ¼ cup (or more) chopped nuts

Preheat oven to 350°. Cream together margarine and brown sugar. Combine dry ingredients. Add eggs to margarine mixture and beat until light. Add pumpkin. Stir in dry ingredients; add rolled oats and vanilla and stir thoroughly. Finally, add fruit and nuts. Drop by teaspoonfuls onto greased cookie sheets and bake 8 to 10 minutes or until lightly browned and top springs back when touched lightly. Cool on wire racks. Yield: approximately 6 dozen.

Rolled-Out Ginger Cookies

- 1 cup margarine, softened
- ¾ cup brown sugar, firmly-packed
- 1 egg
- 1 cup old-fashioned molasses
- 2 tablespoons vinegar
- 1½ teaspoons baking soda
- ½ teaspoon salt
- 1 tablespoon ginger
- 1 teaspoon cinnamon
- 1 teaspoon allspice
- 3 cups whole wheat flour
- 1¾ cups unbleached flour
- ¼ cup soy flour
  Raisins or currants, optional

Cream together margarine and sugar. Beat in egg, molasses, vinegar, soda, salt and spices. Stir in flours. Chill thoroughly. Preheat oven to 375°. On a well-floured surface, roll with a well-floured rolling pin to ⅛ inch . Cut into shapes. If desired, decorate with raisins and currants. Place on greased baking sheet. Bake for 6 minutes or until done. Remove from pan to wire rack for cooling. Decorate with icing and other decorations, if desired. Yield: 8 dozen small to medium cookies.

Cheesecake
Crust

- ⅔ cup vanilla wafer cookie crumbs
- 1 tablespoon soy flour
- 1 tablespoon sunflower seeds
- ½ teaspoon cinnamon
- 2 teaspoons honey
- 2 tablespoons margarine, melted

Mix together crumbs, soy flour, cinnamon, and sunflower seeds. Stir in honey and margarine until all crumbs are moistened. Press crumbs against the sides and bottom of a 9-inch pie plate which holds 4 cups. Reserve any extra crumbs. Chill until ready to use. Yield: 6 to 8 servings.

Filling

- 1 envelope unflavored gelatin
- 1 tablespoon lemon juice
  Peel of ½ lemon
- ½ cup hot milk
- ¼ cup honey
- 2 egg yolks
- 1 8-ounce package cream cheese, softened
- 1 cup creamed cottage cheese, drained, or sour cream
- 1 cup crushed ice

Place gelatin, lemon juice, peel, milk, and honey in an electric blender. Cover and blend. Add egg yolks and cream cheese and blend, covered, for 10 seconds. Add cottage cheese and ice. Cover and blend until smooth. Pour mixture into crumb crust. Any leftover crumbs could be sprinkled on top, or garnished with toasted wheat germ.

Grandma Earle's Apple Bars

- 3 tablespoons margarine, softened
- ¾ cup brown sugar, firmly-packed
- 1 teaspoon vanilla
- 1 egg
- ½ teaspoon salt
- 1 teaspoon baking powder
- 1 teaspoon cinnamon
- 1 cup unbleached or whole wheat pastry flour
- 3 cups chopped apples
- ½ cup chopped nuts

Preheat oven to 350°. Beat margarine, sugar, vanilla, and egg together thoroughly. Mix dry ingredients and stir in until completely blended. Finally, stir in apples and nuts. Pour into a lightly greased 7½ x 9-inch baking pan and bake for 30 minutes or until top springs back when touched lightly. Cool on wire rack. Yield: 12 servings.

Economical Entertaining

Entertain well without anyone else knowing that the budget is being carefully watched. At dinner parties try some economical dishes from foreign lands—Italian pasta or a Chinese chicken dish or an Indonesian Rijsttafel (rice table) plus an interesting salad will make everyone think the hostess (or host) is a gourmet cook, and without a huge cash outlay. A fresh loaf of homemade bread will probably bring more raves than anything else. Soup is often a moneysaver, yet as a first course it seems very elegant. Check the index for interesting foods from the same country or from a number of countries.

Joyce's Stuffed Shells

- 2 12-ounce packages jumbo shell macaroni or cannelloni or manicotti shells
- 2 quarts (64-ounces) Grandma Benvenuto's Tomato Sauce (page 47)
- 4 10-ounce packages frozen chopped spinach or 3 pounds lightly steamed fresh spinach or chard
- 4 eggs, lightly beaten
- 2 pounds small curd cottage cheese or ricotta
- 1 pound shredded mozzarella cheese
- ¼ teaspoon nutmeg
- ⅓ cup freshly grated Parmesan cheese

Cook shells according to package directions until just tender. (Overcooking them will cause them to break apart during stuffing.) Heat spaghetti sauce to simmer. Thaw spinach and drain thoroughly. Mix eggs, cottage cheese, mozzarella, and nutmeg together until well-blended. Stir in spinach and stuff shells with 2 teaspoonsful of the spinach mixture. Preheat oven to 350°. Pour one-fourth of the spaghetti sauce into the bottom of a flat casserole dish that will hold three quarts. Arrange stuffed shells in a single layer on top of the sauce. Pour part of the remaining sauce over shells, leaving enough to repeat process with a second casserole dish. When both casserole dishes are prepared, sprinkle both with Parmesan cheese and bake for 30 minutes or until heated through. One or both of the casserole dishes can be frozen after assembling. Cover ovenproof dish or pan tightly with foil. An hour before needed, preheat oven to 425° and bake frozen casseroles for 40 minutes. Remove foil and bake 20 minutes more or until done. Yield: 12 servings.

Diana's Desperation Burritos

- 2 cups leftover chicken, browned ground beef, tuna, etc.
- ½ cup chopped onion (green onion, if in season)
- 1 16-ounce can refried beans
- ½ 10½-ounce can mushroom soup
- ½ cup taco sauce (more or less, to taste)
- 8 to 12 tortillas
- ¾ pound shredded Colby cheese

Preheat oven to 350°. Mix together first 5 ingredients and heat until warm. Separate tortillas (heat, if necessary to keep from cracking when rolling up). Divide meat mixture among tortillas, spreading the mixture along just one edge. Divide the cheese among tortillas, sprinkling on top of meat mixture. Roll up and place on greased baking sheet. Bake for 20 to 25 minutes or until cheese melts and burritos are heated through. Yield: 8 to 12 servings.

Baked Fish Soufflé

- 1½ pounds fresh or frozen fish fillets, thawed
- 1 teaspoon salt
- ¼ teaspoon freshly ground black pepper
- 1 teaspoon butter or margarine
- 2 egg whites
- ¼ cup mayonnaise
- 3 tablespoons onion, minced (preferably green onions, if in season)
- 1 tablespoon pickle relish
- 1 tablespoon minced parsley
- ¼ teaspoon salt
- 2 to 3 drops bottled red pepper sauce

Preheat oven to 425°. Place fillets in a greased baking dish; sprinkle with salt and pepper and pat with butter. Bake for 10 minutes. Beat egg whites until stiff but not dry. Blend in remaining ingredients and spread over hot fish, covering completely. Continue baking 10 to 15 minutes longer until topping is puffy and fish flakes easily with a fork. Yield: 4 servings.

Sherbos' Seven Layer Dinner

- 2 tablespoons oil
- ½ pound ground beef or turkey
- 1 cup chopped onion
- 2 cups thinly sliced raw potatoes
- ½ cup raw brown rice
- 1 green pepper, chopped
- 2 cups shredded carrots
- ½ cup sliced onion
- 1½ cups diced celery
- ½ cup raw wheat germ
- 4 cups tomato juice or canned tomatoes in juice
  Freshly ground black pepper
  Salt

Preheat oven to 350° or use slow cooker. Brown ground beef and chopped onion lightly in hot oil. Place potatoes in bottom of 3-quart casserole dish or slow cooker. Sprinkle rice on top of potatoes evenly. Follow, in layers, with meat mixture, green pepper, carrots, sliced onion, and celery and top with wheat germ. Taste tomato juice and add salt and pepper to season well. Pour juice over all. Cover tightly and bake 2 hours or until done in oven—8 hours on low in slow cooker. Yield: 8 servings.

Sweet 'N' Sour Pork

- 2 pounds lean pork (shoulder, loin blade chops, or most reasonable cut available)
- ¼ cup water
- 2½ cups (20-ounce can) pineapple chunks
- 2 tablespoons cornstarch
- ¼ cup brown sugar, firmly-packed
- ¼ cup cider vinegar
- 2 tablespoons soy sauce
- ⅓ cup thinly sliced onion rings
- 1 cup green and red pepper rings
- ½ cup bamboo shoots, drained, optional
  Salt

Slice any fat off pork and cut meat into bite-size chunks. Render fat in large skillet. Remove and add meat. Stir-fry pork until browned. Add water; cover and simmer 60 minutes or until tender. Meanwhile, drain pineapple, saving juice. Combine cornstarch and sugar; stir in vinegar until well-blended. Add pineapple juice and soy sauce. Stir into pork and cook, stirring constantly, until sauce is thickened. Add onion and pepper rings; stir lightly. Finally add pineapple chunks and bamboo shoots. Cook 2 to 3 minutes or until heated through. Correct seasonings. Serve over hot rice or chow mein noodles. Yield: 6 to 8 servings.

Chicken Satay

- 2 pounds chicken breasts, cut into bite-size strips
- 3 tablespoons chopped onion
- 1 tablespoon peanut or vegetable oil
- 2 cloves garlic, minced
- ¼ teaspoon ground cardamom
- ⅔ cup plus 1 tablespoon crunchy peanut butter
- 1 teaspoon turmeric
- 2 teaspoons ground coriander
- 1½ teaspoons ground cumin
- 1 teaspoon red pepper flakes, soaked in a small amount of warm water
- 1 tablespoon lemon juice
- 1 teaspoon salt
- 1 tablespoon brown sugar
- ½ cup water

Thread chicken pieces on wooden skewers. Make marinade by stirring together 1 tablespoon peanut butter and remaining ingredients. Place chicken pieces in marinade and leave overnight. Remove skewered chicken and barbecue 3 to 4 minutes outdoors (basting constantly) or broil indoors until browned. Keep chicken hot. To prepare sauce add remaining peanut butter and enough water to remaining leftover marinade to make a sauce of desired consistency. Simmer for 5 minutes and serve hot with the skewered chicken. Yield: 8 servings.

Szechuan Beef (Hot Chinese Dish)

- 2 pounds lean, low-cost beef
- 4 tablespoons soy sauce
- 3 tablespoons dry sherry
- ⅛ teaspoon cayenne pepper
- 2 carrots, sliced on the diagonal
- 1 stalk celery, sliced on the diagonal
- 2 light green chili peppers, seeded and sliced
- 1 sweet green pepper, cut in strips
- 5 large cloves garlic, minced

Trim fat off beef; slice beef into thin, bite-size pieces. Render beef fat in a skillet; stir in beef and cook until brown. Stir in soy sauce and sherry. Cover and simmer until beef is very tender (1 hour or more). Stir in vegetables and cook briefly (they should be crisp). Taste and correct seasonings. Serve over rice. Yield: 6 to 8 servings.

A FAVORITE RECIPE FOR "Blair's Chicken"
With Orange Sauce

1 Broiler-fryer, cut up
½ c. orange sauce
½ c. whole wheat flour
½ c. orange juice
¼ t. dry mustard
½ t. paprika
½ t. salt
½ t. bottled hot pepper sauce
½ c. marmalade
½ c. oil

Blair's Chicken with Orange Sauce

    1 fryer, cut up
    ½ cup whole wheat flour
    ½ cup orange juice
    ¼ teaspoon dry mustard
    ½ teaspoon paprika
    ½ teaspoon salt
    ⅛ teaspoon bottled hot pepper sauce
    ⅓ cup orange marmalade
    ¼ cup vegetable oil
    1 pound Braised Mushrooms

Preheat oven to 325°. Coat chicken with flour. Mix remaining ingredients, except mushrooms, together thoroughly. Place chicken in a shallow baking dish and pour sauce over. Bake for 2 hours, basting regularly. The last 15 minutes add mushrooms and stir in thoroughly. Yield: 4 servings.

Braised Mushrooms

    2 tablespoons margarine
    1 pound mushrooms, washed and patted dry
    Salt
    Freshly ground black pepper

Melt margarine in a large frying pan. Stir in mushrooms and allow to simmer, covered, in their own juice until just tender. Add salt and pepper to taste. Eat as is or use in Blair's Chicken with Orange Sauce recipe.

Indonesian Beef

    Suet or 1 tablespoon vegetable oil
    3 pounds lean beef, cut into bite-size pieces
    1 cup chopped onion
    4 cloves garlic, minced
    1 tablespoon fresh, grated ginger
    ½ teaspoon cinnamon
    ½ teaspoon nutmeg
    ½ teaspoon cardamom
    ¼ teaspoon ground cloves
    1 teaspoon brown sugar
    1 cup beef broth
    2 tablespoons soy sauce
    Salt
    Freshly ground black pepper

Render suet in a large frying pan; add beef cubes and sauté until brown. Add onion and garlic toward end of browning period. Add ginger and other spices, brown sugar, beef broth, and soy sauce. Bring to simmer, cover and simmer 1½ hours until beef is tender. Taste and correct seasoning. Serve with rice and Hot Pepper and Celery Sambal. Yield: 8 servings.

Ham Stuffed Crepes

    3 tablespoons margarine
    5 tablespoons unbleached flour
    2 cups milk
    Salt
    Freshly ground black pepper
    2 cups ground ham
   10 Crepes (page 27)

Melt margarine in a heavy-bottomed saucepan. Stir in flour and allow to cook, stirring regularly, for a few minutes until flour is golden. Pour in milk all at once. Stir with a wire whisk until sauce thickens. Add salt and a good deal of pepper, to taste. Mix one cup of the cream sauce with ham. Divide ham mixture among the crepes and place crepes in a well-buttered casserole dish. Pour remaining sauce over the crepes, cover with aluminum foil, and refrigerate until approximately 40 minutes before serving. Preheat oven to 350°. Bake crepes approximately 40 minutes or until very hot. Leave foil off the last 5 to 10 minutes to brown surface as desired. Yield: 10 crepes.

Grandma Benvenuto's Tomato Sauce

    ¼ cup olive oil
    ½ pound bulk pork sausage
    1 pound ground beef
    3 minced garlic cloves
    ½ green pepper, minced
    1 onion, minced
    2 12-ounce cans tomato paste
    3 28-ounce cans tomatoes
    3 bay leaves
    3 tablespoons salt
    1 tablespoon oregano
    1 tablespoon sugar

In a very large, heavy-bottomed saucepan or Dutch oven heat olive oil. Stir in sausage, reduce heat and cook for 30 minutes. Add ground beef, garlic, pepper, and onion. Turn up heat and brown meat quickly. Place tomato paste and tomatoes in blender and blend until smooth. Pour tomato sauce over meat mixture and bring to boil. Reduce heat and simmer. Add remaining ingredients. Simmer from 1 to 3 hours. Sauce can be used on pasta, on pizza, or in casseroles. It can be stored in refrigerator for up to a week or can be frozen for use later. Yield: approximately 4 quarts.

Indonesian Curried Pork

Pork fat *or* 2 tablespoons vegetable oil
2½ to 3 pounds lean pork, cut into bite-size pieces
¼ cup flour
3 cups chopped onion
5 cloves garlic, minced
2 to 3 tablespoons curry powder
2 cups Coconut Milk (page 60)
2 strips lemon or lime peel
2 strips orange peel
Salt
Freshly ground black pepper

Render pork fat in a large frying pan (or heat oil). Meanwhile, roll pork cubes in flour until well-covered. Brown pork well; add onion and garlic toward end of browning period. Stir in coconut milk and seasonings. Reduce heat, cover, and simmer 1½ hours or more until pork is tender. Skim fat. Taste and correct seasonings. Serve at this point or cool and freeze, well wrapped. Reheat thoroughly before serving with Minted, Parslied Rice and Hot Pepper and Celery Sambal, if desired. Yield: 6 to 8 servings.

Minted, Parslied Rice

5 cups water
1 tablespoon margarine
2 cups long-grained rice
¼ cup chopped mint
¼ cup chopped parsley
Salt
Freshly ground black pepper

Bring water and margarine to boiling point in a heavy-bottomed saucepan. Stir in rice, cover, reduce heat, and simmer 15 to 18 minutes or until water is absorbed and rice is tender. Turn off heat and let stand for about 5 minutes before fluffing with a fork and gently stirring in mint, parsley, and seasonings. If desired, pack rice into a buttered mold and unmold just before serving on a platter garnished with parsley. Yield: 6 to 8 servings.

Hot Chocolate Mix

½ cup cocoa
¾ cup sugar
Dash salt
3 cups nonfat dry milk

Mix ingredients together thoroughly and store in tightly covered container. When hot chocolate is desired, use ¼ to ⅓ cup mix to 1 cup water. Heat, stirring with a wire whisk, until foamy and thoroughly blended. Yield: 2 quarts.

Sangria

1 orange, sliced
1 lime, sliced
1 lemon, sliced
¼ cup granulated sugar
½ cup brandy
1 bottle (24-ounce) Spanish red wine or California Burgundy
2 tablespoons lemon juice
3 cups soda water

Place sliced fruit into a very large pitcher. Mix sugar and brandy together until sugar dissolves and pour over fruit. Let stand at room temperature for an hour. Pour in red wine and lemon juice, stir, and let stand another hour. Just before serving, add ice cubes and soda water. Stir until thoroughly chilled and serve. Yield: 8 servings.

Claret Punch

4 cups ginger ale
2 bottles claret wine
2 6-ounce cans lemonade concentrate
2 cups pineapple juice
1 orange, sliced

Pour ginger ale into a 1-gallon container. Add remaining ingredients, stirring well. Finally, add enough ice cubes to fill the container. Stir until well chilled and serve. Yield: 1 gallon.

Hot Apple Tea

1 quart (4 cups) apple juice
4 teaspoons loose tea leaves
1 lemon, sliced
1 apple, sliced
6 cinnamon sticks or ½ teaspoon cinnamon

Heat apple juice until just boiling; pour over tea leaves in a scalded teapot. Steep 2 to 3 minutes. Serve with lemon and apple slices and garnish with cinnamon. Yield: 6 servings.

Why not serve "tea" at four o' clock some afternoon? Along with freshly brewed tea in china cups, serve tiny sandwiches, a thinly sliced cake, a quick bread (with butter and jam on the side), and a few tempting cookies.

Wine tasting parties are fun. Ask each guest to bring a bottle of good wine for everyone to sample in polished wine glasses. The hosts provide a good selection of cheeses and crackers or breads.

Canning and Freezing

There is no question that a way to save an enormous amount on food is to plant a vegetable garden. For a very small cash outlay, it's possible to grow delicious fresh carrots, Swiss chard, green beans, and tomatoes—all prolific—even in a minuscule plot. Plant family favorites, learn to can and freeze them, and reap huge savings. Eat frozen green peppers during the winter when they are selling at out-of-season prices and experience one of the many joys of gardening.

Hints:

1. Freeze as soon after harvesting as possible.
2. Freeze only ripe, unblemished fruits and tender vegetables.
3. Most vegetables must be scalded, using 1 gallon of water for every pint of vegetables. Bring water to boil in a large kettle with cover; place washed and prepared vegetable into boiling water in a colander or wire basket and submerge until vegetable is heated to the center. (See chart.) Remove from boiling water immediately and plunge vegetable into ice water. Drain and pack into freezer containers. Leave head space for vegetables that pack down.

Sliced Cucumber Pickles

```
 8  cups very thinly sliced cucumbers
 ¼  cup pickling salt
    Ice cubes
 4  cups very thinly sliced small onions
 2  cups cider vinegar
1½  cups sugar
 2  teaspoons celery seed
 1  tablespoon mustard seed
 2  teaspoons ginger
 1  teaspoon turmeric
```

Place cucumber slices in a large bowl; sprinkle with salt and toss gently. Cover with ice cubes and let stand 2 to 3 hours or until cucumbers are thoroughly crisped. Drain and stir in onions. Combine remaining ingredients in a large, heavy-bottomed saucepan. Bring to a boil and allow to boil for 10 minutes. Stir in cucumber and onion slices and allow to return to boiling. Pack at once in hot, sterilized jars, and seal. Process in boiling water bath for 30 minutes. Remove and cool before storing. Yield: 4 pints.

Guide to Freezing Garden Produce

Berries: blackberries, boysenberries, loganberries, blueberries.	Wash in ice water; drain carefully; pack and freeze.
Cherries (tart)	Wash, stem, and pit. Stir ¾ cup sugar into each quart of cherries until sugar dissolves. Package and freeze.
Green or yellow beans	Scald 3½ minutes. Package and freeze.
Greens: collards, Swiss chard, beet or turnip greens, kale, spinach	Use 2 gallons water per pint of greens. Scald all greens except collards and chard stems for 2 minutes. Scald collards and chard stems 3 to 4 minutes. Package and freeze.
Peas	Scald shelled peas 1½ to 2 minutes. Package and freeze.
Peppers	Can be frozen without scalding for use in casseroles and other cooked dishes.
Pumpkin and winter squash	Cut into uniform pieces and either steam or bake at 350° until tender. Scoop pulp from shells, puree, and package. Freeze.
Rhubarb	Cut off leaves and ends. Wash and cut into 1-inch pieces or freeze whole.
Strawberries	Wash in cold water, drain, hull, and slice into thirds. Use 1 cup sugar for every 9 cups berries. Stir carefully to dissolve sugar, pack and freeze.
Summer squash: zucchini, crookneck	Wash, do not peel, cut into 1¼-inch pieces and scald 6 minutes.
Tomatoes	Whole tomatoes or uncooked tomato pulp (to be used in casseroles and other cooked dishes) can be frozen without scalding if used within a few months of freezing.

Canning and Freezing

Emma Rogers' Frozen Coleslaw

- 1 very large head cabbage, shredded
- 1 teaspoon salt
- 1 cup vinegar
- 2 cups sugar (or much less if vinegar isn't tart)
- ¼ cup water
- 1 teaspoon celery seed
- 1 teaspoon mustard seed
- 1 mango, and/or pimiento, cut-up, optional
  Shredded carrots, diced celery, optional

Toss cabbage with salt and drain. Mix together vinegar, sugar, water, celery and mustard seed in a heavy-bottomed saucepan. Bring to the boil and boil for 1 minute. Cool. Pour over drained, shredded cabbage in a large mixing bowl. Package in freezer containers as desired and freeze. Remove approximately ½ hour before serving to thaw and serve garnished with optional ingredients listed above. Yield: 10 servings.

Chowchow

- 1 medium head cabbage, chopped
- 4 cups chopped cucumbers
- 6 green peppers, seeded and chopped
- 4 cups chopped green tomatoes
- ¼ cup pickling salt
- 2 teaspoons dry mustard
- 6 cups cider vinegar
- 2½ cups sugar
- 1 teaspoon turmeric
- 1 teaspoon ginger
- 1 tablespoon mustard seed
- 1 tablespoon celery seed
- 1 tablespoon mixed whole pickling spices

Combine vegetables and mix with salt. Cover and let stand overnight. Drain juices. Mix mustard with 1 tablespoon of vinegar into a smooth paste. Add to remaining vinegar in a large, heavy kettle along with remaining ingredients, except cabbage mixture. Simmer for 20 minutes; add cabbage mixture. Simmer 10 minutes more. Simmer remainder while packing relish into hot, sterilized jars. Fill within ⅛-inch of the top, being certain liquid covers pickles. Wipe jar lid clean and seal with sterilized ring and lid. Repeat until all relish is used. Yield: 6 to 9 pints.

Note: Vegetables can be put through medium-fine blade of grinder, if preferred.

Julia's Bread and Butter Pickles

- 4 quarts medium-size pickling cucumbers, chilled
- 3 to 4 cups small white onions, sliced very thin
- 2 green or red peppers, chopped
- ½ cup pickling salt
- 5 cups cider vinegar
- 5 cups brown sugar
- 1½ teaspoons allspice
- 2 tablespoons mustard seed
- 1½ teaspoons celery seeds
- ½ teaspoon ground cloves or one 1-inch stick cinnamon

Slice chilled cucumbers into the thinnest slices possible. Place vegetables in a bowl and sprinkle salt over all. Cover with a weighted lid and place in refrigerator for three hours. Rinse in ice water. Drain well. Mix vinegar, sugar, and spices together in a large, heavy kettle and bring to the boiling point. Add vegetables gradually with very little stirring. Heat to scalding point but do not permit to boil. Pack pickles in hot sterilized jars. Wipe jar rims clean and seal at once with sterilized rings and lids. Yield: 7 to 8 pints.

Grapefruit Marmalade

- 3 white grapefruit (1 pound each)
- 2 lemons
- 3 cups water
- 1 box fruit pectin
- 10 cups sugar

Remove rind from fruit in quarters; lay flat and shave off about half of the white part; discard. Slice remaining peel into very thin strips. Place peel and water in a heavy pan and bring to boil. Reduce and simmer, covered, 20 minutes or until peel is tender. Chop peeled fruit, discarding seeds, and place pulp and juice into heavy pan with peel. Simmer, covered, 10 minutes. Mix fruit pectin with peel. Bring quickly to a hard boil, stirring constantly. Add sugar; bring to a full rolling boil. Boil hard 1 minute, stirring constantly. Remove from heat; skim off foam with a metal spoon. Pour into hot, sterilized jars, leaving ½-inch space at top. Wipe any spills from jar rim and immediately pour ⅛-inch hot paraffin on top. Yield: 10 half-pints.

Canning and Freezing

Strawberry Jam

2 quarts fully ripe strawberries, washed and drained
1 box fruit pectin
4 cups sugar
  Paraffin

Crush berries with a potato masher or plate, one layer at a time, so that all berries are reduced to pulp. Place berries in a very large, heavy-bottomed saucepan. Stir pectin into pulp. Bring quickly to a full, hard boil, stirring constantly. Stir in sugar; bring back to a full rolling boil that is impossible to stir down and boil hard for 1 minute, continuing to stir constantly. Remove from heat; skim foam with metal spoon. Ladle into hot, sterilized jars, leaving ½-inch space at top. Wipe spills from rim of jar. Cover at once with ⅛-inch melted paraffin. Yield: 8 ½-pint jars.

Zucchini Pickles

2 cups vinegar
2 teaspoons dill seed
¾ cup sugar
1 teaspoon celery seed
¼ cup pickling salt
1 teaspoon turmeric
½ teaspoon ground mustard
2 quarts unpeeled zucchini, sliced into rings
1 quart onions, sliced into rings

Place everything except vegetables in a heavy kettle; bring to a boil. Pour over zucchini and onion and let stand approximately 1 hour. Place again in heavy kettle; bring to a boil; reduce heat and simmer 3 minutes. Pack at once into hot, sterilized jars to within ⅛-inch from the top. Wipe jar rim clean and seal at once with sterilized ring and lid. Repeat with remaining pickles. Yield: 3 pints.

Pumpkin Preserves

4 pounds raw pumpkin, finely diced
6 cups sugar
3 lemons, sliced very thin
4 teaspoons grated gingerroot

Pour 3 cups sugar over pumpkin and let stand, covered, overnight. The next day, add remaining sugar and bring to boil in a heavy kettle. Reduce heat and simmer 1¼ hours. Add lemon slices and ginger. Simmer 1 hour more. Pack into hot, sterilized jars, leaving ½-inch space at top. Wipe any spills from jar rims and immediately pour ⅛-inch hot paraffin on preserves. Yield: 8 half-pint jelly glasses.

Fresh Mint Jelly

1½ cups fresh mint leaves and stems, firmly packed
2¼ cups water
  Juice of 1 lemon (2 tablespoons), strained
  Green food coloring, optional
3½ cups sugar
½ bottle or 1 1¾-ounces box fruit pectin

Wash mint leaves and stems thoroughly. Place in a large saucepan and crush with a potato masher or glass. Add water and bring quickly to a boil. Remove from heat, cover, and let stand 10 minutes. Strain and measure 1¾ cups into saucepan. Add lemon juice and a few drops of food color if desired. Add sugar. Mix well. Place over high heat and bring to a boil, stirring constantly. Stir in fruit pectin. Bring back to a full rolling boil and boil hard for 1 minute, stirring constantly. Remove from heat, skim off foam with metal spoon, and pour quickly into sterilized jars or jelly glasses, leaving ½-inch space at top. Wipe any spills from jar rim and immediately pour ⅛-inch hot paraffin on jelly. Yield: 3¼ cups.

Bittersweet Orange Marmalade

6 medium-size, thin-skinned oranges
2 lemons
2 medium-size, thin-skinned grapefruit
2 cups water
7 cups sugar

Cut whole fruits into ⅛-inch slices, discarding seeds. Cut grapefruit slices into eighths; cut orange and lemon slices into quarters. Combine chopped fruit with water in a large, heavy saucepan. Bring to boiling point, then reduce heat and simmer, covered, until peel is tender and translucent, about 25 to 30 minutes. Add sugar to the pan and stir until dissolved. Increase heat to medium-high and cook, uncovered, stirring often. Boil about 30 minutes or until 2 drops of marmalade run together and sheet off the edge of a cold, metal spoon. Cover and let stand at room temperature for 24 hours. The next day, rapidly return marmalade to boiling, stirring constantly. Skim off any foam with a metal spoon and pour immediately into hot, sterilized jars, leaving ½-inch space at top. Wipe spills from rims and cover at once with ⅛-inch hot paraffin. Yield: approximately 10 half-pints.

One-Day-at-a-Time Pickles

    1 quart small, fresh pickling cucumbers
    2 quarts iced water
    1 cup cider vinegar
 1½ tablespoon kosher salt
    1 cup water
    4 cloves garlic, peeled and sliced
    1 teaspoon pickling spices (without red pepper)
    3 large heads fresh dill *or* 3 teaspoons dill seed

Place unscrubbed, firm cucumbers in iced water for 30 minutes. Scrub off dirt and remove any particles of blossoms. Meanwhile, sterilize one quart jar and lid. In a small, stainless steel pan, bring vinegar, salt, water, garlic, and pickling spices, to a boil. When mixture boils, remove garlic and place cucumbers in sterile jar with dill, packing carefully, so no cucumbers will touch the lid. Pour vinegar solution over cucumbers to within ½-inch of the top of the jar, wipe rim of jar, seal, and process in a boiling water bath for 10 minutes. Store jar in a dark place for at least 2 weeks before serving. Yield: 1 quart.

Note: Recipe can be multiplied by the amount of cucumbers harvested.

Mom's Dilled Zucchini Slices

    2 to 3 pounds fresh, firm zucchini
      about 4¾-inches long
   ¼ cup salt
    2 teaspoons celery seed
    2 teaspoons mustard seed
    4 cloves garlic
 2½ cups water
 2½ cups cider vinegar
    1 cup sugar
   ¼ cup salt
    4 heads fresh dill *or* 1 tablespoon dill seed

Wash zucchini and cut lengthwise into thin slices. Cover with 1-inch water and ¼ cup salt. Let stand for 2 hours. Drain thoroughly. Tie celery and mustard seed with garlic in a cheescloth bag. In a large saucepan, combine water, vinegar, sugar, and salt; add the spice bag and bring to a boil. Remove from heat and add zucchini slices. Let stand another 2 hours. Bring all ingredients to a boil and cook for five minutes. Place dill in the bottom of 4 sterilized pint jars. Place slices and brine in the jars, leaving ¼-inch at the top. Seal and process 10 minutes in a hot water bath. Yield: 4 pint jars.

Note: These are delicious to use fresh, too.

Julia's Rhubarb Chutney

    2 cups cider vinegar
    4 cups brown sugar
    4 cups chopped rhubarb
    4 cups chopped onion
    1 teaspoon salt
    1 teaspoon cinnamon
   ½ teaspoon ground allspice
   ½ teaspoon ground cloves
   ¼ teaspoon freshly ground black pepper
   ¼ cup finely chopped gingerroot

Combine vinegar and brown sugar in a heavy saucepan. Bring to a boil, reduce heat and simmer 5 minutes. Add remaining ingredients and simmer, covered, until fairly thick. Pour into hot, sterilized jars; wipe spills off jar rims and seal immediately with sterilized lids and rings. Yield: approximately 4 pints.

Mom's Beet Relish

    4 cups cooked or canned beets, drained
    1 cup cider vinegar
   ½ cup brown sugar, firmly packed
   ¼ cup grated horseradish
    1 teaspoon salt

Chop beets very fine. Place all ingredients in a saucepan and bring to a boil. Pour immediately into two sterilized pint jars and seal (or cool and serve). Yield: 2 pints.

Canned Tomatoes

   20 pounds (approximately) firm, ripe tomatoes
      (1 pound equals 4 small, 3 medium,
      or 2 large tomatoes)
    7 teaspoons salt
    7 tablespoons lemon juice

Plunge tomatoes into boiling water for 15 seconds, then plunge into ice water. Remove and peel. Leave whole or quarter. Fill sterilized jars with the tomatoes, pressing down until they yield juice and fill in the spaces. Fill to within ½-inch of the top. Run a knife down side of jars in several places to remove air bubbles. Add salt and lemon juice to each quart. Wipe rims and seal jars, tightening bands securely. Place jars on the rack in hot water bath, covered by one or two inches of water. Cover and bring to boiling. Boil gently for 45 minutes. Remove jars and place on wire racks to cool. Check seals. (Use those which don't seal as soon as possible; keep refrigerated.) Store in a cool, dark, dry place. Yield: 7 quarts.

Timesaving Basic Mixes

Why do so many of us buy prepackaged cake mixes, pie crusts, baking powder biscuits, salad mixes, baked goods, etc.? Because they save us time. But they generally don't save us money. Basic mixes, prepared at home, make baking fast and inexpensive.

Basic Quick Bread Mix

9 cups sifted, unbleached flour *or* 10 cups whole
   wheat pastry flour
1/3 cup baking powder
1 teaspoon cream of tartar
1 tablespoon salt
2 cups shortening

Stir together dry ingredients thoroughly. Sift into a very large bowl. Cut in shortening with a pastry blender until the mixture resembles coarse cornmeal. Store in an airtight container in the refrigerator. Do not pack down. Use as called for in the recipes that follow. Yield: approximately 13 cups mix.

Muffins

3 cups Basic Quick Bread Mix
2 tablespoons firmly packed brown sugar
1 cup milk
1 egg, beaten

Preheat oven to 425°. Place Mix and sugar in a medium-size mixing bowl. Stir until well blended. Make a well in the center of the ingredients and pour milk and egg into it. Stir until dry ingredients are just moistened. Fill muffin papers or greased muffin tins about one-half full with batter. Bake for about 20 minutes or until done. Yield: 12 muffins.

Variations: For blueberry muffins, apple muffins, or other fruit muffins, stir 1 cup of desired drained fruit (chop apples and similar fruit) into the muffin batter just before pouring into muffin tins.

Applesauce Bread

3 cups Basic Quick Bread Mix
1/2 cup brown sugar, firmly-packed
1 teaspoon cinnamon
1 cup thick applesauce
1/2 cup milk
1 egg, beaten

Preheat oven to 350°. Grease a 9 x 5 x 3-inch loaf pan thoroughly. Blend Mix, sugar, and applesauce together. Combine milk and egg and stir into applesauce mixture. Stir until well blended. Bake 1 hour or until done. Yield: 1 loaf.

Upside-Down Coffee Cake

2 cups Basic Quick Bread Mix
1/4 cup plus 2/3 cup firmly packed brown sugar
1 teaspoon cinnamon
1/4 cup chopped nuts
1 egg
1/2 cup milk, approximately
1 teaspoon vanilla
1/4 cup margarine

Place Mix, 1/4 cup brown sugar, cinnamon, and nuts into a bowl and mix thoroughly. Break egg into a measuring cup and add enough milk to make 3/4 cup total. Add vanilla, and stir wet ingredients in measuring cup with a fork. Add to the dry ingredients. Stir until thoroughly blended. Preheat oven to 375°. Melt margarine in the bottom of an 8 x 8 x 2-inch cake pan. Stir in remaining sugar, and spread mixture evenly over bottom of pan. Pour batter over margarine mixture carefully and bake 30 minutes or until done. Remove coffee cake immediately from tin by loosening from sides of pan with a knife and inverting onto serving plate. Yield: 12 servings.

Banana Bread

3 cups Basic Quick Bread Mix
1/2 cup honey
1 cup mashed, ripe bananas
2 eggs, well beaten
1/2 cup nuts, optional

Preheat oven to 350°. Grease a 9 x 5 x 3-inch loaf pan thoroughly. Blend Mix, honey, and bananas together. Stir in eggs until well blended. Bake for 1 hour or until done. Yield: 1 loaf.

Banana Bread
Basic Quick Bread Mix
Apple Cider Bread p.5
Muffins

Waffles

1½ cups Basic Quick Bread Mix
  2 teaspoons honey
  1 egg, separated
  1 cup milk

Blend mix, honey, beaten egg yolk, and milk. Beat egg white until stiff and fold in. Pour into prepared waffle iron and bake according to manufacturer's specifications. Yield: 5 waffles.

Pancakes

1½ cups Basic Quick Bread Mix
  1 tablespoon honey
  ¾ cup milk
  ¼ cup raw wheat germ
  1 egg, well beaten

Place mix into a bowl and stir in rest of the ingredients until well blended. Drop batter from a large spoon onto lightly greased, hot griddle. Turn once and serve. Yield: 1 dozen pancakes.

Streusel Topped Apple Bread

  3 cups Basic Quick Bread Mix
  ¼ cup firmly packed brown sugar
  1 teaspoon cinnamon
  ½ teaspoon cloves
  2 eggs
  ¼ cup milk
  5 cups chopped apples
  ½ cup raisins

Preheat oven to 375°. Mix together Mix, brown sugar, cinnamon, and cloves. Beat in eggs thoroughly for at least 1 minute. Stir in milk and blend thoroughly. Add apples and beat 1 more minute. Finally, stir in raisins. Pour batter into a well-greased 9 x 5 x 3-inch loaf pan. Spoon Streusel Topping evenly onto bread batter. Bake for about 1 hour or until done. Yield: 1 loaf.

Streusel Topping

⅔ cup brown sugar
½ cup unbleached flour
  2 teaspoons nuts
  1 teaspoon raw wheat germ
½ teaspoon cinnamon
¼ teaspoon salt
  3 tablespoons cold margarine

Stir together, brown sugar, flour, nuts, wheat germ, cinnamon, and salt. Cut in margarine with a pastry blender until mixture resembles crumbs.

Baking Powder Biscuits

  2 cups Basic Quick Bread Mix
½ cup milk

Preheat oven to 450°. Place mix in a bowl and make a well in the center. Add the milk and stir with fork until mix is well moistened. Form into a ball and turn out onto lightly floured surface. Knead lightly until smooth. Roll out with a floured rolling pin to ½-inch thickness and cut into 2-inch rounds. Place on lightly greased baking sheet and bake 15 minutes or until done. Yield: 1 dozen biscuits.

Note: For drop biscuits, do not knead but simply drop dough by the spoonful onto greased baking sheet and bake.

Quick Pizza

  2 cups Basic Quick Bread Mix
⅓ cup milk
  2 cups tomato sauce
  1 teaspoon oregano
½ teaspoon sweet basil
  1 clove garlic, minced
¼ cup minced onion
  1 cup shredded mozzarella cheese
¼ cup grated Parmesan or Romano cheese
    Toppings: anchovies, green peppers, browned ground beef, pastrami, olives

Preheat oven to 425°. Stir milk and Mix together in a small bowl until dough forms. Turn onto a lightly floured board and knead lightly. Roll out dough with a well-floured rolling pin and place on a well-greased, 14-inch baking sheet. Turn up edges of dough to hold in filling. Mix together tomato sauce, oregano, garlic, and onion and spread onto dough evenly. Add favorite topping either before or after sprinkling on cheese, as desired. Bake 10 to 15 minutes or until crust is done. Yield: One 14-inch pizza.

Karin's Pumpkin Dessert

    1 cup Basic Quick Bread Mix
    ½ cup old-fashioned rolled oats
    ⅔ cup brown sugar, firmly packed
    ¼ cup plus 2 tablespoons firm margarine
    2 cups pumpkin puree (16-ounce can)
    1 13-ounce can evaporated milk
    2 eggs
    1 cup brown sugar
    ½ teaspoon salt
    1 teaspoon cinnamon
    ½ teaspoon ginger
    ¼ teaspoon cloves
    ⅔ cup chopped nuts

Preheat oven to 350°. Mix together Basic Mix, oats, ⅔ cup brown sugar, and ¼ cup margarine until crumbly. Press into a 10 x 13-inch baking pan. Bake 8 minutes. Beat together pumpkin, milk, eggs, sugar, salt, cinnamon, ginger, and cloves. Pour over hot oat mixture and bake fifteen minutes. Mix nuts and remaining brown sugar, and margarine. Sprinkle over hot pumpkin mixture and bake 15 to 20 minutes, or until knife inserted in the center comes out clean. Cool and serve with Spiced Whipped Cream, if desired. Yield: 12 to 16 servings.

Spiced Whipped Cream

    1 cup whipping cream
    1 tablespoon sugar
    1 teaspoon grated orange rind
    ½ teaspoon cinnamon

Chill cream, beaters, and bowl. Beat cream until as thick as desired. Stir in sugar and flavorings. Serve immediately.

Applesauce-Bran Cookies

    3 cups Basic Quick Bread Mix
    1 cup bran flakes
    1 cup firmly packed brown sugar
    ½ teaspoon allspice
    ½ teaspoon nutmeg
    1 teaspoon cinnamon
    1 teaspoon vanilla
    2 eggs, beaten
    1 cup thick applesauce
    ½ cup raisins or currants

Preheat oven to 350°. Mix dry ingredients together thoroughly. Stir in vanilla, eggs, applesauce, and, finally, raisins. Drop by teaspoonfuls onto well-greased baking sheets. Bake for 15 minutes or until done. Yield: 4 dozen cookies.

Basic Pastry Mix

    12 cups sifted, unbleached flour (or half whole
         wheat pastry flour)
    1½ tablespoons salt
    4   cups shortening

Sift flour with salt into a very large bowl. Cut in shortening with a pastry blender or fork until the mixture is the consistency of coarse cornmeal. Store in a tightly covered container in a cool place. Yield: 18 cups (about nine 2 crust 8-inch pies).

Pie Crust

Using the chart, measure required amount of Basic Pastry Mix into a bowl. Sprinkle water in slowly, tossing mixture with a fork. When dough is just moistened, form into a ball. Divide in half if for two crusts, and place half on a well-floured cloth. With a well-floured rolling pin, roll the crust into a circle extending at least an inch beyond outside edge of pan. Fit pastry into pan gently. Fill with desired filling and repeat directions for top crust. Press edges together. Flute edge of pie shell. For baked, unfilled pastry shell, prick bottom of crust with fork and bake at 425° for 10 to 12 minutes.

Size of Crust	Ice Water (Tablespoons)	Pastry Mix (Cups)
one 8-inch	1-2	1¼
two 8-inch	2-3	2
one 9-inch	2-3	1½
two 9-inch	3-4	2¾

Note: Measure pie pan from inside rim to inside rim. The typical 9-inch pie pan holds about 4 cups filling; and 8-inch pan typically holds about 3 cups. Tart shells can be baked in muffin tins.

Make and freeze extra pie crust shells; they'll be like store-bought but at much less expense.

Large cannisters, coffee cans, or restaurant-size mayonnaise or mustard jars can be perfect storage places for basic mixes.

To prevent hard pieces of brown sugar from forming, store in an airtight container with a slice of apple. This will keep the sugar moist. In order to salvage your purchase, use a grater to break down any hardened pieces of brown sugar.

Welsh Lemon Tarts

    5 cups Basic Pastry Mix
    7 tablespoons ice water
    4 tablespoons margarine
    ⅓ cup brown sugar, firmly packed
    2 large egg yolks
    1 tablespoon grated lemon rind
    2 teaspoons brandy
    ⅛ teaspoon salt
    1½ cups small curd cottage cheese
    ⅓ cup currants
      Whipped cream, optional

Place Pastry Mix into a mixing bowl. Sprinkle water over and toss with a fork. Form a ball from dough; knead lightly. Divide into two parts and roll out half on a lightly floured board with a floured rolling pin. With a 3½-inch cookie cutter or jar lid, cut dough into eight rounds. Press rounds gently into muffin tins or fluted tart pans. Repeat to make 16 tart shells. Preheat oven to 425°. In a small bowl, beat margarine until soft with an electric mixer. Beat in sugar until light and fluffy; add yolks, rind, brandy, and salt. Beat thoroughly. Stir in cottage cheese and beat until mixture is almost smooth. Finally, add currants. Spoon mixture into pastry shells. Bake for 10 minutes and lower heat to 350°. Bake 15 to 20 minutes more or until filling is golden. Cool completely on wire racks before carefully removing from tins. Serve with whipped cream, if desired. Yield: 16 tarts.

Cheese Appetizers

    2 cups Basic Pastry Mix
    ½ teaspoon garlic powder
    1 tablespoon baking powder
    1 cup grated Parmesan or Romano cheese
    ½ cup milk
      Flour

Mix dry ingredients together thoroughly. Add milk and stir—mixture will be sticky. Stir until mixture cleans the bowl. Preheat oven to 400°. Turn out onto a very well-floured board. Roll mixture into a ball on floured surface until workable. Roll out with a well-floured rolling pin until ¼-inch thick. Cut into strips, approximately 1 x 3-inches. Place strips on well-greased baking sheets and bake approximately 10 minutes or until lightly browned. Serve hot as an appetizer or cold as a snack or with soup. Can be frozen and reheated in aluminum foil, if desired. If stored, keep in a tightly covered tin. Yield: 4 dozen "sticks."

Basic White Sauce Mix

    2⅔ cups non-instant powdered milk
    1½ cups unbleached or whole wheat flour
        (or a combination)
      2 teaspoons salt
      1 cup margarine
        Freshly ground black pepper

Mix together milk, flour, and salt. Cut in margarine with a pastry blender until mixture resembles crumbs. Refrigerate in a tightly covered container until needed. To make 1 cup sauce, pour 1 cup cold milk into a small, heavy-bottomed pan. Thoroughly stir in ½ cup of the mix. Stir over medium heat until mixture is thickened and bubbly. Taste and correct seasonings. Use as is or in any recipe calling for a white or cream sauce. Yield: mix for 12 cups sauce.

Quick Spinach-Stuffed Zucchini

    1 very large or 2 medium-size zucchini
    1 10-ounce package frozen spinach
    ½ cup White Sauce
    ⅛ teaspoon nutmeg
      Salt
      Freshly ground black pepper
    ¼ cup grated Parmesan cheese

Slice zucchini in half lengthwise; steam until barely tender. Scoop out pulp and reserve. Preheat oven to 350°. Steam spinach until thoroughly hot; drain. Gently stir in white sauce and pulp from zucchini, adding nutmeg and salt and pepper, if needed. Spoon creamed spinach mixture into zucchini and sprinkle with Parmesan cheese. Place on greased baking sheet or in a casserole. Bake 30 minutes or until heated through. Yield: 4 servings.

To add inexpensive protein to a recipe calling for milk, mix in a tablespoon of nonfat dry milk powder, per cup of milk; there will be no change in the outcome of the recipe. To an appropriate recipe calling for water, consider adding ¼ to ½ cup nonfat dry milk per cup of water.

Timesaving Basic Mixes

Flaked Coconut, Coconut Cream, and Coconut Milk

1 coconut

With an ice pick and hammer, punch a hole in two of the coconut eyes. Drain the liquid and reserve. Crack the coconut shell into four or five pieces. If meat will not come out of the shell easily, place, shell side down, over electric burner set at low heat for about one minute. Protect hands with a potholder or towel, and lift the meat from the shell. Scrape away the thin, dark layer with a vegetable peeler. Cut the meat into cubes and place them in a blender or food processor. Pour the reserved coconut liquid over the coconut meat with two cups very hot water. Blend until meat is flaked as desired. Pour liquid out of blender through a sieve. Press to extract as much liquid as possible. This is coconut cream. Refrigerate. Pour another cup of hot water over flaked coconut and sieve again. The thinner liquid is coconut milk. Use cream or milk immediately or within 24 hours. Freeze coconut or liquid if not using right away. Yield: 2 cups flaked coconut, 2 cups cream, 1 cup milk.

Indonesian Dessert

 2 tablespoons soft margarine or butter
²/₃ cup sugar
 6 tablespoons sifted, unbleached flour
 1 teaspoon cinnamon
⅛ teaspoon salt
 6 eggs, separated
1½ cups coconut cream
 4 tablespoons coconut
   Whipped Cream, optional

Preheat oven to 350°. Cream butter and sugar together thoroughly. Stir in flour, cinnamon, and salt. Add egg yolks, one at a time, beating thoroughly after each addition. Gradually stir in Coconut Cream. Beat egg whites until stiff but not dry and fold into yolk mixture. Pour custard into buttered 2-quart baking dish. Sprinkle Coconut on top. Set dish in a larger, shallow pan of hot water so that the water comes a little more than halfway up the side of the baking dish. Bake until set, about 45 minutes. Serve chilled with whipped cream, if desired. Yield: 12 servings.

Economical Yogurt

1½ cups instant nonfat dry milk
   Lukewarm water (120°)
 3 tablespoons good quality plain yogurt (commercial or homemade), fresh

Place dry milk in a sterilized quart jar. Blend in 1 cup lukewarm water. When thoroughly mixed, fill the container almost to the neck with additional lukewarm water. Stir well. Finally, stir in yogurt gently but thoroughly. Place plastic wrap on lip of jar and put cover on. Wrap well in several towels and place somewhere warm for 6 to 8 hours. Do not disturb for at least 6 hours, then check to see if it is thick as pudding. Yield: 1 quart, 2 pints, 4 cups.

Alternative Methods: Use yogurt maker, following directions. Or, in an oven that will maintain an even 115°, place the milk mixture into smaller sterilized jars such as baby food jars, cover and place in a pan filled to the jar necks with 115° water; leave in oven until yogurt is of desired consistency. Other incubators are an electric saucepan or frying pan that can keep an even low temperature no higher than 120°, or the pilot light on a gas stove.

Cucumber, Tomato, and Yogurt Salad

 2 cups plain yogurt
 1 large cucumber, chopped
 2 ripe tomatoes, chopped
 6 to 8 scallions, chopped
   Freshly ground black pepper to taste
½ teaspoon cumin seed
   Salt to taste
   Dash of cayenne pepper, optional
   Paprika

Beat yogurt until smooth. Toast cumin seed for 2 to 3 minutes in a heavy frying pan and crush. Stir cucumber, tomatoes, scallions, black pepper, and a pinch of cumin into yogurt; add salt to taste. Add cayenne if desired. Garnish with paprika and another pinch of cumin. Chill until ready to serve. Yield: 6 servings.

The Cook's Helpers

Glossary

Blanch   to drop slowly into boiling water for a few minutes then immediately place in ice water to stop cooking process; time varies with the vegetable. Pour boiling water over tomatoes and similar fruits and vegetables to make removal of skins easier.

Braise   to brown meat in vegetable oil and simmer, covered, with a small amount of additional liquid.

Mince   to cut up into very fine, tiny pieces.

Non-hydrogenated foods   foods which have not been processed with hydrogen to turn oil content into solid fat. Non-hydrogenated peanut butter can be recognized by the oil which rises to the top.

Non-instant powdered milk   more nutritious than instant.

Nutritional yeast   another name for brewer's yeast; an inexpensive source of protein and vitamin B complex. Can be consumed raw (in salads, juice, etc.), unlike baking or active yeast.

Old-fashioned molasses   unsulphured, dark molasses.

Puree   to mash cooked fruits or vegetables into a pulp, usually in a blender or sieve.

Sauté   to cook quickly in a small amount of oil, stirring or turning frequently.

Simmer   to cook just below boiling point; bubbles rise gently to the surface.

Unbleached flour   creamy white flour which has not been bleached with chemicals.

Wheat germ   part of the grain from which the new plant grows. Raw wheat germ contains high quality protein and B vitamins. Can be used in cooking process or sprinkled raw on a variety of foods.

Whole wheat flour   flour ground from the whole grain, containing endosperm, bran, and germ; milled from hard wheat.

Whole wheat pastry flour   more finely ground than whole wheat flour; milled from soft wheat.

Dollar-Saving Substitutions

Veal   chicken or turkey breast in many recipes

Ham   picnic ham or a meaty ham bone, if applicable

Beef tenderloin and similar cuts   ground chuck in many recipes

Ground beef   ground turkey or lamb in many recipes; substitute ground pork for some of the ground beef; try ground, cooked soy-beans, pinto beans, lentils, etc. as a substitute

Canned salmon   canned mackerel in many recipes

Ground cloves   allspice

Mace   nutmeg

Raisins   dates, currants, dried elderberries

Walnuts   ground roasted peanuts, hickory nuts (pick them yourself), and any other nuts at a lower cost or that can be harvested.

1 cup buttermilk   1 cup yogurt, 1 cup milk plus 1 tablespoon vinegar (in baked goods)

1 cup sour cream   1 cup plain yogurt in many recipes

Sharp Cheddar cheese   mild Cheddar, Colby, Longhorn

1 quart milk   1⅓ cup nonfat dry milk plus 3¾ cups cold water (for added nutrition at a low cost, use more dry milk)

1 tablespoon fresh herb   1 teaspoon dried herb

Hints: A Baker's Dozen

Thirteen Budget Saving Hints

1. Start "shopping the ads." Every week, check the newspaper ads from several supermarkets that have the best prices throughout the store. If the prices are right, plan complete menus around the week's meat and other specials.

2. Shop when there is time to compare prices, sizes, and brands. Use a well-organized, thorough shopping list.

3. Clip and save coupons regularly—but only for products ordinarily purchased. When a local store offers double-coupon savings, it's almost always best to shop there that week. Keep a large envelope handy for coupons received in the mail or clipped from magazines and newspapers; before doing the weekly shopping, always look through the envelope to see which can be used.

4. Watch at the check-out counter to make certain charges are correct—particularly when the clerk has to figure out the cost of one item when it is priced in multiples, for example, 6 for 98¢. When buying all 6, be certain to stack them together.

5. Unbranded foods can be as nutritious as name brands, but ingredients may not be as uniform in size or color. Unbranded meat is USDA inspected, just as the regular meats on the counter are. In nearly every case, unbranded foods cost less than even store name brands.

6. Convenience foods are only that—convenient. The customer pays to have a machine do something he or she could just as easily do. Make bread crumbs, add almonds to green beans, glaze carrots, prepare salad dressings, instead of buying the prepacked product. Be certain to check the chapter "Timesaving Basic Mixes" in this cookbook.

7. Buy foods that are consumed in great quantity by the case near harvesttime when the store has a special and the price is low. Consider buying flour in 25-pound sacks and rice in the largest quantity that can be stored.

8. Slow cookers are more economical than the oven; the oven is more economical than stove burners in the use of energy.

9. Match the size of the saucepan with the electrical element on a stove. Whenever possible turn off the element before the food is totally cooked, and the stored-up heat (especially in heavy-bottomed saucepans) will finish the cooking without using energy. Don't overcook vegetables; they are less nutritious and money is wasted.

10. Try to use the oven to its fullest by cooking several dishes at the same time and then freezing those not needed for later. Try not to be an "oven peeper"—up to 20% of the heat is lost through frequent opening of the oven door.

11. Whenever possible, buy spices and herbs in bulk from a gourmet shop, specialty store, or health food store.

12. Budget-watchers should shop at garage sales, flea markets, etc., for kitchen utensils and pots and pans. Someone else's second-hand cast-iron utensils will be another person's treasures. Cast-iron frying pans and the like should be "seasoned" before using if they have not been taken care of properly in the past. This is done by scouring the utensil thoroughly, rinsing well, drying, and then greasing well with an unsalted oil. Heat the utensil in a hot oven for 20 to 30 minutes.

13. USDA "Good" meats are just as nutritious as "Choice" grades of meat. "Good" meats have less fat, therefore are less tender, but actually have more protein per weight than higher-priced grades. Many of the less tender, but less expensive, cuts of meat can be prepared very successfully by moist-cooking (braising, pressure-cooking, stewing, etc.) Meat that costs more per pound may actually cost less if it has little bone.

Book I Index

Book II

Meatless Meals
COOKBOOK

by Donna A. Paananen

CONTENTS

Book I   Budget Saving Meals Cookbook

Book II   Meatless Meals Cookbook

Book III   Ideals Family Cookbook

Photograph opposite:
Caponata, p. 9

Appetizers and Savory Snacks

MOM'S HOT OLIVE CHEESE PUFFS

Yield: 2 dozen

- 1 c. grated sharp Cheddar cheese
- 3 T. butter, softened
- ½ c. whole wheat pastry flour
- ¼ t. paprika
- ¼ t. salt
- 24 pimiento stuffed olives, well drained

Blend the cheese and butter together thoroughly. Sift flour with seasonings and add to cheese mixture. Combine thoroughly with pastry blender or fork. Drop dough onto waxed paper by teaspoonfuls. Wrap dough around each olive, covering completely. At this point you can freeze the wrapped olives (on a pan and when frozen, place in plastic bags), or bake immediately in a 400° oven on an ungreased baking sheet for 10 to 15 minutes or until lightly browned. Serve hot.

HERB SPREAD OR DIP

Yield: 2 cups

- 1¼ c. cottage cheese
- 1 6-oz. pkg. cream cheese (at room temperature), cut into chunks
- 2 T. chopped green onions
- 2 T. chopped parsley
- 2 T. chopped chives
- ⅛ t. thyme
- ¼ t. basil
- ¼ t. oregano
- ¼ c. plain yogurt (optional)
  Salt

Place cottage cheese and cream cheese into a blender. If mixture is too thick to blend, add yogurt. Add the rest of the ingredients and blend until mixture is smooth. Taste and add salt. Refrigerate several hours before serving. Goes well with Grandma's Onion and Poppy Seed Soda Crackers.

MARINATED MUSHROOMS AND CHICK-PEAS

Yield: 1⅔ cups

- 1 c. cooked chick-peas (garbanzo beans), drained
- ⅔ c. thinly sliced fresh mushrooms
- ¼ c. olive oil, or vegetable oil
- 2 T. cider vinegar
- 2 t. minced onion
- 1 t. basil
- 1 small garlic clove, minced
  Salt
  Freshly ground black pepper
  Parsley, minced (for garnish)

Place chick-peas and mushrooms into a small bowl. In a separate container, mix the rest of the ingredients, adding salt and pepper to taste. Pour marinade over chick-peas and mushrooms, tossing gently. Chill until serving time, tossing from time to time to marinate evenly. Serve garnished with a dusting of parsley.

CAROLYN'S GUACAMOLE

Yield: approximately 2/3 cup

- 1 ripe avocado, mashed
- 2 t. lime juice
  Onion salt
  Garlic salt
- 1 T. mayonnaise or sour cream

Mix all the ingredients together thoroughly; taste and correct seasonings. Add more mayonnaise if mixture doesn't "bind" well. Use as a dip with corn chips or as a sandwich spread.

SUNCHOKE STUFFED MUSHROOMS

Yield: 20 appetizers

20 large mushrooms, washed and patted dry
1 T. butter or margarine
¼ c. minced onion
1 large sunchoke (Jerusalem artichoke), scrubbed and grated
½ t. lemon juice
⅛ t. basil
⅛ t. oregano
Freshly ground black pepper
Salt
1 2-oz. pkg. feta cheese, mashed

Remove stems from caps of mushrooms. Chop stems and sauté them in butter with the onion and grated choke; add lemon juice. When onion begins to soften, add herbs; add salt and pepper to taste. Remove from heat. Meanwhile, rub butter onto each mushroom cap and place on lightly greased baking sheet. Preheat oven to 350°. Stuff each mushroom cap with choke mixture, top with mashed cheese, and bake 10 to 15 minutes or until mushrooms are cooked and cheese is melted. Serve immediately while hot.

ANTIPASTO

Choose from among the following to make an excellent, meatless antipasto:

Green or red pepper strips or circles
Olives
Mozzarella cheese cubes
Marinated garbanzo beans and mushrooms
Stuffed or plain celery ribs
Carrot sticks
Radish flowers
Caponata
Zucchini or patty pan squash circles (unpeeled)
Cucumber slices or sticks
Cauliflowerets
Cherry tomatoes
Pickled hot peppers
Hard-boiled egg slices or deviled eggs

Arrange choices attractively on a tray or on individual dishes and serve before meal with bread, if desired.

SAMOSA (INDIAN "PASTY")

Yield: 2 dozen

2 c. whole wheat pastry flour, sifted
2 T. butter, melted
1 T. ground coriander
¾ t. salt
½ c. warm water
1 lb. (about 3 medium) potatoes
1½ c. fresh or frozen green peas
1 T. vegetable oil
1 c. minced onion
1 yellow chili, seeded and chopped (or 1 or 2 green chilies)
1 t. chopped fresh ginger
1 t. cumin seed
2 T. chopped coriander leaves
1 t. curry powder
1 T. lemon juice or dry mango powder
2 T. whole wheat pastry flour
¼ c. water
Vegetable oil for deep frying

Mix flour thoroughly with butter, coriander, and salt. Add warm water slowly until a stiff but smooth ball of dough forms. Turn out onto lightly floured board and knead for about 5 minutes. Cover with a damp cloth and let rest for about 30 minutes. Meanwhile, scrub and quarter potatoes. Place in steamer basket and steam 20 to 25 minutes. Add green peas and steam 5 minutes or until potatoes are tender. Cool. When potatoes are cool enough, cut into small cubes. Sauté onion in a large skillet in the vegetable oil for about 2 minutes. Add the chili, all the seasonings, the potatoes, and the peas and cook about 5 minutes, stirring regularly. Let cool. Divide dough into twelve equal parts; shape into twelve balls. Roll into circles as thin as possible on lightly floured board with floured rolling pin. Cut circles in half. Divide filling among semi-circles, placing filling in the center. Brush edges of the semi-circles with the 2 tablespoons pastry flour mixed with ¼ cup water and seal carefully. Samosas should be shaped like quarter circles and have no loose edges. Heat vegetable oil to 360° for deep frying; fry samosas until golden. Drain on paper towels and serve immediately. Yogurt with fresh mint chopped into it is a good accompaniment.

LYNN'S CURRY-CHEESE CRACKERS

Yield: 30 crackers

1 c. whole wheat pastry flour
¼ t. salt
¼ t. dry mustard
¾ t. curry powder
Dash of cayenne pepper
⅓ c. butter or margarine
½ c. grated sharp Cheddar cheese
1 egg, beaten
1 T. cold milk

Preheat oven to 400°. Combine first five ingredients. Cut in butter with a pastry blender until mixture resembles fine crumbs. Stir in cheese, egg, and milk. When mixture holds together, turn out onto floured board and roll to 1/16-inch thickness. Cut with floured 2-inch round cookie cutter; place on lightly greased baking sheets, and bake 6 to 8 minutes or until golden. Remove immediately to wire racks to cool. Store in airtight containers.

GRANDMA'S ONION AND POPPY SEED SODA CRACKERS

Yield: Approximately 7 dozen small crackers

3 c. whole wheat pastry flour
½ c. butter or margarine, chilled
½ c. minced onion
½ c. poppy seed
1 t. baking soda
¼ c. water
1 t. salt
2 t. cream of tartar
¼ c. cold milk (approximately)

Cut butter into flour with a pastry blender until mixture resembles crumbs. Add onion and poppy seed and mix well. Dissolve baking soda in water. Add soda mixture and remaining ingredients in order listed, stirring to form a dough. Turn out onto lightly floured surface. Preheat oven to 400°. Knead well for about 10 minutes. Roll out to ⅛-inch thick on a lightly floured surface with lightly floured rolling pin; cut with cookie cutters to desired shapes (or into squares or rectangles). Place on well-greased baking sheets, prick with fork if desired, and bake 6 to 8 minutes or until lightly browned. Remove from tins and let cool on wire racks. Store in tightly covered tins.

STUFFED CELERY

Yield: 12 to 15 celery ribs

12 to 15 celery ribs, washed
Paprika (optional)

Trim end pieces of celery ribs, mince, and set aside. Add minced celery end pieces to stuffing. Smooth cheese stuffing into celery ribs; garnish with paprika, if desired. Cover and chill or serve immediately.

CHEDDAR CHEESE STUFFING

4 oz. Cheddar cheese, grated
4 oz. softened cream cheese
1 t. prepared mustard
Dash of hot bottled pepper sauce

Combine all ingredients, mixing well.

ROQUEFORT STUFFING

1 4-oz. pkg. Roquefort or blue cheese
4 oz. softened cream cheese
1 t. Worcestershire sauce

Combine all ingredients, mixing well.

CHILI BEAN DIP

Yield: 2 cups

2 c. cooked kidney beans, drained, save juice
4 t. tomato juice
1 T. cider vinegar
1 t. Worcestershire sauce
2 or 3 garlic cloves
2 t. chili powder (to taste)
Dash of cayenne pepper or liquid red pepper sauce
⅓ c. cubed Cheddar cheese
Salt
Freshly ground black pepper
Chives (for garnish)

Place first seven ingredients into blender; cover and blend on high until smooth. Add bean cooking juice if mixture is too thick. Add cheese; blend until smooth. Taste and add seasonings. Pour into the top of a double boiler or a very heavy saucepan and heat until hot (or bake in a 350° oven for 15 to 20 minutes or until thoroughly heated through). Sprinkle chives on top. Serve with corn chips, vegetables, pita bread, etc.

Photograph opposite: Chili Bean Dip

SESAME AND/OR CELERY CRACKERS

Yield: Approximately 6 dozen

¾ c. sesame seed (*or* twice as many if you're making sesame crackers only)
½ t. (or more) celery seed
3½ c. pastry flour, sifted
1 c. (2 sticks) margarine or butter
1½ t. salt
½ c. ice water

Toast sesame seed in a heavy frying pan over low heat, stirring regularly, until they are lightly browned. Let cool. Meanwhile, cut margarine into flour with a pastry blender or fork until mixture resembles crumbs. Add salt. Divide mixture in half if you're making both kinds of crackers. To half of the mixture add the cooled sesame seeds; to the other half add the celery seeds. Slowly stir in ¼ cup ice water to each half until dough is thoroughly moistened and will form a ball. Cover and chill for about 30 minutes. Preheat oven to 400°. Lightly dust two 11 x 7-inch baking sheets with flour. With a well-floured rolling pin, roll out dough directly onto baking sheets. (To get dough into corners evenly, use a floured drinking glass.) Patch if necessary and make certain dough is even from one end of baking sheet to the other. Cut dough into triangles, rectangles, or 2-inch squares. Prick dough with a fork. Bake 10 to 12 minutes or until crackers are lightly browned. Remove from baking sheets immediately, and allow to cool on wire racks. Store in tightly covered tins.

WHOLE WHEAT WALNUT BREAD WITH WALNUT CHEESE SPREAD

Yield: 2 loaves bread and approximately 1 lb. cheese spread

WHOLE WHEAT WALNUT BREAD

1 pkg. active dry yeast
¼ c. lukewarm water
2 c. cooled scalded milk
2 T. butter, melted
2 T. honey
2 t. salt
6 c. whole wheat flour
Butter
1 c. whole walnuts

Sprinkle yeast on water in a large mixing bowl and stir until yeast is dissolved. Add milk, butter, honey, salt, and 1 cup flour. Stir thoroughly until well blended. Stir in 3 more cups of flour, one at a time, mixing thoroughly after each addition. Add the fifth cup of flour, beating until mixture is stiff. Sprinkle a board with the last cup of flour and knead dough with floured hands until dough is smooth (about 10 minutes). Don't underknead. Place dough in a well-buttered bowl, turn once, cover, and let rise in a warm place (85°) until two fingers inserted in dough leave an indentation. Punch down, work in the walnuts. Shape into two round loaves and let rise until doubled in bulk on a well-greased baking sheet (for about 1 hour). Bake in a 375° oven for about 45 minutes or until done. Let cool on wire racks.

WALNUT CHEESE SPREAD

(make at least 1 day in advance)

1 4-oz. pkg. Brie, softened
1 4-oz. pkg. Camembert, softened
1 4-oz. pkg. Liederkranz, at room temperature
4 oz. cream cheese, softened
2 to 3 T. kirsch or cherry liqueur
½ c. whole walnuts, toasted in a frying pan

Beat the cheeses together until smooth; add kirsch and continue beating until well blended. Stir in walnuts. Let ripen 24 hours before serving with Walnut Bread.

CAPONATA
(EGGPLANT APPETIZER)

Yield: 8 ample servings

½ c. olive oil, *or* ¼ c. olive and
    ¼ c. vegetable oil
6 c. (1 large) eggplant, washed and cubed
1 c. diced celery
2 c. chopped onion
1 large garlic clove, minced
2 c. tomato sauce
¼ c. red wine vinegar
1 T. honey
2 T. capers, drained
⅔ c. stuffed olives, drained
    Freshly ground black pepper
    Salt

Heat oil over medium heat in a large skillet; sauté eggplant until golden and tender. Remove with slotted spoon. Add more oil if necessary. Stir in celery, onion, and garlic and sauté until tender and golden. Stir in tomato sauce and eggplant. Simmer, covered, for 10 minutes. Add remaining ingredients, except salt. Simmer, covered, 15 minutes or until mixture is thick and well done. Stir occasionally. Taste, add salt, and correct seasonings. Cool and then chill, covered, at least 4 hours, preferably overnight. Can be frozen or kept for several days in the refrigerator. Serve cold with toast rounds, crusty bread, or crisp crackers.

RYE BREAD STICKS

Yield: 4 dozen

2 pkgs. active dry yeast
2½ c. warm water
¼ c. brown sugar, well-packed
½ c. soft margarine
1 t. salt
4 c. sifted medium rye flour
2 T. caraway seed
4 c. whole wheat flour (approximately)
1 egg yolk beaten with 1 T. milk
    Caraway seed

Sprinkle yeast on warm water in a large mixing bowl; add brown sugar and stir until yeast is dissolved. Add all ingredients except whole wheat flour and egg yolk mixture and beat until smooth. Cover and let rise in a warm place (85°) about 45 minutes. Stir in whole wheat flour slowly; then turn dough out onto lightly floured board and knead until smooth (about 10 minutes). Divide dough into quarters; cut each quarter into 12 equal pieces. Shape each piece into a stick about 6 inches long. Place about 2 inches apart on greased baking sheets. Cover with towels and let rise in a warm place about 30 minutes or until doubled in bulk. Preheat oven to 400°. Brush sticks with egg yolk mixture and sprinkle with more caraway seeds as desired. Bake 15 minutes or until done. Remove from baking sheets and cool on wire racks. Store in airtight tins or freeze until needed.

Note: For thinner bread sticks, divide each quarter into more than 12 pieces. To make a rye "party loaf," divide the dough into fewer pieces. You must have similar sized "sticks" on the same baking sheet.

Soups and Stews

DIANE'S GAZPACHO

Yield: 8 to 10 servings

6 ripe tomatoes, blanched, peeled and chopped
1 large cucumber, deseeded, and chopped (peeled if necessary)
1 sweet green pepper, deseeded and chopped
1 sweet red pepper, deseeded and chopped
½ sweet onion, peeled and chopped
6 large garlic cloves, minced
1 small piece fresh chili pepper
1 c. (more or less to taste) tomato juice
½ c. olive or vegetable oil
2 t. salt
  Freshly grated black pepper

Thoroughly mix together all ingredients. Taste and correct seasonings. Serve ice cold.

WALKER-STALKER CREAM OF PARSLEY SOUP

Yield: 6 servings

2 c. chopped fresh parsley
½ c. chives (or onions), finely chopped
¼ c. butter or margarine
3 c. vegetable or garlic broth
1 c. water
2 T. whole wheat flour
2 c. milk
⅔ c. nonfat powdered milk
½ c. water
  Salt
  Freshly ground black pepper
⅔ c. freshly grated Parmesan cheese
⅔ c. grated Cheddar cheese
  Parsley

Place chives, parsley, butter, and broth in a large skillet or saucepan. Simmer until parsley is dark and limp (approximately 15 minutes). In a small bowl, stir water and flour together until a smooth paste is formed. Add to cooked parsley and stir until smooth and thickened. Add milk and powdered milk and continue stirring until smooth. (Add more water if too thick.) Salt and pepper to taste. Approximately 5 minutes before serving, add cheeses. Cook until cheeses are melted. Correct seasonings. Garnish with fresh parsley, if desired.

LENTIL SOUP

Yield: 6 to 8 servings

1¾ c. dried lentils, washed, drained, and picked over
6 c. vegetable cooking liquid or broth
2 T. butter or margarine
1 c. chopped onion
½ c. chopped celery
⅔ c. chopped carrot
¼ lb. soy "bacon" bits (optional)
2 to 3 large cloves garlic, minced
¼ c. chopped parsley
½ t. thyme
1 bay leaf
1 T. butter
  Lemon juice
  Salt
  Freshly ground black pepper
  Optional garnishes: hard-boiled eggs, parsley, or sour cream

In a large kettle, bring lentils and broth to a boil. Cover and turn off heat. Melt 2 tablespoons butter in a large frying pan and add onion, celery, carrot, "bacon" bits, garlic, parsley, thyme, and bay leaf. Cover and let simmer over low heat approximately 10 minutes. Add the vegetables to the lentil mixture and simmer covered for 1½ hours. Put mixture through a food mill or blender. Heat to serving temperature and stir in 1 tablespoon butter. Add lemon juice, salt, and pepper to taste. Garnish as desired.

Photograph opposite:
Diane's Gazpacho

FRENCH TOMATO SOUP

Yield: 4 to 6 servings

1 T. butter or margarine
2 c. chopped onion
2 T. soy "bacon" bits
5 to 6 ripe tomatoes, chopped
1 strip lemon peel
4 c. Vegetable or Garlic Broth (p. 12, 15)
¼ c. chopped parsley
1 sprig thyme or ⅛ t. dry thyme
2 basil leaves or ½ t. dry basil
Salt
Freshly ground black pepper
Parsley and basil, chopped
Whole wheat garlic croutons

In a very large frying pan, melt butter. Add onion and sauté 5 to 6 minutes or until tender. Add "bacon" bits, tomatoes, peel, broth, and herbs. Bring to a boil; cover, lower heat, and simmer for about 20 minutes or until tender. Put soup through blender, if small bits of tomato skin remain, through a sieve. Add salt and pepper to taste. Serve hot; garnish with parsley, basil, and croutons.

GARLIC BROTH

Yield: 6 to 8 servings

14 to 16 garlic cloves, peeled and chopped
2 qts. water or vegetable cooking liquid
2 whole cloves
½ bay leaf
2 T. minced parsley
1 leaf sage or ¼ t. dried sage
½ t. thyme or ¼ t. dried thyme
Freshly ground black pepper
Salt
⅔ c. grated Swiss, Parmesan or Romano cheese
Whole wheat bread rounds, toasted until dry

Place garlic, water, and next 5 ingredients into a large soup kettle; bring to a boil. Cover, lower heat, and let simmer for 30 minutes or until garlic is tender. Add pepper and salt to taste. Serve hot, garnished with toasted whole wheat bread rounds and grated cheese, or use this broth as the basis for other soups.

COLD LENTIL SOUP

Yield: 4 servings

1 c. chopped onion
2 T. vegetable oil
½ c. lentils, rounded
2½ c. Vegetable Broth (p. 15)
1 t. ground coriander
Freshly ground black pepper
Salt
½ c. chopped chive

Sauté onion in vegetable oil in a large frying pan or heavy bottomed pan. Stir in lentils; coat well with oil. Pour in Vegetable Broth; add coriander. Bring to a boil, turn down heat and let simmer, covered, for 1½ hours or until lentils are very tender. Add salt and pepper to taste during the last minutes of cooking. Put lentil mixture in blender or through sieve. When mixture is smooth, chill thoroughly. Serve very cold, garnished with chives.

BEAN AND SPLIT PEA SOUP

Yield: 6 to 8 servings

2 c. navy beans, soaked overnight in 7 c. water
1 c. dry white wine
½ c. chopped celery
1 c. chopped onion
½ c. sliced carrot
¼ c. chopped parsley
2 large garlic cloves, chopped
1 whole clove
2 bay leaves
½ t. thyme
¼ t. ground allspice
1 c. green split peas
1 T. lemon juice
Freshly ground black pepper
Salt

Bring beans and soaking liquid to a boil in a large soup kettle (not aluminum). Add all the rest of the ingredients except lemon juice, pepper, and salt. Simmer 1½ hours; then add lemon juice, and salt and pepper to taste. Continue cooking until beans are tender. (If you do not wish to have the split peas disintegrate into the stock, put them into soup during the last hour of cooking.)

MINESTRONE

Yield: 8 ample servings

    2 qts. water or vegetable cooking liquid
 10 to 12 large garlic cloves, peeled and
       chopped
    1 c. chopped onion
    2 whole cloves
    1 leaf sage or ¼ t. dried sage
    ½ t. thyme or ¼ t. dried thyme
    ½ bay leaf
    6 parsley sprigs
    ¼ t. oregano or ⅛ t. dried oregano
    2 t. basil or 1 t. dried basil
    2 c. cubed potato
    2 c. sliced carrot
    6 ripe tomatoes, cut into sixths, or
       3 c. canned tomatoes with juice
    2 c. sliced zucchini
    ½ c. whole wheat shell macaroni
    ⅔ c. cooked kidney beans
       Freshly ground black pepper
       Salt
       Freshly grated Parmesan or Romano
       cheese

Heat water to boiling; add garlic cloves, onion, and seasonings except salt and pepper. Lower heat and let simmer for 30 minutes. Add potatoes, carrots, and ripe tomatoes, and simmer 15 minutes. Add zucchini, macaroni, and canned tomatoes; simmer until macaroni is just tender (15 to 20 minutes). Add kidney beans and heat thoroughly. Taste and add salt and pepper as desired. Serve immediately and garnish with Parmesan or Romano cheese.

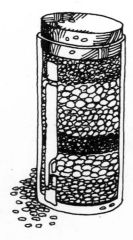

GREEK CABBAGE SOUP

Yield: 8 to 10 ample servings

    1 T. olive oil
    1 c. chopped onion
    1 to 2 large garlic cloves, chopped
    2 qts. water or vegetable cooking liquid
    1 bay leaf
    1 lb. tomatoes, chopped, or
       2 c. canned tomatoes and juice
    2 lbs. cabbage, shredded
    ½ t. freshly ground black pepper
 1½ t. salt
    2 T. minced parsley

Sauté the onion and garlic in oil in a Dutch oven for about 5 minutes. Add water and bring to a boil. Lower heat, add bay leaf, tomatoes, and cabbage. Simmer until cabbage is tender (45 minutes or more, as desired). Add salt and pepper in the last minutes of cooking. Serve hot; garnish with parsley.

RED AND BLACK-EYED BEAN SOUP

Yield: 6 servings

    6 c. water or vegetable cooking liquid
    1 c. dried kidney beans
    ½ c. dried black-eyed peas
    2 c. sliced onion
    2 garlic cloves, minced
    ½ t. thyme
    ½ t. marjoram
    1 c. cubed potato
    1 c. sliced carrot
    1 c. sliced celery
       Freshly ground black pepper
       Salt

Boil water in a large, heavy bottomed kettle; drop in kidney beans and black-eyed peas; let boil 2 minutes. Cover, turn off heat, and let stand for two hours. Stir in onion, garlic, thyme, and marjoram, and let simmer 1½ to 2 hours or until beans are just tender. Add potato, carrot, and celery (and tomato juice or more water if soup is too thick), and cook about 30 more minutes or until vegetables are tender. The last minutes of cooking, add salt and pepper to taste.

MOM'S VEGETABLE STEW

Yield: 3½ quarts

2½ qts. water
2 c. diced carrot
1 c. diced potato
1 c. sliced onion
1½ c. fresh or frozen green beans, cut
3 or 4 garlic cloves, minced
1 fresh or ½ c. canned tomato, chopped
3 T. fresh basil, chopped, or 1 T. dried basil
Freshly ground black pepper
1 to 2 t. salt
½ c. whole wheat spaghetti, broken, or elbow macaroni
1 c. pimiento-stuffed olives, halved
2 c. cooked kidney beans
½ c. freshly grated Parmesan cheese

Bring water to boil in a large soup kettle; add next eight ingredients. Lower heat, cover and cook 10 to 15 minutes or until vegetables are just tender. Stir in salt, spaghetti, and olives. Cook until spaghetti is just barely tender, stirring occasionally. Add kidney beans and heat until piping hot. Correct seasonings. Serve immediately and garnish with Parmesan cheese.

FAMOUS RECIPE VEGETABLE SOUP

Yield: 8 servings

8 c. water or vegetable cooking liquid
½ c. dried yellow split peas
½ c. dried green split peas
½ c. dried barley
½ c. dried baby lima beans
1 bay leaf
1 whole clove
4 large garlic cloves, minced
1 c. chopped onion
2 T. minced parsley
2 c. sliced fresh or frozen green beans
1 c. sliced carrot
Freshly ground black pepper
Salt
½ c. whole wheat egg noodles, pasta, or alphabet noodles

Photograph opposite:
Mom's Vegetable Stew

Heat water to boiling in a large, heavy soup kettle. Meanwhile, rinse and pick over dried legumes. Add all the ingredients except salt and noodles; turn down heat, simmer, covered, stirring occasionally. Add more water if you desire a thinner soup. When the soup has simmered an hour, taste; add salt as desired, then stir in noodles. Continue to simmer until ingredients are tender, 15 to 30 minutes longer. Taste and correct seasonings.
Note: Add chopped celery ribs, fresh or dried mushrooms, chopped potatoes, leeks, tomatoes, or whatever you have on hand.

VEGETABLE BROTH

Yield: About 2 quarts

2 T. margarine or vegetable oil
1 c. chopped onion
2 to 3 large garlic cloves, chopped
2 qts. water or vegetable cooking liquid
1 c. sliced carrot
1 c. chopped celery
½ c. chopped turnip (optional)
½ c. chopped parsnips
1 c. shredded lettuce, chard, collards, or other greens
4 sprigs parsley
½ bay leaf
½ t. thyme
¼ t. marjoram
⅛ t. white pepper
⅛ t. cayenne
Salt

Heat margarine in a Dutch oven; add onion and garlic and sauté about 5 minutes. Add water, bring to boil; lower heat and add all the ingredients except salt. Let simmer 1½ hours; taste, add salt, correct seasonings, and continue cooking up to one half hour more or until all the ingredients are very tender. Strain the broth and use it as the basis for other soups or dishes. (Strained broth can be frozen for later use.)
Note: You can add any other vegetables or their parings to this broth—potato skins, green peppers, leeks—whatever you have on hand will add to the flavor.

CAROLYN'S SCANDINAVIAN FRUIT SOUP

Yield: 10 to 12 servings

½ lb. raisins
½ c. dried apricots, well-packed
½ lb. pitted prunes
3 qts. water
2 apples, sliced
1 orange, sliced
1 stick of cinnamon
1 1-lb. can dark, pitted cherries (including juice)
1 c. canned peaches with juice
Any other fruits or juices on hand
2 to 3 T. tapioca

Soak raisins, apricots, and prunes in water overnight; pour into heavy-bottomed cooking pan. Add remaining ingredients and simmer, covered, 1½ hours or until well-flavored. Chill and serve cold. Can be made several days in advance and kept refrigerated until serving time.

BLACK BEAN SOUP

Yield: 6 servings

3 T. margarine or butter
1 c. chopped onion
4 garlic cloves
2 c. black beans, soaked overnight in 6 c. water or vegetable cooking liquid
½ c. chopped celery (with leaves)
6 sprigs parsley
½ c. chopped carrot
1 bay leaf
Freshly ground black pepper
Salt

Melt margarine in a heavy soup kettle or Dutch oven. Add onion and garlic; sauté until onion is transparent. Stir in rest of ingredients in order except salt. Add salt the last 30 minutes of cooking. Cook 2 to 3 hours or until beans are tender (depends upon type and age of black beans). Put through sieve or blend in blender, if desired. Heat to serve and garnish with hard-boiled egg slices, soy "bacon" bits, or minced onion.

AVGOLEMONO SOUP
(Greek egg and lemon soup)

Yield: 8 servings

8 c. well-flavored Vegetable Broth (p. 15)
1¼ c. brown rice, washed and picked over
Freshly ground black pepper
Salt
2 whole eggs
2 to 4 T. fresh lemon juice
4 T. chopped parsley or chives

Bring vegetable broth to a boil; add rice, cover and simmer until rice is tender (45 to 50 minutes). Taste; add pepper and salt; remove from heat. Beat eggs well and add lemon juice; continue beating. Take a ladleful of soup; stir it into the egg mixture. Beat thoroughly. Pour the egg mixture into the soup slowly, stirring constantly. Reheat soup and cook until it thickens. *Do not let the soup boil or the eggs will curdle.* Taste and correct seasonings. Garnish with parsley or chives and serve immediately.

CARROT SOUP

Yield: 8 servings

3 T. margarine or butter
4 c. sliced carrot
1 c. sliced onion
⅛ t. thyme
8 c. Vegetable or Garlic Broth (p. 12, 15)
⅓ c. brown rice
Salt
Freshly ground black pepper
2 T. thinly sliced margarine or butter

Melt 3 tablespoons margarine in a large, heavy bottomed pan or Dutch oven over low heat. Stir in carrot, onion, thyme, and pepper. Cover and let cook about 10 minutes, stirring occasionally. Add broth; simmer mixture and add rice. Let cook until rice is tender (45 to 50 minutes). Put mixture in blender or through a sieve. When mixture is smooth, add salt and pepper to taste. Bring the soup to serving temperature, stir in 2 tablespoons butter and serve immediately.

Sandwiches

TOFU, OLIVE, AND SPROUT SANDWICHES

Yield: 4 sandwiches

1 c. tofu
1 small garlic clove, minced
3 T. raw wheat germ
3 green onions, chopped
1 rib celery, chopped
¾ t. minced fresh basil
¾ t. minced fresh rosemary
½ t. minced fresh fennel
¾ t. minced fresh oregano
1 T. mayonnaise
8 pimiento stuffed olives, chopped
  Dash of freshly ground black pepper
8 slices bread or toast
  Margarine or butter
½ t. chili powder (optional)
1 c. alfalfa sprouts, packed down

Mash tofu and mix in remaining ingredients in order up to bread. When thoroughly blended, taste and correct seasonings. Butter 4 slices of bread, sprinkle with chili powder, if desired. Divide spread among unbuttered bread slices; top with alfalfa sprouts, and assemble sandwiches.

LENTIL TOSTADAS

Yield: 6 servings

1½ c. dried lentils, washed and sorted
  3 c. water or vegetable cooking liquid
  1 bay leaf
½ c. chopped onion
  1 small whole clove
  1 T. chopped parsley
⅛ t. dried thyme
  1 large garlic clove, minced
1½ t. chili powder
⅛ t. ground cumin

  Dash of freshly ground black pepper
  Salt
6 tortillas

In a large, heavy kettle combine all ingredients except salt and tortillas. Cover and quickly bring to a boil. Reduce heat; simmer, covered, until lentils are tender, approximately 1 hour. Remove clove and bay leaf and mash lentil mixture thoroughly by hand or in blender. When completely blended, taste and correct seasonings. Sauté tortillas briefly in a small amount of oil; drain on paper towels or heat in oven. Keep warm until ready to serve. Top with lentil mixture; garnish as desired.

Note: May garnish with shredded lettuce or spinach; chopped tomato, chopped chive or green onion; Guacamole, or avocado slices, and grated Chedder cheese or yogurt.

CAROLYN'S GOLDEN TEMPLE SANDWICH

Yield: 4 open-faced sandwiches

4 slices bread, toasted on one side
4 large slices Mozzarella, sharp Cheddar, Muenster, or other cheese
  Minced onion
½ c. sliced fresh mushroom
½ c. chopped tomato
  Guacamole (p. 4)
1 to 2 c. alfalfa sprouts

Layer cheese slices on untoasted side of bread; add onion to taste, mushroom, and tomato. Place under broiler and grill until cheese melts. Immediately top with Guacamole and alfalfa sprouts. Serve.

BEAN TOSTADA

Yield: 6 servings

- 4 c. water or vegetable cooking liquid
- 2 c. dry pinto beans
- 2 c. chopped onion
- 2 garlic cloves, minced
- 1 yellow hot pepper or 2 small green, chopped
- ½ t. crushed hot red peppers (dry)
- ½ t. sweet red pepper flakes
- 4 T. fresh oregano *or* 2 T. dried
- 1 T. ground coriander seed
- 1 T. cumin seed
- 1 t. paprika
- ⅛ t. cayenne pepper
- 4 large ripe tomatoes, chopped *or* 2 c. canned tomato
  Dash of freshly ground black pepper
- 1½ t. salt
- 6 stone ground corn tortillas

Bring water to boil; add beans, cover and cook for two minutes. Turn off heat and let stand for two hours. Add remaining ingredients except salt and simmer 2 to 3 hours or until beans are tender. Add salt the last 15 to 20 minutes. Taste and correct seasonings. Just before serving, heat tortillas in oven or sauté briefly in a small amount of oil and drain on paper towels. Keep warm until ready to serve. Spoon bean mixture on top of tortillas. Garnish with shredded lettuce, chopped tomatoes, grated Cheddar or Monterey Jack cheese or yogurt.
Note: Use as pita filling or on whole wheat bread or toast.

VEGETARIAN SUBMARINE

Yield: 1 large submarine sandwich

- 1 large whole wheat submarine sandwich roll, sliced lengthwise
- 3 to 4 large cheese slices
- ¾ c. hot, sautéed mushroom and onion
  Shredded lettuce
- 1 tomato, sliced
  Pickle and raw onion slices, if desired

Place cheese on bottom half of roll and place under broiler until cheese melts. Top with sautéed mushroom and onion, lettuce, tomato slices, pickles, and raw onion. Replace top of roll; slice into individual servings. (May broil top part of roll in aluminum foil while melting cheese on bottom half.) Serve hot.

AVOCADO 'N EGG SANDWICHES

Yield: 4 sandwiches

- 8 thin slices whole wheat bread
  Butter or margarine
- 1 ripe avocado
- 4 hard-boiled eggs, chilled
- ½ c. mayonnaise, chilled
  Dash of freshly ground black pepper
  Dash of salt
  Crisp lettuce

Spread small amount of butter on bread slices. With a fork or pastry blender, mash eggs and avocado together. Add mayonnaise and pepper. Taste and add salt. (If making ahead, add lemon juice to prevent avocado from discoloring.) Spread mixture on half the buttered bread; add lettuce and assemble sandwiches.
Note: Alfalfa sprouts may be substituted for the lettuce.

TOFU SALAD SANDWICH

Yield: 4 sandwiches

- 1 c. tofu
- 1 small garlic clove, minced
- 3 T. raw wheat germ
- 1 T. chopped parsley
- ¼ t. turmeric
- ¼ t. dry mustard
- ¼ t. celery seed
- ½ t. chopped fresh oregano
- ½ t. chopped sweet basil
- ½ t. crushed dill weed
- 1 T. mayonnaise
- 4 green onions, chopped
- 2 ribs celery, chopped
- ¼ t. paprika
  Dash of freshly ground black pepper
  Dash of salt
- 8 slices toast or bread
  Margarine or butter
- 1 c. alfalfa sprouts, packed down

Mash tofu thoroughly. Mix in remaining ingredients in order up to the bread, until spread is well-blended. Taste and correct seasonings. May be chilled until serving time. Butter four slices of toast; spread tofu mixture on unbuttered slices; top with alfalfa sprouts. Assemble sandwiches.

Photograph opposite:
Bean Tostada

Breads and Breakfasts

SIX-LOAVES-AT-A-TIME PROTEIN BREAD

Yield: Six 1½-pound loaves

- 6 pkgs. dry yeast
- 6 c. lukewarm milk
- ¾ c. honey
- 3 eggs, beaten
- ¾ c. soy flour, sifted
- 2 c. non-instant powdered milk
- ¾ c. raw wheat germ
- ⅓ c. nutritional yeast
- 2 T. salt
- 12 to 15 c. (nearly 4 lbs.) whole wheat flour or graham flour
  Vegetable oil

In a very large container, mix together yeast, milk, and honey. Let stand in a warm place for 5 minutes. Stir in eggs and remaining ingredients, adding only 3 cups of whole wheat flour at this time. Beat thoroughly. Stir in additional flour until a soft dough is formed. Turn dough out onto a well-floured, large surface, and knead until smooth (this may take up to 15 minutes). Place dough in a large, well-greased container. Cover with damp towel and let rise in a warm place (85°) until doubled in bulk, one hour or more. Punch down, let rest for 10 minutes, covered. Divide dough into six loaves and place in well-greased tins, large juice or coffee cans, or directly on baking sheets. Cover loaves with damp towels and let rise again in a warm place about 45 minutes or until doubled in bulk. Bake in a 350° oven 45 minutes to 1 hour, or until done. Remove immediately from pans and place on wire racks to cool. Brush top crust with butter if softer crust is desired.

PITA OR POCKET BREAD

Make above recipe. Take out as much dough as you like, divide it into balls approximately 2 inches in diameter. On a lightly floured surface, roll out each ball with a lightly floured rolling pin, forming rounds about ¼ inch thick. Sprinkle lightly with flour, cover with a cloth, let rise. Preheat oven to 450°. Lightly oil baking sheets as needed and place in oven to heat. When bread rounds have risen, slip them gently onto baking sheets, sprinkle tops with cold water, and bake for 6 to 10 minutes. Bread is done if it sounds hollow when tapped. Remove from baking sheets immediately and place on wire racks to cool.

DINNER ROLLS

From Six-Loaves-At-A-Time dough, set aside desired amount of dough, roll out about 1/3 inch thick, and brush with melted butter. Cut out with round cutter. Crease center with a knife. Fold in half, place on greased baking sheet and let rise. Bake in a 350° oven for about 20 minutes. "Cloverleaf" rolls can be made by dividing desired amount of dough into small balls and placing 3 or 4 balls in each cup of well-greased muffin tins. Let rise and bake in a 350° oven for about 20 minutes.

PIZZA

Make Six-Loaves-At-A-Time recipe. After the dough has risen the first time, take out enough to spread onto a well-greased pizza pan or baking sheet. Brush top of the dough with vegetable oil. Fill as desired with your favorite tomato sauce (consider adding mashed tofu, soy "beef" bit, and/or minced onions and garlic to your sauce). Spread plenty of grated mozzarella or other cheese on top, add chopped green peppers, mushrooms, sliced olives, etc., and sprinkle oregano and/or freshly grated Parmesan cheese over the entire surface. Bake in a 425° oven for approximately 25 minutes or until done.

SOURDOUGH HI-PROTEIN BREAD

Yield: 2 Loaves

STARTER

2 c. lukewarm water
1 pkg. active dry yeast
2 c. whole wheat flour

Place water in a glass mixing bowl. Sprinkle with yeast and stir with a wooden spoon until yeast is dissolved. Add flour and beat until smooth. Cover with a towel and let stand in a warm place (85°) for 48 hours. Stir once or twice a day with a wooden spoon. Remove enough dough for the recipe; stir equal amounts of flour and water (usually 1 cup flour and 1 cup lukewarm water) into the starter. Let ferment about 5 hours, then cover and refrigerate in a clean, wide-mouthed glass container. (Do not put cover on tightly; the jar might crack during fermentation.) Used regularly and replenished about once a week, sourdough starter can be kept indefinitely. Separation of the starter is normal; just stir with a wooden spoon thoroughly before using.

This sourdough method allows you to let your starter grow. Every few days, let the mixture return to room temperature and add equal parts water and flour; let it ferment, then return to refrigerator. If you have a large amount of sourdough starter on hand, you can make double or even triple-sized recipes. For a different flavor, experiment with rye and oat flours.

Note: Always have starter at room temperature before using in a recipe.

SOURDOUGH BREAD

1¼ c. lukewarm milk
1 pkg. active dry yeast
3 T. honey
2 t. salt
1½ c. Sourdough Starter (at room
    temperature)
¼ c. soy flour, sifted
¼ c. nutritional yeast
¼ c. non-instant powdered milk
½ c. raw wheat germ
4½ c. (approximately) whole wheat flour

Pour milk into a large mixing bowl; sprinkle yeast on top. In order given, stir in remaining ingredients except whole wheat flour. When thoroughly mixed, add flour; dough will be soft. Cover with a cloth and let rise in a warm place (85°) for one hour or until doubled in bulk. Turn dough out on heavily floured surface and knead 10 minutes or until smooth, adding flour as necessary. Shape into loaves and place in two well-greased 9 x 5-inch loaf tins. Cover and allow to rise again in a warm place 45 minutes or until almost doubled in size. Place loaves in a 350° oven and bake 35 minutes or until done. Remove bread from tins to cool on wire racks. Brush tops of loaves with butter if soft crust is desired.

Note: This recipe can be used to make pita bread or dinner rolls; see variations under "Six-Loaves-At-A-Time Protein Bread."

BAKED WHOLE WHEAT DOUGHNUTS

Yield: 2 dozen or more

2 pkgs. active dry yeast
¼ c. lukewarm water
1½ c. lukewarm milk
⅓ c. honey
¼ t. cinnamon
1 t. nutmeg
1 t. salt
2 eggs
½ c. shortening or margarine
¼ c. soy flour
1 T. nutritional yeast
¼ c. wheat germ
4 to 5 c. whole wheat flour
Melted butter or margarine

In a large mixing bowl, dissolve yeast in warm water. Add milk, honey, spices, salt, eggs, shortening, soy flour, yeast, wheat germ, and 1½ cups of the flour. Blend 30 seconds on low speed, scraping bowl constantly. Beat 2 minutes at medium speed. Stir in remaining flour until soft dough is formed. When well mixed, cover; let rise in a warm place until double, 50 to 60 minutes. Turn dough out onto well-floured, cloth-covered board. Roll gently with well-floured rolling pin until dough is ½ inch thick. Cut with floured doughnut cutter. Put leftover scraps together and continue making doughnuts until all dough has been used. Place doughnuts on well-greased baking tins, brush with melted butter. Cover. Let rise in a warm place about 20 minutes or until double. Preheat oven to 425°. Bake 8 to 10 minutes or until golden. Immediately brush with melted butter and shake in brown cinnamon sugar or icing sugar or serve plain.

PARATHA

Yield: 8 to 10 parathas

Fried, whole wheat bread from India

2 c. whole wheat flour
½ t. salt
2 T. ghee (clarified butter)*
Cold water
Additional melted ghee

Sift the flour and salt together into a large mixing bowl. Work in the butter with fingertips until mixture resembles coarse meal. Pour ⅓ cup water over the mixture; mix well. Add more water slowly until a workable dough is formed. Knead well on a lightly floured surface (10 to 15 minutes). Gather dough up into a ball, place in a bowl and cover. Set aside 1 hour. Knead again. Shape into 8 to 10 balls. Roll each ball into a 6 or 7-inch round. Brush top lightly with melted ghee. Fold round in half and brush again. Fold once more into a rough triangle shape, roll lightly with rolling pin. (You can set them aside up to 4 hours at room temperature, covered with a damp towel, before frying.) Heat a large griddle or skillet and lightly brush with ghee. Fry parathas on both sides, continously brushing with butter, until golden, crisp, and flaky. Serve warm as they are or make a sandwich with them. They may be cooked ahead and reheated in an ungreased pan for a short time on each side.

*To clarify butter (ghee), melt butter in a saucepan over medium heat, skimming off foam constantly. Remove from heat and strain the clear liquid. Discard the residue in the bottom of the pan. Can be made ahead and stored in the refrigerator.

DATE NUT BREAD

Yield: 1 loaf

1¼ c. boiling water
2 c. cut-up dates
½ c. old-fashioned molasses
⅓ c. honey
1 T. melted butter
1 egg
1 t. vanilla
2½ t. baking powder
2¾ c. whole wheat pastry flour
½ t. salt
¼ c. raw wheat germ
¼ c. non-instant powdered milk
1 c. chopped nuts

Mix boiling water and dates together in a large mixing bowl; let stand until lukewarm. Preheat oven to 350°. Add molasses, honey, butter, egg, and vanilla to dates. In a separate bowl, mix all dry ingredients except nuts. Combine with date mixture and blend thoroughly. Stir in nuts. Pour into greased bread pan and bake for about an hour or until top springs back when lightly pressed.

WHOLE WHEAT CRUMPETS

Yield: 12 crumpets

½ c. milk
½ c. boiling water
1 ⅝-oz. cake yeast
1 t. honey
¾ t. salt
1¾ c. sifted whole wheat pastry flour
2 t. baking powder
3 T. hot tap water
½ c. raisins or chopped apples (optional)
½ t. cinnamon (optional)
4 or more tuna fish (or similar type) cans with tops and bottoms removed, and washed well

Mix milk and boiling water together in a large mixing bowl. Cool to lukewarm (90°). Stir in yeast and honey and let stand in warm place for 10 minutes. Stir in salt and flour. Mix well, cover with a towel, and let rise in a warm place (84° - 86°) until very bubbly and almost doubled in bulk (about 30 to 40 minutes). Mix baking powder with the hot tap water. Stir into batter and let rise again, covered, in a warm place until doubled in bulk (about 30 minutes).

Heat a lightly greased griddle or very large skillet until a drop of water jumps when sprinkled on it. Place as many lightly greased tuna fish can rings on the griddle as you have and spread small amount of batter evenly into the bottom of them. Cook *slowly* until brown on bottom and dry on top. Remove rings. Turn and let brown quickly on the other side. Repeat until all batter is used up. To serve, split with a fork; then toast. (For best results place under broiler, uncooked sides up.) Eat while hot.

Photograph opposite:
Date Nut Bread

MRS. ROGERS' OATMEAL BREAD
Yield: 3 loaves

2 c. rolled oats
4 c. boiling water
1 c. sorghum or molasses
1 T. margarine
1 T. salt
1 pkg. dry yeast
¾ c. warm water
1 T. honey
1 c. raw wheat germ
½ c. soy flour, sifted
7 c. (approximately) whole wheat flour
½ c. bran
¼ c. nutritional yeast

Place oats in a large bowl; pour boiling water over and add sorghum, margarine, and salt. Set aside to cool. In a small bowl, combine yeast, warm water, and honey. When oat mixture is cool, stir in wheat germ, flours, bran, nutritional yeast, and yeast mixture; blend thoroughly. Dough will be soft. Cover with a towel and place in a warm place overnight. The next morning, stir the dough down. Place on a well-floured surface, adding flour as necessary, and knead ten minutes or until smooth. Form dough into 3 loaves on a well-floured surface and place into three well-greased 8½ x 4½ x 2⅝-inch loaf pans. Let rise again. Bake 35 minutes in a 350° oven. Remove immediately and cool on wire racks.

RYE POPOVERS
Yield: 1 dozen

¾ c. medium rye flour
¾ c. whole wheat pastry flour
¼ t. salt
2 eggs, well beaten
1 c. milk

Preheat oven to 450°. Sift dry ingredients together. Add eggs and milk to the flour mixture and make a smooth batter. Beat with electric mixer until batter is full of air bubbles. Meanwhile, grease two 6-cup muffin tins and place into oven to heat. Fill each cup 2/3 full. Bake 15 minutes; reduce heat to 350° and bake an additional 15 minutes until popovers are golden.
Note: If you wish a higher popover, substitute unbleached flour for the whole wheat flour.

GRANOLA
Yield: 9 to 10 cups

6 c. rolled oats
½ c. bran
2 c. raw wheat germ
1½ c. raw nuts and/or ground roasted, unsalted soybeans
¼ c. sesame seeds
½ c. soy flour, sifted
¼ c. nutritional yeast
½ c. honey
½ c. vegetable oil
1 t. salt
1 c. raisins
1 c. unsalted, roasted sunflower seeds

Preheat oven to 275°. Combine all ingredients except raisins and sunflower seeds; mix well. Spread evenly and not too thickly on two large baking sheets. Bake until golden (about 45 minutes), stirring approximately every 15 minutes. When cool, add raisins, seeds, and any optional ingredients of your choice. Store in tightly covered container in the refrigerator. Serve as a breakfast cereal with milk, yogurt, fruit, etc. or as an ingredient in cookies, breads, or snack items.

APRICOT-NUT BREAD
Yield: 1 loaf

1½ c. unbleached flour
1½ c. whole wheat flour
1 T. baking powder
¼ t. baking soda
1 t. salt
¼ c. margarine
1 c. milk
½ c. honey
¼ c. brown sugar
½ c. chopped walnuts
½ c. chopped dried apricots
2 T. raw wheat germ
2 T. chopped walnuts

Preheat oven to 350°. Sift dry ingredients together into a large mixing bowl. Melt margarine. Cool slightly and add milk, honey, and sugar. Stir milk mixture into dry ingredients. Stir ½ cup nuts and apricots into the batter. Spoon batter into a well-greased 9 x 5 x 3-inch loaf pan. Sprinkle wheat germ on top, then sprinkle with nuts. Bake for about an hour or until a toothpick inserted in the middle comes out clean. Let cool about 10 minutes before removing from pan. Finish cooling on wire rack.

WHOLE WHEAT BLINTZES

Yield: 6 to 8 servings

3 eggs
1 c. whole wheat pastry flour, sifted
¼ c. non-instant powdered milk
¼ c. raw wheat germ
1¼ c. milk
3 T. vegetable oil
Fresh strawberry sauce, bananas, yogurt, blueberries, etc. for topping

In a medium bowl, beat eggs lightly; mix dry ingredients together and combine with eggs until just blended. Add milk and oil. Cover and let rest in refrigerator for 45 minutes to one hour.

Heat a crepe pan or other 6 to 8-inch skillet. When a drop of water sprinkled onto pan bounces, grease lightly with small amount of butter. Pour small amount of batter into pan, moving it from side to side to cover bottom. Cook on only one side until top is set and underside is done. Drain on toweling and continue process until all batter is used.

Divide Filling among blintzes, placing in center of the browned side of the blintz. Fold blintz similarly to an envelope. Fold two opposite sides over filling, fold one end up and the other end down over all. In a large skillet, melt small amount of butter. Cook blintzes until golden with the folded side down, turn to brown the other side. Add more butter as needed. Keep warm until all are cooked. Serve immediately with desired topping.

FILLING

2 c. cottage cheese, drained dry
1 egg
2 T. honey
½ t. vanilla

In a large bowl mix together cottage cheese, egg, honey, and vanilla. Beat with an electric beater at high speed until smooth.

MIXED GRAIN CEREAL

Yield: Approximately 3¾ lbs.

1 lb. rolled oats
1 lb. flaked or rolled wheat
1 lb. rolled rye
½ lb. raw or toasted wheat germ
¼ lb. bran

Mix all ingredients together thoroughly and store in a tightly covered tin. Use as a breakfast cereal, adding raw or dried fruit, milk, honey, and/or yogurt; or use in cookie recipes that call for oatmeal.
Note: Nuts and any other grain that appeals to you can be added to or substituted for the above.

CELESTE'S CHEESE AND BEER BREAD

Yield: 2 loaves

1½ c. beer
⅔ c. water or vegetable cooking liquid
½ c. vegetable oil
6 c. (approximately) whole wheat flour or graham flour
½ c. brown sugar, well-packed
½ c. raw wheat germ
2 t. salt
2 pkgs. active dry yeast
1 egg
2 c. grated sharp Cheddar cheese

Heat beer, water, and oil in a small pan until very warm (about 120°). In a large bowl, combine beer mixture, 2½ cups flour, and remaining ingredients, except cheese. Beat thoroughly with electric mixer for about 2 minutes at medium speed. With a wooden spoon, stir in remaining flour until soft dough is formed. Turn out onto well-floured surface; knead until smooth (about 10 minutes). Place in a greased bowl; turn once. Cover with a towel and let rise in a warm place (about 85°) until doubled in size (1 hour or more).

Line two 9 x 5-inch loaf tins with aluminum foil; grease thoroughly. When dough has risen, punch down, divide in half, and flatten each half on well-floured surface. Pour 1 cup Cheddar cheese into the center of each flattened surface and roll up carefully into well-shaped loaves. Place in prepared tins. Cover and let rise again until doubled in size (45 to 60 minutes). Preheat oven to 350°. Bake loaves 40 to 50 minutes or until done. Remove from tins immediately and place on wire racks to cool. If soft crusts are desired, brush with melted butter.
Note: If you desire higher loaves, substitute some unbleached flour for the whole wheat flour.

MOM'S BRAN MUFFINS

Yield: 12 muffins

1¼ c. bran
¼ c. raw wheat germ
1 c. whole wheat flour
½ c. raisins
½ t. salt
1 t. baking soda
1 t. baking powder
¾ c. milk
⅓ c. honey
2 T. vegetable oil
1 egg, beaten

Preheat oven to 400°. Stir together first 7 dry ingredients and set aside. Mix together milk, honey, oil and egg. Add to dry ingredients and stir just until moistened. Spoon into well-greased muffin cups or paper liners and bake about 15 minutes or until done.

MRS. SCHULKE'S BASIC BUCKWHEAT PANCAKE MIX

BASIC MIX

Yield: About 6 cups starter

1½ c. buckwheat flour
1½ c. whole wheat pastry flour
⅓ c. nutritious yeast
1 c. soy flour
3 T. baking powder
1¼ c. raw wheat germ
2 t. salt
½ c. non-instant powdered milk

Thoroughly mix together all ingredients. Store in freezer or refrigerator.
Note: Whole wheat pastry flour can be substituted for buckwheat flour.

BUCKWHEAT PANCAKES

Yield: 12 Pancakes

1¼ c. sweet or sour milk
1 egg
2 T. vegetable oil
1½ c. Mrs. Schulke's Basic Buckwheat Pancake Mix

Combine liquid ingredients and add to pancake mix, stirring only until ingredients are blended. Spoon onto a lightly greased, hot griddle.

Photograph opposite:
Mom's Bran Muffins

PRUNEOLA

Yield: About 3 pounds

6 c. rolled oats or a mixture of grains
1 c. raw wheat germ
½ c. sesame seeds
1 c. chopped nuts
1 c. raw sunflower seeds
½ c. vegetable oil
⅓ c. honey
12 oz. pitted prunes, chopped

Preheat oven to 300°. Combine first five ingredients in a large bowl. Mix honey and vegetable oil together in a small pan and heat until just below a boil. Stir oil mixture into dry ingredients. Spread mixture very thinly on two very large flat baking pans or cookie sheets. Bake, stirring occasionally, for 25 minutes or until mixture is golden. Remove from pans into a large bowl and immediately stir in prunes. Let cool. Store in large container with tight cover. Eat as a cereal with milk, fruit, nuts, or yogurt added.

ZUCCHINI-BRAN BREAD

Yield: One 9 x 5-inch loaf or
Two 7 x 4-inch loaves

¼ c. soy flour
2 T. nutritional yeast
1½ c. bran
2⅔ c. whole wheat flour
1 T. baking powder
½ t. baking soda
1 t. salt
1½ t. cinnamon
¼ t. ginger
¾ c. honey
⅓ c. vegetable oil
½ c. milk
2 eggs, beaten
2 c. grated zucchini
¼ c. chopped nuts
½ c. raisins

Preheat oven to 325°. Stir first 9 dry ingredients together. In a separate bowl, stir together honey, oil, milk, and eggs. Add honey mixture to dry ingredients; stir in zucchini, nuts, and raisins. Pour into well-greased 9 x 5-inch loaf pan or two 7 x 4-inch pans and bake 60 minutes or until golden (less time for smaller loaves). Cool 10 minutes in pan and then turn out onto wire racks to finish cooling.

Main Dishes
American

GARDEN HARVEST CASSEROLE

Yield: 6 to 8 servings

1 c. sliced and unpeeled eggplant
1 c. thinly sliced carrots
1 c. sliced green beans
1 c. diced potatoes
2 medium tomatoes, quartered
1 small yellow squash, sliced
1 small zucchini, sliced
1 medium onion, sliced
½ c. chopped green pepper
½ c. chopped cabbage
3 cloves garlic, crushed
3 sprigs parsley, chopped
  Freshly ground black pepper
1 c. beef bouillon
⅓ c. vegetable oil
2 t. salt
¼ t. tarragon
½ bay leaf, crumpled

Mix vegetables together and place into a shallow baking dish (13 x 9 x 2 inch). Sprinkle parsley and grind pepper over all. At this point you can refrigerate until ready to bake. Preheat oven to 350°. Pour bouillon into a small saucepan; add oil, salt, tarragon, and bay leaf. Heat to boiling; correct seasonings. Pour over vegetables. Cover baking dish with aluminium foil; bake 1 to 1½ hours or until vegetables are just tender and are still colorful. Carefully stir vegetables occasionally; but to preserve color, don't lift cover off for very long.

Note: You can substitute other vegetables if they are in harvest and they appeal to you.

JACKIE'S STUFFED ACORN SQUASH

Yield: 4 servings

2 acorn squash
  Butter
1½ c. frozen peas
½ c. grated sharp Cheddar cheese
  Salt to taste
  Freshly ground black pepper to taste

Slice squash in half lengthwise; remove seeds and membrane. Place squash, cut side down, in a baking pan. Add about ½ inch water and bake in a 350° oven 45 minutes to 1 hour. When squash is just tender, turn and butter the inside. Divide peas among squash, sprinkle cheese on top, and salt and pepper to taste. Add more water, if necessary; cover with aluminum foil and heat through. Serve hot.

Note: May also add steamed pearl onions to the dish or use mixed vegetables, creamed chard or spinach, or whatever vegetable appeals.

LAYERED DINNER

Yield: 6 to 8 servings

1 c. sliced carrot
1 c. sliced potatoes
1 c. sliced celery
¾ c. brown rice
  Salt to taste
  Freshly ground black pepper to taste
1 c. sliced onion
3 c. canned tomatoes and juice
½ c. raw wheat germ

Preheat oven to 350°. Place layers as listed into a buttered 2-quart casserole. Salt and pepper the rice layer as desired. Sprinkle wheat germ on top. Cover with a tight-fitting cover or heavy foil; bake 2 hours or until vegetables are tender and rice is done. Add more juice, if necessary. Remove cover the last 10 minutes of baking to toast top, if desired.

LOUISIANA RED BEANS AND RICE

Yield: 6 servings

- 8 c. water or vegetable cooking liquid
- 2 c. (1-lb.) dried red kidney beans, rinsed and sorted
- 4 large cloves garlic
- 1 c. chopped onion
- ¼ c. soy "bacon" bits (optional)
  Freshly ground black pepper to taste
  Salt to taste
- 2 c. cooked brown rice

In a heavy bottomed kettle soak beans in 5 cups water overnight. Add another 3 cups water and the remaining ingredients, except salt. (Or bring beans to a boil in 8 cups water; boil 2 minutes and turn off heat. Cover and let sit for 2 hours; then proceed with the recipe.) Simmer beans slowly 3 to 4 hours or until beans are very tender and a thick sauce has formed. Add salt to taste in the last 20 minutes of cooking. Serve over hot brown rice.

STUFFED GREEN PEPPERS

Yield: 8 servings

- 4 green peppers
- 1 T. vegetable oil
- 1½ c. chopped onion
- 1 clove garlic, chopped
- 2 large ripe tomatoes, chopped
- 1½ c. cooked brown rice
- 1 t. chili powder
  Salt to taste
  Freshly ground black pepper to taste
- ¾ c. grated sharp Cheddar cheese

Slice peppers in half; remove stalks and seeds. Steam until just tender. Sauté onion and garlic in oil until onion is translucent. Add tomatoes; heat until mixture is well blended and tender. Mix with rice. Add seasonings to taste. Preheat oven to 375°. Place peppers in a lightly greased baking dish. Spoon mixture into pepper cases, sprinkle grated cheese on top. Cover and bake for 30 minutes or until cheese melts. If desired, put dish under broiler for a few minutes to brown slightly. Serve hot.

French

MAKE-AHEAD SOUFFLÉ

Yield: 6 servings

- 1 T. butter
- 2 to 3 shallots or 1 T. minced onion
- 1½ c. chopped spinach, chard, or broccoli
- 1 T. lemon juice
- 6 large eggs, separated
- 6 T. butter or margarine
- 6 T. whole wheat flour
- 1 t. salt
  Freshly ground black pepper
- 1½ c. milk
- ¼ c. instant powdered milk
  Freshly grated Parmesan cheese

Melt butter in heavy saucepan and add minced shallots. Cook about 3 minutes, stirring once or twice. Add vegetables and lemon juice and cook over low heat, stirring frequently until liquid has evaporated (about 10 minutes). Set aside. In heavy saucepan (or over boiling water in the top part of a double boiler), melt butter and blend in flour and seasonings thoroughly. Add milks all at once and cook, stirring constantly with a wire whisk, until mixture is smooth and thickened. Remove from heat; beat egg yolks until thick. Slowly stir yolks into milk mixture; stir in vegetables and set aside. With clean, dry beaters, beat egg whites until stiff but not dry. (They should hold soft peaks.) Gradually stir yolk mixture into whites, folding carefully with rubber scraper until well-blended. Butter soufflé dish lightly and sprinkle with Parmesan cheese. At this point the soufflé can be refrigerated for up to 8 hours or even frozen, unbaked. Preheat oven to 350°. Bake the soufflé, uncovered, for 45 minutes, or until puffed and golden brown. (Do not open oven door until time is up.) Allow longer cooking time if frozen.

JENNIFER'S CARROT FLAN

Yield: 8 servings

1 Double Pastry Crust (p. 60) (made in a 10-inch flan tin)
¾ lb. new carrots, scraped
1 to 3 T. honey
1 T. soft butter
1 2-inch piece of orange peel
3 eggs
1¼ c. carrot steaming liquid, cooled
½ c. non-instant powdered milk

Preheat oven to 400°. Place crust in oven for 10 minutes, prick bottom if bubbles form. When crust firms, remove from oven. Reduce heat to 375°. Meanwhile, using a steamer-rack and 2 cups water, steam carrots until tender. Put steamed carrots in blender; add remaining ingredients and blend until smooth. Taste and correct seasonings. Pour carrot mixture into flan crust; bake until just firm (30 to 40 minutes). Serve warm.

SPINACH-ONION-MUSHROOM CREPES

Yield: 10 crepes

2 T. butter or margarine
¾ c. chopped onion
1 8-oz. can mushrooms, sliced
1 10-oz. pkg. chopped spinach, steamed
2 c. milk
¼ t. salt
¼ c. non-instant powdered milk
2 T. butter
3 T. whole wheat flour
1 4-oz. pkg. Swiss cheese, grated
¼ c. raw wheat germ
⅓ c. Parmesan cheese
10 Whole Wheat Crepes (p. 33)

Sauté onion and mushrooms in butter until onion is tender. Stir in steamed spinach; make certain all liquid in the pan has evaporated. Turn off heat. Mix together milk, salt, and non-instant powdered milk in a heavy-bottomed saucepan. Heat almost to a boil. Meanwhile, melt butter in a heavy skillet, stir in flour, and cook for about 2 minutes, stirring constantly. Do not allow mixture to scorch. Add hot milk all at once; continue stirring with a wire whisk until sauce comes to a boil. Boil for about 1 minute, stirring constantly. Remove from

heat, taste and correct seasonings. Stir in Swiss cheese. Add ½ cup of Swiss cheese sauce into onion/spinach mixture stirring well. Preheat oven to 350°. Spoon layer of sauce over the bottom of an 11½ x 7½-inch baking dish. Divide filling among 10 crepes; roll each crepe. Place crepes, seam side down, close together in baking dish. Spoon remaining sauce over and sprinkle with wheat germ and Parmesan cheese. Cover with foil and bake about 40 minutes or until heated through. Uncover the last 10 minutes to brown top.

OMELET

Yield: 2 servings

3 eggs
1 T. milk
Dash of liquid red pepper sauce
¼ t. salt
1 T. butter or margarine

Beat all ingredients except butter with a whisk or rotary beater until foamy and "stringy." Heat a heavy, round-bottomed 9-inch omelet pan or skillet; when skillet is hot, a few drops of water will bounce off surface. Melt butter or margarine; coat to the top edge of the pan and quickly pour in egg mixture. "Scramble" the eggs for a moment, move omelet around to allow it to climb up the sides slightly and set. It should take only a minute to make an omelet. When it is ready, roll or fold it gently and turn out onto plate.

Note: If desired, add one or more of the following to the omelet, before cooking, during, or just before folding.

    Steamed asparagus
    Sautéed mushroom
    Sautéed zucchini
    Chopped chives and parsley
    Tender sorrel leaves
    Steamed baby Brussels sprouts
½ **c. grated Colby, Cheddar, or Swiss cheese**
    Diced green pepper
    Onion, minced
    Sautéed leeks, minced
    Steamed spinach or chard
    Any combination of minced, fresh herbs

Photograph opposite:
Jennifer's Carrot Flan

RATATOUILLE

Yield: 6 to 8 servings

2 cloves garlic, minced
1 c. thinly sliced onion
⅓ c. olive oil or a combination with
  vegetable oil
1 medium eggplant, peeled and diced
3 medium zucchini, sliced
2 green peppers, sliced
3 c. quartered tomatoes
1 t. oregano or ½ t. dried
1 t. sweet basil or ½ t. dried
  Salt to taste
  Freshly ground black pepper to taste

Sauté garlic and onion in oil over medium heat until transparent. In a large frying pan, Dutch oven, or casserole that can be used on top the stove, layer onion with the remaining ingredients, seasoning each layer with salt, pepper, and herbs. Cover and simmer 40 minutes or until vegetables are tender. If there is too much liquid, uncover and cook until it reduces. Serve hot or cold.

STUFFED CABBAGE PROVENCALE

Yield: 6 servings

1 large Savory cabbage, chilled
1 t. vegetable or olive oil
1 c. chopped onion
2 large cloves garlic, minced
1 c. fresh whole wheat bread crumbs
2 T. milk
¼ c. chopped parsley
½ c. roasted buckwheat groats (kasha)
¼ c. raw wheat germ
1 egg
¼ t. thyme
  Freshly ground black pepper to taste
  Salt to taste

Wash and trim cabbage; remove several outer leaves, chop, and reserve. Steam cabbage over medium heat for 15 to 20 minutes or until leaves are pliable. Remove cabbage (reserving steaming liquid); place stem side down in the center of a large piece of cheesecloth. Carefully separate leaves until core is visible. Cut out core and chop. Sauté onion, garlic, and the chopped outer leaves and core of the cabbage in oil in a large

frying pan over medium heat until onion is soft. Turn off heat. Meanwhile, moisten bread crumbs with milk. Add crumbs, parsley, buckwheat groats, and wheat germ to onion mixture. Stir well and when pan is fairly cool, season to taste, and add egg. Place half of the buckwheat mixture in the center of the cabbage; distribute the rest in layers, with cabbage leaves as top layer. Reshape cabbage; brush well with olive oil. Bring cheesecloth up around cabbage and tie on top so that the cabbage holds its shape. Place cabbage in a lightly oiled deep baking dish with a tight-fitting cover (or use aluminum foil). Pour hot vegetable sauce over cabbage. Cabbage can be refrigerated at this point to be baked later or bake immediately covered in a 375° oven for 1 hour (longer if the dish has been refrigerated). Remove cover and baste cabbage; bake for 20 minutes more or until tender. Remove cheesecloth before serving, spoon Vegetable Sauce over cabbage.

VEGETABLE SAUCE OR GRAVY

1 T. vegetable oil
2 c. chopped onion
1 c. chopped carrot
2 T. whole wheat flour
2 c. liquid from steaming cabbage and/or
  water
¼ c. chopped parsley
½ bay leaf
  Freshly ground black pepper to taste
  Salt to taste

Sauté onion and carrot in oil in a large frying pan over medium heat until onion is soft. Add flour and stir until well mixed and lightly browned. Add liquid and seasonings; stir until mixture thickens. Lower heat, cover, and simmer 15 minutes more. Use when hot.

MUSHROOM AND ONION BUFFET QUICHE

Yield: 8 to 10 servings

- 1 lb. Swiss cheese, grated
- ¼ c. whole wheat flour
- ½ c. non-instant powdered milk
- ½ t. salt
  Freshly ground black pepper to taste
- 1 c. milk, scalded (150°)
- 3 eggs, beaten
- 3 T. margarine
- 1 T. vegetable oil
- 2 lbs. onion, minced
- 1 lb. mushrooms, sliced
- 1 t. lemon juice
- 2 T. dry white wine
- 1 unbaked whole wheat pie crust

Preheat oven to 325°. Combine grated cheese with flour, powdered milk, salt, and pepper. Let scalded milk cool; when cool, beat in eggs. Meanwhile, heat margarine and oil together in a very large skillet over medium heat until butter is melted; stir in the onion and cook until translucent. Stir in the mushrooms, lemon juice, and wine. Cover and simmer over low heat for about 8 minutes. Stir onion mixture into cheese mixture; when blended stir in egg mixture thoroughly. Place pie crust in an 11½ x 7½-inch baking dish. Pour onion-cheese mixture into the crust and bake for 40 minutes or until a table knife inserted in the center comes out clean and top is golden.

SPINACH OR CHARD QUICHE

Yield: 4 to 6 servings

- 1 10-oz. pkg. chopped spinach or Swiss chard
- 1 c. milk
- ½ lb. Swiss cheese, grated
- 2 T. whole wheat flour
- ¼ c. non-instant powdered milk
- ¼ t. salt
  Freshly ground black pepper to taste
- 3 eggs, beaten
- 1 T. minced onion
- 1 unbaked 10-inch pie crust

Preheat oven to 325°. Steam spinach until tender (6 to 8 minutes). Scald milk (150°) in a heavy saucepan. Combine cheese, flour, milk, salt, and pepper until the cheese is coated with flour. Stir cheese mixture into the scalded milk; add steamed spinach, and finally stir in the beaten eggs and onion. When thoroughly combined, pour mixture into pie crust and bake for 30 to 40 minutes or until a table knife inserted in the center comes out clean. This quiche can be reheated after it has been baked. Garnish with thin slices of tomato.

WHOLE WHEAT CREPES

Yield: Approximately 20

- 4 eggs
- 1 c. whole wheat pastry flour, sifted
- 1 c. milk
- ¼ c. non-instant powdered milk
- 1 T. vegetable oil
- 1 t. salt
  Butter

Beat all ingredients together with a wire whisk or rotary beater until smooth. Grease a heavy, round-bottomed crepe or omelet pan or a skillet thoroughly with butter. Place the pan over medium-high heat. When pan is hot, water drops will bounce off. Ladle batter into pan; tilt so batter covers bottom. Cook until bottom of crepe is lightly browned, turn and brown other side lightly. Place crepes on paper towels to cool until ready to use. Butter pan at regular intervals when necessary. Extras can be frozen. Crepes can be used as is, stuffed with vegetables, cheese, or a hard-boiled egg-cottage cheese-soy "beef" bits filling, rolled, and baked.

Indian and Pakistani

BLACK-EYED PEA CURRY

Yield: 6 servings

- 2 c. water or vegetable cooking liquid
- 2 10-oz. pkgs. frozen black-eyed peas
- 2 T. vegetable oil
- ½ t. cumin seeds
- 1½ c. chopped onion
- ¼ t. ground turmeric
- 1 t. ground coriander
- 1 t. ground cumin
- 1 c. Joyce's Favorite Tomato Sauce (p. 36)
  Cayenne pepper to taste
  Salt to taste
- 3 T. tamarind paste *or* 2 T. lemon juice

In a large kettle, bring water to a boil. Add the frozen peas, bring to a boil again. Cover, and simmer gently for 15 minutes. Drain, reserving ¾ cup liquid and set aside peas, covered. In a large heavy frying pan or Dutch oven, heat oil over medium heat. Toast cumin seeds in oil for a few minutes and stir in onion. Sauté onion until golden. Add turmeric, coriander, and ground cumin, heat to blend spices thoroughly. Pour in tomato sauce; let simmer for about 5 minutes, stirring occasionally. Stir in black-eyed peas, ¾ cup of cooking liquid, cayenne, salt, and the tamarind paste. Bring to a boil, cover, and simmer 25 to 35 minutes or until peas are coated with sauce. Stir often. Serve immediately.

CAULIFLOWER IN YOGURT SAUCE

Yield: 4 to 6 servings

- 1 large cauliflower
- 1 t. lemon juice
- 2 c. chopped onion
- 1 c. yogurt
- ¼ c. chopped coriander leaves
- ¼ t. ground cloves
- ½ t. ground cardamom
- 1 T. curry powder
- 1 T. chopped fresh ginger
- 2 T. vegetable oil
  Salt to taste

Freshly ground black pepper to taste
Tomato slices
¼ c. chopped coriander leaves

Pour lemon juice over cauliflower; steam over medium heat for about 10 minutes. Mix together the next 7 ingredients thoroughly. Heat oil in a frying pan and stir in yogurt mixture. Simmer gently about 6 minutes; remove from heat and cool. Taste; add salt and pepper. Gently rub yogurt sauce over steamed cauliflower. Place in a saucepan with about 1 cup of steaming liquid poured into the bottom. Cover and simmer until cauliflower is tender (about 30 minutes). Baste cauliflower occasionally. Serve hot. Garnish with tomato slices and coriander leaves.

THE MEINERS' GINGERED CARROTS AND PEAS

Yield: 4 to 6 servings

- 1 2-inch piece fresh ginger, peeled
- 3 T. water
- 3 T. vegetable oil
- ¼ t. black mustard seed
- 6 fenugreek seeds
- ¼ t. turmeric
- 1 c. chopped coriander leaves, firmly packed
- 1 green or yellow chili, deseeded and chopped
- 1 lb. shelled fresh or frozen green peas
- 1½ lbs. young carrots, scrubbed and sliced
- 1 t. ground coriander
- 1 t. ground cumin
- 1 t. curry powder
- 3 T. water
- 1 t. salt

Place ginger and water in blender; blend until smooth. Heat vegetable oil in a large skillet over medium heat. Stir in mustard and fenugreek seeds; when seeds begin to pop, carefully stir in ginger mixture and turmeric. Sauté for about 2 minutes, stirring frequently. Add coriander leaves and chili. Sauté, stirring constantly, approximately 2 more minutes, adding more oil if necessary. Stir in peas and carrots; simmering for about 5 minutes, stirring frequently. Add remaining ingredients; stir thoroughly and gently. Cover, lower heat, and simmer for about 30 minutes, stirring occasionally. Serve hot.

Photograph opposite:
Black-Eyed Pea Curry

MILD EGGPLANT CURRY

Yield: 4 to 6 servings

2 c. chopped onion
3 T. vegetable oil
¾ t. chopped fresh ginger
Dash of cayenne pepper
1¼ t. ground coriander
½ t. turmeric
1 ripe tomato, chopped
2 c. tomato sauce
1 large eggplant (1½-lb.), washed and chopped
2 t. lemon juice
Salt to taste
¼ c. coriander leaves, chopped, or Italian parsley

Sauté onion in vegetable oil in a large skillet over medium heat; add ginger, cook until onions are golden. Stir in spices, tomato, and sauce; simmer until sauce is smooth. Stir in eggplant, cover thoroughly with sauce. Cover and simmer until eggplant is tender (30 to 40 minutes). Stir occasionally; if mixture becomes dry, add a little water. Stir in lemon juice. Taste and add salt; correct seasonings as desired. Serve with brown rice or pulao. Garnish with coriander leaves.

PULAO ("FANCY" RICE)

Yield: 4 to 6 servings

1 1-inch stick cinnamon
3 whole cardamoms
4 whole cloves
¼ c. slivered almonds
3 T. vegetable oil
2 c. brown rice, rinsed and picked over
5 c. water
⅓ c. yellow raisins
Salt to taste

Sauté cinnamon, cardamoms, cloves, and almonds in oil in a large skillet over medium heat until almonds are golden. Stir in rice and fry about 3 minutes. Add water and raisins and stir; bring to a boil. Reduce heat; cover and simmer on low until done (about 45 to 50 minutes). Stir in salt to taste and serve.

Italian

JOYCE'S FAVORITE TOMATO SAUCE

Yield: 4 to 5 cups sauce

1 6-oz. can tomato paste
4 to 5 c. seeded Italian plum tomatoes
1 medium green pepper, minced
1 small onion, minced
1 to 2 bay leaves
Fresh sweet basil (optional), to taste
1 t. fennel
1 t. salt
1 clove garlic, minced
1 T. olive oil

Place tomato paste and tomatoes in blender; blend until smooth. Turn mixture into a heavy-bottomed stainless steel pan; bring just to boil. Reduce heat, add remaining ingredients, and simmer, uncovered, 1 hour or until sauce is well flavored. Remove bay leaf and taste. Correct seasonings. Use immediately or freeze until needed. Recipe can easily be doubled, depending upon available tomatoes.

CAROLYN'S SICILIAN SPINACH AND RICOTTA PASTA

Yield: 4 servings

1 lb. spinach, thoroughly washed
½ lb. whole wheat egg noodles
1 c. ricotta or small curd cottage cheese
⅓ c. freshly grated Parmesan and/or Romano cheese
⅓ c. butter or margarine
Salt to taste
Freshly ground black pepper to taste

Steam spinach (or cook with just the moisture clinging to the leaves from the washing) over medium heat for 7 to 10 minutes. Drop the noodles into boiling water and stir. Cook until just tender. Mix ricotta with grated cheese. When spinach is tender, stir into ricotta mixture; add salt and pepper to taste. When noodles are tender, drain and butter thoroughly. Pour sauce over noodles, toss gently, and serve. Pass around extra grated cheese.

MARGARET'S EGGPLANT SPAGHETTI

Yield: 5 servings

⅓ c. vegetable oil
1 eggplant, cut into ½-inch cubes
⅓ c. finely chopped onion
1 clove garlic, minced
2 t. parsley flakes or 1 T. minced
  fresh parsley
1 28-oz. can Italian style tomatoes
1 6-oz. can tomato paste
1 10½-oz. can tomato purée
⅓ c. dry red wine
1 4-oz. can mushrooms, drained or 1 c.
  fresh mushrooms, braised
2 t. crushed oregano
1 t. salt
1 lb. whole wheat spaghetti, cooked until
  just tender and drained
  Parmesan cheese freshly grated
  Parsley, minced (optional)

Heat oil in Dutch oven over medium heat. Cook eggplant, onion, and garlic for 8 minutes or until onion is tender. Add remaining ingredients, up to spaghetti; stir to break up the tomatoes. Reduce heat, cover, and simmer at least 45 minutes. Pour over hot spaghetti, garnish with Parmesan cheese and parsley, if desired, and serve immediately.

LASAGNE

Yield: 6 to 8 servings

1 c. chopped onion
1 lb. mushrooms, chopped
1 lb. zucchini, chopped
2 T. butter
1 large clove garlic, minced
½ t. dried mint or 1 t. fresh, (optional)
½ t. rosemary
½ t. oregano
  Salt to taste
  Freshly ground black pepper to taste
4 c. Joyce's Favorite Tomato Sauce (p. 36)
1 T. vegetable oil
1 lb. whole wheat-spinach lasagne
  noodles
1 lb. ricotta or cottage cheese
1 lb. Mozzarella cheese, grated
1 T. minced parsley
½ c. freshly grated Romano and/or
  Parmesan cheese (optional)

Sauté onion, mushroom, and zucchini in butter until mushrooms begin to lose juices. Add garlic, mint, rosemary, oregano, salt, and pepper; continue cooking until vegetables are tender. Stir in tomato sauce and simmer, stirring regularly, until sauce is well-flavored and thick. Taste and correct seasonings. Boil lasagne noodles in about 6 quarts boiling water to which 1 tablespoon vegetable oil has been added. Cook until just tender (5 to 7 minutes); drain. Separate slices so they won't stick together during assembling. Preheat oven to 350°. Mix together Mozzarella and ricotta cheese with parsley. Lightly grease an 8 x 12 x 2-inch baking dish. Spoon tomato sauce on the bottom. Layer with lasagne noodles, ricotta mixture and sauce, ending with the tomato sauce. Sprinkle on Parmesan cheese, if desired. Bake, uncovered, 30 minutes or until heated through. Let stand 5 minutes before cutting into squares. Can be made ahead and baked at serving time, or served cold the second day.

PESTO OVER WHOLE WHEAT OR SPINACH NOODLES

Yield: 4 to 6 servings

1 c. minced fresh basil or 1/3 c. dried
½ c. minced parsley
1 large clove garlic
½ c. freshly grated Romano and/or
  Parmesan cheese
¼ c. almonds or walnuts
¼ t. salt
  Freshly ground black pepper to taste
¼ c. olive oil
1 lb. whole wheat or spinach noodles
¼ c. butter

Place basil, parsley, garlic, cheese, almonds, salt, and pepper in blender; blend until smooth. Add olive oil gradually (in a thin, steady stream) until mixture is the consistency of soft butter. You can refrigerate at this point until needed. Cook noodles until just tender; drain and toss in butter. Add approximately ¾ of the almond mixture (Pesto) and toss again. Serve immediately. Pass remaining Pesto and additional Romano and/or Parmesan cheese.

TOFU-NOODLE BAKE

Yield: 4 to 6 servings

- 1 T. vegetable oil
- ¾ c. minced onion
- 2 cloves garlic, minced
- 1 rib celery, minced
- ¼ c. minced green pepper
- 1 c. tofu, drained and patted dry
- ½ c. cottage cheese, drained
- 1 egg, slightly beaten
- 1 T. whole wheat flour
- 1 T. minced parsley
- 1 t. oregano
- 1 T. minced chives
- Salt to taste
- Freshly ground black pepper to taste
- ½ lb. whole wheat noodles
- 1 c. Joyce's Favorite Tomato Sauce with sweet basil, (p. 36)
- ¼ c. raw wheat germ
- ¼ c. freshly grated Parmesan cheese

In a medium-sized skillet, sauté onion, garlic, celery, and green pepper until onion is translucent. Mash tofu and mix in cottage cheese, egg, flour, parsley, oregano, and chives. Combine tofu mixture with onion mixture; add salt and pepper to taste. Cook noodles in boiling water until just tender; drain. Preheat oven to 350°. Grease a 2-quart casserole; spread half the cooked noodles evenly over the bottom of the casserole. Cover with tofu/onion mixture. Spread remaining noodles on top. Pour tomato sauce over noodles, and sprinkle wheat germ and Parmesan cheese over all. Bake for about 40 minutes or until heated through and bubbly.

CAROLYN'S SPAGHETTI

Yield: 6 servings

- 1½ lb. whole wheat spaghetti
- Salt
- 2 T. olive oil
- 1 c. chopped onion
- 1½ lb. ripe tomatoes, chopped
- ½ t. marjoram
- Freshly ground black pepper to taste
- ½ c. soy "bacon" bits
- 1 c. freshly grated Parmesan and/or Romano cheese

Bring a large pan of water to a boil; add spaghetti, salt to taste and let boil until just tender (about 8 to 10 minutes). Sauté onion in olive oil until transparent. Stir in tomatoes, marjoram, and pepper. Simmer briskly, stirring regularly, for about 10 minutes until spaghetti is tender. Drain spaghetti. Add "bacon" bits to tomato sauce; taste, and correct seasonings. Pour sacue over spaghetti, sprinkle on grated cheese, and serve immediately.

Middle Eastern

SPANAKOPITTA (SPINACH PIE)

Yield: 24 servings

- 2 lbs. (or 2 10-oz. boxes) fresh spinach or Swiss chard, chopped
- ½ c. butter or margarine, melted
- 10 sheets filo pastry
- ½ lb. feta cheese or Gruyere or Cheddar
- 1 c. small curd cottage cheese
- 3 eggs, well beaten
- Freshly ground black pepper to taste
- Freshly grated nutmeg
- Salt to taste

Steam spinach until just tender (5 to 8 minutes). Preheat oven to 375°. Butter an 11 x 17-inch jelly roll or similar baking pan. Brush butter on each of 5 filo sheets, place on bottom of pan. (Keep remaining filo sheets thoroughly covered with a damp cloth.) Drain spinach and stir in feta cheese, cottage cheese, eggs, pepper, nutmeg, and salt. Place the spinach mixture on the filo sheets in baking dish; make certain to spread filling almost to the edges of the pastry. Place remaining filo sheets on top, brushing butter on each sheet as you assemble. (You can bake this dish later; it keeps well in the refrigerator wrapped in foil.) Cover baking sheet with foil and bake for about thirty minutes. Remove foil and continue baking until Spanakopitta is golden. Cut into squares or diamonds and serve immediately.

Photograph opposite:
Spanakopitta

SANDRA'S DOLMAS
(STUFFED GRAPE LEAVES)

Yield: Approximately 25 dolmas

¼ lb. grapevine leaves (approximately 25)
   either from a jar, in brine, or picked
   fresh, unwashed, and frozen
6 to 8 cloves garlic
   Juice of ½ lemon
1 T. minced mint (optional)
   Filling

Rinse preserved vine leaves thoroughly to drain off most of the salt; if leaves are not pliable, pour boiling water over; let soak 15 to 20 minutes. Drain again; pour cold water over them. If still too salty, repeat process. A similar method works for fresh-frozen grapevine leaves. Wash thoroughly; pour boiling water over several times until limp. Remove stems. Choose a filling; divide filling among the leaves and place on rib side, near stem edge. Turn stem edge and sides in toward rib and over filling, roll tightly so no filling can cook out. When ready to cook, place leftover or broken vine leaves on the bottom of a heavy saucepan, pour in a small amount of water, pack dolmas tightly in layers, alternating the directions of the layers, and sprinkle each layer with lemon juice. Push garlic cloves among dolmas; add mint, if desired. Place a plate upside down on top of dolmas, and simmer, covered, 1½ to 2 hours or until tender. Serve hot. Leftovers can be served cold.

FILLING #1

1 c. cooked brown rice
½ c. minced green onion
3 T. minced parsley
½ t. allspice
¼ c. currants
¼ c. chopped walnuts
2 cloves garlic, minced
   Freshly ground black pepper to taste
   Salt to taste

FILLING #2

1 c. cooked brown rice
½ c. minced green onion
2 T. minced fresh mint
½ t. cinnamon

2 T. minced parsley
½ t. allspice
2 cloves garlic, minced
   Freshly ground black pepper to taste
   Salt to taste

FILLING #3

1 c. cooked brown rice
½ c. soy "beef" bits
3 T. minced fresh mint
½ c. minced onion
4 T. minced parsley
½ t. allspice
   Salt to taste
   Freshly ground black pepper to taste

FILLING #4

¾ c. cooked brown rice
½ c. ground or chopped cooked chick-peas
3 T. minced parsley
½ t. allspice
1 clove garlic, minced
1 T. minced fresh mint leaves
½ c. minced onion
   Salt to taste
   Freshly ground black pepper to taste

Mix together the ingredients of whichever filling you choose. Taste and correct seasonings. Fill vine leaves.
Note: For a crowd, make all four fillings. Fill one pound of vine leaves with the fillings, and simmer them all in a large, heavy pan.

MARY'S KASHA

Yield: 4 servings

1 egg, slightly beaten
1 c. kasha (buckwheat groats)
2 c. boiling Vegetable Broth (p. 15) or other
   vegetable cooking liquid.
   Salt to taste
   Freshly ground black pepper to taste

Mix egg and kasha together. Pour into a hot iron frying pan, stirring until kernels separate. When mixture is dry, pour into boiling liquid. Cover, reduce heat and let simmer 20 minutes or until tender. Add salt and pepper to taste. Serve with braised mushrooms, sautéed onions, toasted almonds, or vegetable gravy.

Mexican

LYNN'S QUICK CORN AND CHILI CASSEROLE

Yield: 4 to 6 servings

- 2 1-lb. cans cream-style corn
- 4 eggs, beaten
- ¾ c. cornmeal
- 2 cloves garlic, minced
- 4 T. vegetable oil
- 2 to 3 yellow chilies or 2 or more green chilies to taste, minced
- 2 c. grated sharp Cheddar cheese

Preheat oven to 350°. Mix together corn, eggs, cornmeal, garlic, and vegetable oil. Place half of the corn mixture into a greased 2-quart casserole. Sprinkle on chilies and cheese; pour remaining half of corn mixture on top. Bake 45 minutes or until mixture is firm and lightly golden. Serve immediately.

ENCHILADAS

Yield: 8 servings

FILLING

- 1 T. vegetable or olive oil
- 1 large clove garlic, minced
- ½ c. chopped green onion
- 3 T. chopped pimiento-stuffed olives
- 2 t. chili powder
- 1 c. cooked red beans, undrained
- ½ c. soy "beef" bits
  Salt to taste
  Freshly ground black pepper to taste
- 8 stone-ground tortillas
  Vegetable oil
- 1½ c. grated sharp Cheddar cheese
  Ripe olives, sliced

Sauté garlic and onion in oil until onion is tender. Stir in olives, chili powder, and beans. When mixture is thoroughly blended and hot, remove from heat; add soy bits, and season to taste. Set aside. Make Sauce. Fry tortillas in oil until lightly browned but still pliable. Drain on paper towels. While still hot fill each with ⅛ of the bean filling. Roll up carefully. Preheat oven to 350°. Pour ¾ of the tomato sauce into the bottom of an 11½ x 7½-inch baking dish. Place tortillas on top, seam side down, and cover with re-

maining Sauce. Sprinkle with cheese and olives. Bake about 25 minutes or until heated through.

SAUCE

- 1 T. vegetable or olive oil
- 1 c. chopped onion
- ½ green pepper, chopped
- 2 large cloves garlic, chopped
- 1 yellow or green chili pepper, chopped
- 4 c. canned tomatoes and juice
- 1 6-oz. can tomato paste
- 1 T. chili powder
  Salt to taste

Sauté onion, green pepper, garlic, and chili pepper together in oil until onion is tender. Add tomatoes, tomato paste, and chili powder. Let simmer, uncovered, about ½ hour. Season to taste.

BULGUR WHEAT CHILI

Yield: 4 to 6 servings

- 1 T. vegetable oil
- ½ c. onion
- ⅔ c. bulgur wheat
- 1⅓ c. water or vegetable cooking liquid
- 1 c. tomato sauce
- 2 c. cooked kidney, red, or pinto beans
- 1 T. chili powder
- ½ t. oregano
- ½ t. sweet basil
  Freshly ground black pepper to taste
  Salt to taste
  Sharp Cheddar cheese, grated (optional)

In a large frying pan, sauté onion in vegetable oil. Stir in bulgur and let toast slightly. Add water; cover, and let simmer 10 to 15 minutes or until bulgur becomes tender. Add remaining ingredients; salt and pepper to taste. Heat to serving temperature. (Chili tastes better if it can be refrigerated for several hours or overnight, allowing seasonings to blend.) Garnish with cheese, if desired.

Note: If you prefer more beans than cracked wheat in your chili, reduce the amount of wheat and cooking liquid or double the beans and tomato sauce. Correct seasonings.

Oriental

SUKIYAKI

Yield: 4 to 6 servings

2 c. green onion, cut into 3-inch lengths
1 c. celery, diagonally cut into 2-inch slices
½ lb. mushrooms, washed and thinly sliced
1 5-oz. can water chestnuts, drained and thinly sliced
1 5-oz. can bamboo shoots, drained and slivered
1 lb. fresh mung bean sprouts
5 c. spinach or chard leaves, chopped into medium-sized pieces
½ lb. tofu, cut into 1-inch cubes
2 T. honey
½ c. soy sauce
½ c. Vegetable Broth (p. 15)
1 to 2 T. vegetable oil

Arrange vegetables attractively on a large platter or tray. Mix honey, soy sauce and broth together in a small pitcher. At the table in an electric wok or skillet, heat vegetable oil over medium heat. Stir in onion with chopsticks or large spoon and fork and stir-fry 1 minute. Stir in about ¼ cup sauce (electric skillet will require more than wok) and let heat. Push onion aside. Add remaining vegetables, in order given, stir-frying for 1 minute and pushing aside. When all ingredients have been heated through, serve with brown rice. Pass soy sauce.

Photograph opposite:
Sukiyaki

TEMPURA UNLIMITED

Yield: 4 to 6 servings

Vegetables for frying
1 c. whole wheat flour, sifted
2 T. rice flour
½ t. salt
1 egg, beaten thoroughly
1¼ c. ice water
4 c. vegetable oil plus sesame oil (approximately)

Select well-chilled vegetables, such as carrot, onion, cauliflower, parsnips, broccoli, and green pepper. Thoroughly scrub vegetables and cut into long sticks, flowerets, or rings. Mix flours and salt together in a medium-sized bowl. Pour in egg and water gradually, beating continuously. When mixture is smooth, refrigerate. Dust vegetables with whole wheat flour, if slippery, then dip into batter. To fry, pour 3 inches of vegetable oil into deep fryer. Add sesame oil to taste. Heat to 350°. Place a few batter-dipped vegetables into the hot oil. Deep-fry for 5 to 10 minutes or until batter is golden. Drain on paper towels and serve immediately with soy sauce and brown rice.

FRIED RICE

Yield: 4 servings

2 to 3 T. vegetable oil
½ c. chopped green onion
½ c. chopped carrot
½ c. chopped celery
½ c. chopped green pepper
1 c. fresh or frozen small green peas
¼ c. soy sauce
4 to 5 c. leftover cooked brown rice
1 egg, slightly beaten
1 c. fresh bean sprouts
¼ c. soy "bacon" bits

Heat oil in wok or electric frying pan; stir-fry onion, carrot, celery, and green pepper until vegetables are tender-crisp. Stir in peas and soy sauce and add brown rice; cook until thoroughly hot. Move rice and vegetables to one side, pour in egg (add a little oil where egg will be poured), and stir-fry until scrambled. Add bean sprouts, stir mixture together and heat through. Sprinkle on "bacon" bits and serve immediately.

Vegetable Side Dishes

MOM'S SWEET 'N SOUR YELLOW BEANS

Yield: 4 to 6 servings

1 lb. yellow beans (approximately 4 cups), fresh or frozen
2 T. brown sugar, well-packed
2 t. cornstarch
¼ c. cider vinegar
Salt to taste
Freshly ground black pepper to taste

Slice yellow beans as desired. Steam until tender (about 10 minutes). In a heavy-bottomed saucepan, mix together brown sugar and cornstarch. Add vinegar. Simmer over medium heat, stirring constantly. When sauce is thickened and clear, pour over hot beans. Add salt and pepper to taste; toss gently until all beans are coated with sauce. Serve hot or cold.

STIR-FRIED CABBAGE OR BRUSSELS SPROUTS

Yield: 4 servings

2 T. vegetable oil
1 c. chopped onion
1 large clove garlic, minced
1 lb. cabbage or Brussels sprouts, chilled and chopped
1 T. soy sauce (or to taste)
Salt
Freshly ground black pepper
3 T. water
1 T. cornstarch

Heat oil in a large frying pan; sauté onion and garlic until transparent. Add cabbage or sprouts, increase heat, and stir constantly for 3 or 4 minutes. Add soy sauce, salt, and pepper to taste. Continue to cook and stir constantly another 3 to 4 minutes. Combine water and cornstarch until smooth. Pour into cabbage mixture and stir until cornstarch mixture is clear. Serve immediately while piping hot.

MOM'S DILLED GREEN BEANS

Yield: 4 servings

1 T. vegetable oil
2 to 3 T. water
2 c. sliced fresh or frozen green beans
½ c. bean sprouts
¼ c. chopped green onion
1 T. chopped pimiento (optional)
1 T. cider vinegar
½ t. dill weed
Freshly ground black pepper to taste
Salt to taste

Heat oil in wok or electric skillet; add water (less for wok) and green beans. Cook until tender (approximately 6 to 7 minutes). Add remaining ingredients, toss lightly and heat through. Serve immediately.

MARY'S CAULIFLOWER IN CHEESE SAUCE

Yield: 4 to 6 servings

2 c. milk
¼ t. salt
2 T. butter or margarine
3 T. whole wheat flour
1 c. grated Herkimer or strong, white Canadian Cheddar cheese
1 T. lemon juice
1 large whole cauliflower

In a heavy bottomed sauce pan, mix together milk and salt. Heat almost to a boil. Meanwhile, melt butter in a heavy skillet, stir in flour, sauté for about 2 minutes, stirring constantly. Do not allow mixture to scorch. Add hot milk all at once; stir with a wire whisk until sauce comes to a boil. Boil for about 1 minute, stirring constantly. Remove from heat, taste, and correct seasonings. Stir in cheese. Pour lemon juice over cauliflower and steam until tender (20 to 25 minutes). Pour cheese sauce over hot cauliflower and serve immediately.

ONE SKILLET EGGPLANT DINNER

Yield: 4 servings

1 medium eggplant, sliced into ¼-inch
  circles
  Vegetable oil
1 medium green pepper, sliced
1 small onion, minced
1 clove garlic, minced
2 c. tomato sauce
  Oregano
  Sweet basil
  Freshly ground black pepper
1 c. grated Cheddar or colby cheese
¼ c. freshly grated Parmesan cheese

Pour enough vegetable oil into a large fry-ing pan to coat. Fry eggplant gently until browned on both sides. Add more oil as necessary. Turn down heat, add vegetables, pour tomato sauce over all. If tomato sauce does not contain herbs, add oregano and sweet basil to taste. Add black pepper if needed. Sprinkle cheeses on top. Cover tightly and let simmer until eggplant is tender (30 minutes or less.) Serve with pasta or as desired.

AUNT RUTH'S ONION CASSEROLE

Yield: 4 to 6 servings

1 lb. small onions, peeled
1 c. water
¾ c. tomato juice mixed with ¼ c.
  steaming liquid
1 T. cornstarch
½ c. whole wheat bread crumbs
  Butter or margarine
  Freshly ground black pepper to taste

In a saucepan steam onions in 1 cup water until barely tender, 8 to 10 minutes. Mix tomato juice and cornstarch together; heat in a casserole dish that can be used on top of the stove. When tomato juice mixture has thickened, stir in onions until all are coated. (If tomato sauce seems too thick, dilute with a little more water.) Sprinkle bread crumbs on top, dot with butter; season with pepper. Can be made ahead and baked later at this point. When ready to bake, preheat oven to 350°. Cover and bake about 40 minutes or until onions are tender and heated through. To brown the crumbs, remove the cover the final minutes of baking.

PARSNIP-STUFFED ZUCCHINI

Yield: 6 servings

3 medium-size zucchini, sliced
  lengthwise
3 medium-size parsnips, cubed
2 T. chopped onion
  Butter or margarine
  Salt to taste
  Freshly ground black pepper to taste

In a small amount of water, steam zucchini and parsnips until tender (6 to 8 minutes). Mash parsnips with onion; add butter, salt, and pepper to taste. Scoop centers out of the zucchini; add to parsnip mixture. Correct seasonings. Fill zucchini with parsnip stuf-fing. Can be made ahead and baked at serving time. Preheat oven to 400°. Place the zucchini in a well-greased baking dish, cover and bake 15 to 20 minutes or until thoroughly heated and tender.

HOLLANDAISE SAUCE FOR VEGETABLES

Yield: About 1 cup

½ c. margarine or butter
3 egg yolks at room temperature
1½ T. lemon juice
¼ t. dry mustard
¼ t. salt
  Freshly ground black pepper

In a small saucepan, melt butter until bubbly. Place egg yolks, lemon juice, mustard, and seasonings into blender container; cover and blend on low until yolks are frothy. Pour in half the butter in a very slow, steady stream until creamy. Then turn blender to high and add remaining butter slowly. Taste and correct seasonings. Serve immediately on steamed vegetables such as Brussels sprouts, broccoli, zucchini. If reheated, warm the sauce gently over hot water, stirring carefully.

BROCCOLI CASSEROLE

Yield: 8 servings

3 to 4 c. chopped broccoli
⅓ c. finely chopped onion
4 T. margarine
3 T. whole wheat pastry flour
½ c. vegetable cooking water or broth
¾ c. grated Cheddar cheese
3 eggs, well-beaten
½ c. whole wheat bread crumbs
1 T. butter or margarine

Preheat oven to 325°. Melt 4 tablespoons margarine in a large skillet over medium heat; stir in onion and broccoli; sauté covered, until broccoli is barely tender. (If using frozen broccoli, drop about 20 ounces into a small amount of boiling water, cover, and cook quickly. Add to skillet and use the cooking water later in the recipe.) Stir flour into the onion-broccoli mixture and let cook a minute or so. Add cooking water or broth; stir until thickened. Lower heat and quickly stir in cheese until well blended. Remove from heat and gradually stir in eggs. Pour into a well greased 1½ to 2-quart casserole. Pour crumbs over and dot with butter. Bake for 30 minutes or until done.

DELUXE GREEN BEANS

Yield: 6 servings

3 c. sliced fresh or frozen green beans
2 T. margarine or butter
⅓ c. chopped onion
2 T. whole wheat flour
½ t. salt
  Freshly ground black pepper to taste
1 c. dairy sour cream
½ c. grated Cheddar cheese

Steam beans until tender (about 10 minutes). Preheat oven to 350°. Melt butter in a small, heavy-bottomed pan; add onion and sauté until tender. Stir in flour, salt, and pepper. When thoroughly mixed, add the sour cream very carefully and heat. Do not boil. Taste and correct seasonings. Stir sour cream mixture into hot beans; pour beans into a greased 1-quart casserole. Top with cheese. Bake about 15 minutes or until cheese melts and beans are heated thoroughly. Serve.

Photograph opposite:
Deluxe Green Beans

ZUCCHINI AND CHEESE CASSEROLE

Yield: 6 servings

2 lbs. zucchini (about 6 medium)
½ lb. sharp Cheddar cheese
  Salt to taste
  Freshly ground black pepper to taste

Preheat oven to 350°. Scrub and grate zucchini; grate cheese. Grease a 2-quart casserole dish. Place a layer of zucchini on the bottom and cover it with a layer of cheese. Salt and pepper to taste. Keep on layering until you have six layers, the cheese on top; continue to salt and pepper to taste. Bake, covered, for approximately 40 minutes or until done.

BERNICE ROTH'S RED CABBAGE

Yield: 6 to 8 servings

1 head red cabbage, chopped
¾ c. chopped onion
1 T. vegetable oil
⅛ t. allspice
1 raw apple, chopped
¼ c. dry white wine or vermouth
1 T. brown sugar
  Salt to taste
  Freshly ground black pepper to taste

In a large frying pan, stir-fry cabbage and onion in vegetable oil until cabbage is just tender. Add allspice and raw apple and continue to stir until apple is hot. Add wine and brown sugar; taste and season as desired. When thoroughly heated, serve.

JOYCE'S FRIED CAULIFLOWER

Yield: 6 servings

1 head cauliflower, broken into flowerets (or can use zucchini or artichoke hearts)
1 egg, well-beaten
½ t. salt
¼ c. unbleached flour
¼ c. water

Pour 1 inch of olive oil into a small, deep iron pan. Stir remaining ingredients except cauliflower together; coat the flowerets in the batter. Fry cauliflowerets a few at a time, for a few minutes in hot oil; drain thoroughly on paper towels. Keep cooked vegetables on a warm platter in oven until serving time. (This dish can be made ahead. Reheat before serving for about 10 minutes in a 400° oven.)

Salads

ROASTED PEPPER SALAD

Yield: 6 servings

6 large green peppers (or 3 red and 3 green)
¼ c. olive or vegetable oil
1 T. wine vinegar
1 large clove garlic, minced
⅛ t. salt
Freshly ground black pepper to taste
Parsley, minced

Place peppers under broiler; turn regularly until they are blistered thoroughly. Wrap peppers in a damp towel and set aside until cool. Peel and cut peppers into quarters or sixths, discard seeds and membranes. Mix oil, vinegar, garlic, salt, and pepper together in a medium-sized mixing bowl; add peppers and let marinate, covered, in the refrigerator for at least 3 to 4 hours. Occasionally, stir gently. When ready to serve, drain, arrange on a serving dish, and garnish with parsley, if desired.

ROGER'S RAITA (INDIAN CUCUMBER, TOMATO, AND YOGURT SALAD)

Yield: 6 servings

2 c. plain yogurt
1 large cucumber, chopped
2 ripe tomatoes, chopped
6 to 8 scallions, chopped
Freshly ground black pepper to taste
½ t. cumin seed
Salt to taste
Dash of cayenne pepper (optional)
Paprika

Beat yogurt until smooth. Toast cumin seed for 2 to 3 minutes in a heavy frying pan and crush. Stir cucumber, tomatoes, scallions, black pepper, and a pinch of cumin into yogurt; add salt to taste. Add cayenne if desired. Garnish with paprika and another pinch of cumin. Chill until ready to serve.

SUNCHOKE SALAD

Yield: 4 to 6 servings

1 lb. sunchokes (Jerusalem artichokes)
2 t. lemon juice
½ c. minced onion
2 T. minced green pepper
2 ribs celery, minced
1 carrot, grated
½ c. mayonnaise
1 t. prepared mustard
Freshly ground black pepper to taste
Salt to taste
Garnishes: Paprika; hard-boiled egg slices; minced parsley

Scrub chokes and steam until tender (about 12 minutes.) Chill. Peel chokes and slice into a medium-sized serving dish. Sprinkle with lemon; add remaining ingredients except pepper, and salt, and the garnishes. Toss gently; add salt and pepper to taste. Garnish and serve cold.

LIMA BEAN SALAD

Yield: 4 to 6 servings

1½ c. dried lima beans
3 c. water
⅔ c. chopped green onion
2 hard-boiled eggs, chopped
Freshly ground black pepper to taste
Salt to taste
Parsley, chopped
½ c. pitted black olives

Soak beans in water overnight; the next day simmer 2 to 2½ hours or until beans are tender. Add more water if needed. Drain, and cool the beans. Mix with remaining ingredients; pour your favorite vinegar and oil dressing over; chill until served.

QUICK WINTER SALAD

Yield: 10 to 12 servings

1 1-lb. can garbanzo beans, drained
1 small bunch radishes, sliced
1 T. olive oil
1 1-lb. can kidney beans, drained
3 ribs celery, chopped
1 T. wine vinegar
1 1-lb. can lima beans, drained
1 green pepper, chopped
2 to 4 mushrooms, sliced
2 T. lemon juice
½ t. paprika
  Salt to taste
  Freshly ground black pepper to taste
  Salad greens
  Parsley, chopped

Mix garbanzos, radishes, and olive oil together. In separate bowl, mix kidney beans, celery, and wine vinegar. In third bowl mix together lima beans, green pepper, mushrooms, and lemon juice. Sprinkle paprika on top. Chill bowls for about 1 hour. Taste each; add salt and pepper to taste. Drizzle a small amount of olive oil on the lima beans; put a small amount of vinegar or lemon juice on the garbanzos. Put each bean mixture into a separate section on a large serving tray. Garnish with salad greens and dust with parsley.

GARDEN MACARONI SALAD

Yield: 6 to 8 servings

2 c. cooked whole wheat macaroni, chilled
½ c. chopped tart apples
½ c. mayonnaise
1 c. freshly shelled large green peas
½ c. diced celery
2 hard-boiled eggs
1 green pepper
  Freshly ground black pepper to taste
  Salt to taste
  Crisp lettuce (optional)

In a large serving bowl, mix together macaroni, apples, mayonnaise, peas, and celery. Dice one egg and half of the green pepper; stir into salad. Taste and add salt and pepper as desired. Slice the other egg; garnish salad with egg slices and diced green pepper. Serve on lettuce leaves, if desired.

CLASSIC GREEN SALAD

Yield: 8 servings

8 c. fresh, washed, crisp young greens*
1 clove garlic, split
⅓ c. sliced radishes
  Parsley
  Chives

Tear greens into bite-size pieces. Rub garlic clove against the inside of a salad bowl. Add greens to bowl. Garnish with radishes, parsley, and chives. Pour about half of the dressing over salad; toss well and serve.

*Note: Choose from spinach, chard, various lettuces, curly endive, watercress, mustard and turnip greens, and collards.

GARLIC DRESSING

Yield: 1 cup

¾ c. olive and/or vegetable oil
¼ c. wine vinegar
½ t. salt
  Freshly ground black pepper to taste
1 clove garlic, minced (optional)

Mix all ingredients together thoroughly. Taste and correct seasoning.

CUCUMBERS IN SOUR CREAM

Yield: 6 servings

2 large cucumbers, peeled, and sliced
2 T. sour cream
1½ T. mayonnaise
3 T. chopped fresh dill or 2 T. dill seed
  Freshly ground black pepper to taste

Mix all ingredients together in a serving dish; refrigerate for at least 1 hour before serving. Taste and correct seasonings.

CHEF'S SALAD

Yield: 6 large servings

1 clove garlic
½ c. olive oil or a vegetable-olive oil combination
1 c. whole wheat bread cubes
2 heads crisp Romaine, washed and dried
4 green onions, chopped
¾ c. slivered Swiss or other cheese
3 ripe tomatoes, quartered
½ t. dry mustard
 Dash of Worcestershire sauce
2 T. wine vinegar
 Freshly ground black pepper to taste
1 t. salt
1 coddled egg
 Juice of 1 lemon
¼ c. freshly grated Parmesan cheese

Mash garlic clove into oil and let flavors blend as long as possible, preferably overnight. Sauté bread cubes in 2 tablespoons of the garlic oil, drain; set aside and cool on paper towels. Coddle egg 1½ minutes in simmering water. Tear lettuce into bite-sized pieces; place in a large salad bowl. Add onion, cheese, and tomatoes. Pour the remaining garlic oil on salad; toss lightly until coated well. Add dry mustard, Worcestershire sauce, and wine vinegar; toss again. Season with pepper and salt; break coddled egg onto salad. Squeeze lemon onto egg; sprinkle with Parmesan cheese. Toss again and garnish with bread cubes.

MOM'S CARROT AND RAISIN SALAD

Yield: 6 to 8 servings

3 c. grated raw carrots
1 c. seedless raisins
1 T. honey
6 T. mayonnaise
¼ c. milk
1 T. fresh lemon juice
¼ t. salt

Toss carrots and raisins together. Blend remaining ingredients and pour over carrots and raisins. Stir carefully and thoroughly. Chill to blend flavors.

GREEK SALAD

Yield: 6 servings

⅓ c. olive oil or vegetable oil
 Juice of one lemon
2 T. chopped fresh oregano or 1 T. dried
4 T. minced parsley
 Freshly ground black pepper to taste
 Salt (optional)
1 head crisp lettuce, torn into bite-sized pieces
1 green pepper, seeds and membrane removed and sliced lengthwise
2 to 3 tomatoes, cut into sixths
½ c. crumbled feta cheese
12 black olives
1 red onion, sliced into rings
1 hard-boiled egg, sliced

Combine oil, lemon juice, and seasonings. Taste and correct seasonings. Pour into a cruet. Remove seeds and membranes from green pepper; slice lengthwise. On individual serving plates, place lettuce, pepper, and tomatoes. Divide cheese, olives, and onion slices among the plates. Garnish with egg. Pour a small amount of the oil and lemon juice mixture on each salad, pass the rest.

CUB SCOUT'S FRUIT SALAD

Yield: 12 servings

2 pears, cored and chopped
1 bunch grapes, seeds removed
2 oranges, peeled and chopped
2 apples, cored and chopped
2 c. canned pineapple chunks
¾ c. raisins (optional)
¾ c. shredded coconut
2 bananas, chopped
 Lemon juice
¼ c. tofu
¼ c. plain yogurt
1 c. cherry yogurt

Sprinkle apples and banana with lemon juice. In a very large serving bowl, mix all the fruits together. Mix together the tofu and yogurt in a blender until smooth. Stir together with cherry yogurt; pour over fruit. Toss gently. Serve cold.

Photograph opposite:
Greek Salad

MOM'S BULGUR SALAD

Yield: 4 to 6 servings

    1 c. bulgur wheat (cracked wheat)
    2 c. boiling water
      Salt to taste
    ½ c. chopped green onion
    ½ c. diced or grated carrot
    ½ c. diced celery
    2 tomatoes, sliced into sixths
    ½ c. alfalfa sprouts
    ⅔ c. minced parsley
      Freshly ground black pepper to taste

Pour boiling water over wheat in a small bowl; cover and let stand about 30 minutes. Drain. Place fluffed bulgur into a large serving bowl. Let cool completely. Salt lightly to taste. Add remaining ingredients. Pour dressing over the salad and correct seasonings. Serve cold; may be garnished with lettuce leaves.

DRESSING

    6 T. olive oil
    2 t. wine vinegar
      Salt to taste

Mix all ingredients together well.

STUFFED TOMATO LUNCHEON SALAD

Yield: 6 servings

    6 ripe tomatoes
    6 ribs celery, minced
    1 green pepper, minced
    1 c. peanuts or chopped walnuts
    ⅓ c. plain yogurt
      Salt (optional)
      Freshly ground black pepper to taste
      Paprika
      Shredded lettuce

Slice six gashes into each tomato approximately halfway down. Scoop out as much tomato as desired. Mix together celery, green pepper, nuts, and yogurt. Taste; add salt and pepper. Divide stuffing among tomato cases; sprinkle with paprika. Chill until serving time. Serve on top of shredded lettuce.

LENTIL SALAD

Yield: 12 servings

    5 c. water, vegetable cooking liquid,
      or broth
    1 lb. dried lentils
    1 c. chopped red onion
    4 garlic cloves, peeled and chopped
    1 rib celery, chopped
    1 carrot, chopped
    1 t. thyme
    1 t. sweet basil
    1 t. oregano
    ½ c. chopped parsley
    5 green onions, minced
    1 green pepper, chopped

Bring water to a boil in a large kettle; add remaining ingredients, except green onion and green pepper. Turn heat down, cover, and simmer 1½ hours or until lentils are tender. You may need to add a little water as lentils cook. Pour dressing over cooked lentils. Let cool and refrigerate. Add salt and pepper as desired and garnish with onions and green pepper before serving.

VINEGAR AND OIL DRESSING

    ½ c. vegetable oil
    3 T. wine vinegar
    1 T. prepared mustard
      Freshly ground black pepper to taste
      Salt to taste

Combine ingredients, mixing well.

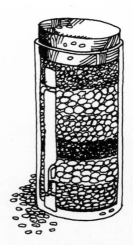

Desserts

SESAME SEED COOKIES

Yield: 3 dozen cookies

1¾ c. whole wheat flour
¼ c. soy flour
1 t. baking powder
¼ t. salt
½ c. margarine
¾ c. brown sugar, firmly packed
1 egg
2 T. toasted sesame seeds
1 T. water
2 T. raw sesame seeds

Mix flours, baking powder and salt together. Cream sugar with margarine; beat in egg and stir in toasted sesame seeds. Add flour mixture alternately with water. Chill dough 3 to 4 hours. Drop dough by teaspoonfuls onto greased cookie sheets. Flatten with a glass dipped in flour. Sprinkle extra raw sesame seeds on top. Bake in a preheated 375° oven for 10 minutes or until lightly browned around edges.

PUMPKIN PIE

Yield: 10-inch pie

2 c. pumpkin purée
⅔ c. brown sugar
½ t. salt
1 t. cinnamon
¾ t. ginger
½ t. nutmeg
⅛ t. cloves
3 eggs, beaten
1 6-oz. can evaporated milk
1¼ c. milk
1 t. nutritional yeast
1 10-inch unbaked pastry shell

Preheat oven to 400°. Combine pumpkin, sugar, salt and spices. Add eggs, milk, and nutritional yeast; mix well. Pour into pastry shell. Bake about 50 minutes or until knife inserted in center comes out clean.

GRAHAM-MILK CRACKERS

Yield: 5 dozen medium crackers

4 c. whole wheat pastry flour or graham flour
¾ c. butter or margarine, chilled
⅔ c. brown sugar, firmly packed
1 t. cinnamon
2 T. nutritional yeast
1½ t. salt
1 t. baking powder
1 c. milk, cold

With a pastry blender or fork, blend flour and butter together until mixture resembles crumbs. Add rest of dry ingredients and mix well. Add milk slowly until mixture forms a smooth ball. Preheat oven to 400°. Knead dough until smooth, 5 to 10 minutes. Roll out ⅛-inch thick on a floured cloth with a floured rolling pin. Cut into desired shapes with cookie cutters (or into squares, diamonds, or rectangles). Place on well-greased baking sheets, prick a design with a fork, if desired, and bake 6 to 8 minutes or until lightly browned. Remove from sheets and let cool on wire racks. Store in tightly covered tin.

CRUNCHY PEANUT BUTTER TREATS

Yield: 2 dozen balls or 6 "cups"

¾ c. crunchy granola
½ c. non-instant powdered milk
½ c. non-hydrogenated chunky peanut butter
¼ c. honey

In a small bowl; mix together the ingredients until thoroughly combined. Form into balls or spread in 2½-inch paper liners placed in muffin tins. Chill.

RHUBARB (OR APPLE) CRUMBLE

Yield: 8 servings

4 c. chopped rhubarb (or tart apples, cored, but unpeeled, or a combination of both)

1 t. lemon juice (if more tartness or flavor is desired)

½ c. honey (more or less, depending upon tartness of fruit)

Preheat oven to 350°. Place rhubarb in a 9-inch, 1¼-inch deep pie plate. Pour honey over all. Pour Topping on fruit. Bake for 30 minutes or until fruit is tender when tested with a fork.

Note: You can have fun experimenting with this easy-to-make crumble. For example, mix raisins with the fruit, mix raw sunflower or sesame seeds or chopped nuts into the topping, etc.

TOPPING

¼ c. brown sugar
¼ c. whole wheat flour
¼ c. raw wheat germ
¼ c. oatmeal
1 T. soy flour
1 t. nutritional yeast
1 t. cinnamon
¼ c. margarine or butter

Mix together dry ingredients. Cut in margarine until mixture resembles crumbs.

GREEN TOMATO MINCEMEAT

Yield: Approx. 1 gallon

8 c. chopped green tomatoes
8 c. chopped tart apples
6 c. raisins, chopped
5 c. sugar (or much less, to taste)
2 heaping t. cinnamon
1 t. ground cloves
1 t. allspice
2 t. grated orange peel
1 lemon (grated peel and juice)
½ c. cider vinegar
Salt to taste

Combine all ingredients in a large, heavy saucepan. Simmer 2 hours, stirring frequently, or until mixture is of desired consistency. Correct seasonings. Freeze or can. Can be used as an ice-cream topping, in pies, or in mincemeat bread.

GINGERSNAPS

Yield: 3 dozen cookies

1½ c. whole wheat pastry flour
¼ c. brown sugar, firmly packed
1 t. baking powder
1½ t. ginger
¼ c. wheat germ
¼ t. salt
¼ c. butter or margarine
1 egg
3 T. old-fashioned molasses

Mix dry ingredients together. With a pastry blender, cut in butter until mixture resembles crumbs. Add the egg and molasses and stir well with a fork. Let chill one half hour. Preheat oven to 375°. Flour a pastry cloth well and with a covered, well-floured rolling pin, roll the dough out about ⅛ inch thick. Cut with small round cookie cutter, and place on a greased baking sheet. Bake for 5 to 10 minutes or until done. Remove immediately to a wire rack for cooling.

GREEN TOMATO MINCE PIE

Yield: 1 pie

3 to 4 c. Green Tomato Mincemeat
1 recipe double pie crust

Preheat oven to 425°. Line 9-inch pie plate with crust. Spoon mincemeat into crust. Roll out dough for top, making design in center through which steam can escape. Place top crust on prepared pie, firmly pressing dough together around edges. Trim and flute edges as desired. Bake for 8 minutes. Lower heat to 325° and continue baking for 20 minutes or until crust is lightly browned.

YOGURT ORANGE SHERBET

Yield: About 1 pint

1 6-oz. can frozen orange juice concentrate
1 to 2 c. plain yogurt (to taste)

Pour juice concentrate into mixing bowl. Stir in yogurt until you like the taste. Pour into ice cube tray or other freezer bowl. Serve when firm. If you won't be using it right away, cover the sherbet as soon as it is frozen.

Photograph opposite:
Rhubarb (or Apple) Crumble

RHUBARB CAKE
Yield: 12 to 16 pieces

5 T. butter or margarine
¾ c. brown sugar, firmly packed
1 egg
½ c. yogurt or buttermilk
¼ t. salt
1 c. whole wheat flour
2½ t. baking powder
¼ c. non-instant powdered milk
¼ c. raw wheat germ
1½ c. chopped rhubarb (or apple)

Preheat oven to 350°. Cream butter and sugar together; beat in egg until fluffy. Add yogurt. Mix dry ingredients together and stir into egg mixture, beating until thoroughly blended. Stir in rhubarb. Pour into lightly greased 8 x 8-inch cake pan. Sprinkle Topping evenly over batter. Bake for 30 to 40 minutes or until top springs back when pressed lightly.

TOPPING

¼ c. brown sugar
¼ t. cinnamon
¼ c. raw wheat germ
⅓ c. chopped nuts

Mix ingredients with a fork.

DATE NUT BARS
Yield: 12 to 16 bars

¾ c. brown sugar, firmly packed
¼ c. margarine or butter
2 eggs
¾ c. whole wheat flour
¼ c. raw wheat germ
½ t. baking powder
½ t. salt
1 c. pitted and chopped dates
½ c. chopped nuts
½ t. vanilla

Preheat oven to 350°. Cream sugar and margarine. Beat in eggs until light and fluffy. Stir dry ingredients together; add gradually to egg mixture, beating well. Stir in dates, nuts, and vanilla. Pour into well-greased 9 x 9-inch cake pan. Bake 30 minutes, or until top springs back when touched lightly. Cut into squares while hot.

MOLASSES-WHEAT GERM COOKIES
Yield: 3 to 4 dozen cookies

¾ c. margarine
¾ c. brown sugar, firmly packed
¼ c. old-fashioned molasses
1 egg
½ c. non-instant powdered milk
1½ c. whole wheat pastry flour
¾ c. raw wheat germ
2 t. baking powder
½ t. cloves
1 t. cinnamon

Cream margarine and sugar together; add molasses. Beat in egg. Mix dry ingredients together and add to batter. Stir well. Chill about one hour. Preheat oven to 350°. Roll dough into 1-inch balls and place on lightly greased baking sheet. Press flat with the smooth bottom of a glass dipped in flour. If desired, raisins may be used to decorate the cookies.

Bake for 10 to 12 minutes or until lightly browned. Remove after a few moments from baking sheet to wire rack to finish cooling.

PUMPKIN AND RAISIN COOKIES
Yield: 5 dozen cookies

1 c. cooked pumpkin or winter squash, mashed
⅔ c. brown sugar
½ c. vegetable oil
1 large egg
2 c. whole wheat flour
2 t. baking powder
1 t. cinnamon
¼ t. cloves
¼ t. nutmeg
½ t. salt
1 t. baking soda dissolved in 1 t. milk
1 c. raisins
½ c. chopped nuts or raw sunflower seeds
1 t. vanilla

Preheat oven to 350°. Thoroughly combine pumpkin, sugar, oil, and egg. (Use blender if pumpkin is lumpy.) Stir together flour, baking powder, spices, and salt. Add to pumpkin mixture along with dissolved soda and mix well. Stir in raisins, nuts, and vanilla. Drop by teaspoonfuls on lightly greased cookie sheets. Bake 10 to 12 minutes or until done. Cool on wire rack.

INDIAN PUDDING

Yield: 4 servings

1½ c. milk
2 T. cornmeal
1 egg, beaten
¼ c. old-fashioned molasses
2 T. brown sugar
½ t. cinnamon
¼ t. salt
¼ t. ginger
¼ t. nutmeg
½ c. wheat germ

Preheat oven to 325°. In a medium-sized heavy pan over medium heat, scald milk (150°). Gradually stir in cornmeal. Cook for approximately 8 minutes, stirring frequently, until mixture is well cooked and thickened. Remove from heat. Combine the rest of the ingredients. Stir the milk mixture into the other ingredients, mixing well. Pour into lightly greased 1½-quart baking dish. Place in a large pan half filled with hot water. Bake for about 1 hour or until table knife inserted in center comes out nearly clean. Serve hot or cold, plain or with yogurt.

EASY CHEESY APPLE PIE

Yield: 6 to 8 servings

5 to 6 apples, sliced and cored (don't peel)
2 T. apple juice or water
2 T. honey (if using sweet apples, omit honey)
¼ c. raisins
¼ c. currants (or more raisins)
2 c. rolled oats
¼ c. unsalted peanuts
½ c. chopped walnuts
¼ c. sunflower seeds (optional)
½ t. salt
¼ lb. grated Cheddar cheese

In a heavy, tightly covered pan over low heat, cook apples, juice, and honey for about 15 minutes or until apples are just beginning to get soft. Preheat oven to 350°. Pour apple mixture into a 9-inch pie plate. Pour currants and raisins on top. Mix together the rest of the ingredients except cheese and pour on top of pie. Bake for 10 minutes or until topping is browned. Pour grated cheese on top of pie and bake for an additional 5 to 10 minutes or until all cheese has melted. Best served hot.

STEAMED CARROT PUDDING

Yield: 8 to 10 servings

1 c. whole wheat flour
1 t. baking soda
¾ c. brown sugar, firmly packed
1 t. allspice
1 t. cinnamon
1 t. nutmeg
1 c. seedless raisins
1 c. coarsely chopped walnuts or other nuts
1 c. grated carrot
1 c. grated potatoes
2 eggs, beaten
2 T. margarine or butter, melted and cooled

Stir together dry ingredients. Add raisins and nuts. Stir carrots, potatoes, eggs, and butter together and add dry ingredients. Spoon into a well-greased 1½ quart mold. Cover mold tightly with waxed paper held on by a rubber band. Place into steamer or pan with a rack. Fill pan with hot water so that mold is only half submerged. Steam, covered, on top of stove over medium heat for 1½ hours or until done. Batter will rise and be firm to the touch when done. Remove from pan when cool.

BROWN RICE CUSTARD PUDDING

Yield: 6 to 8 servings

4 eggs
1 t. vanilla
1 t. nutmeg
1 qt. whole milk
½ c. non-instant powdered milk
2 T. honey
¼ c. raw wheat germ
½-1 c. cooked brown rice
½ c. raisins
⅛ t. salt

Preheat oven to 325°. Beat eggs well, stir in vanilla and nutmeg. In a large, separate bowl, beat milks together until smooth. Add honey. Stir in the rest of the ingredients, mixing well. Stir in the eggs gently but thoroughly. Pour into a well-greased, 2-quart baking dish; sprinkle nutmeg on top. Put baking dish in a large baking pan nearly filled with hot water and bake for about 45 minutes or until knife inserted in the center comes out clean.

THE MEINERS' TOFU "CHEESE" CAKE

Yield: 8 to 10 servings

GRAHAM CRACKER CRUST

1 c. finely crushed graham cracker
  crumbs
3 T. melted margarine

Combine crumbs and margarine; reserve 1 tablespoon for topping. Press remaining crumbs in the bottom of a 9-inch round cake pan. Bake in a 350° oven for 6 minutes; cool.

FILLING

1 lb. 4-oz. medium firm tofu (soybean
  curd)
2 eggs
½ c. brown sugar, packed
2 T. lemon juice
1 1-inch piece lemon peel
1 t. vanilla
2 ripe bananas
1 20-oz. can crushed pineapple, drained

Preheat oven to 325°. Drain tofu, pat dry with paper towels. Place eggs, sugar, juice, peel, and vanilla in blender. Break tofu and bananas into chunks and add half to blender. Cover and blend until smooth. Add remaining banana and tofu chunks to blender; cover and blend again until smooth. Stir in drained pineapple (don't blend) and pour into cooled crust. Sprinkle reserved crumbs on top. Bake for 1 hour or just until center jiggles slightly when pan is gently shaken. Cool on a wire rack and chill until serving time.

CARROT CAKE

Yield: One 9" x 9" cake

1¼ c. whole wheat pastry flour
2 t. baking powder
1 T. nutritional yeast
½ t. cinnamon
⅛ t. salt
¾ c. vegetable oil
1 c. brown sugar, firmly packed
2 eggs
1 c. finely grated carrots

Preheat oven to 350°. Thoroughly mix together flour, baking powder, yeast, cinnamon and salt. In a large mixing bowl, combine the sugar and oil, mixing well. Add eggs one at a time, beating well after each addition. Add dry ingredients gradually. Finally, add grated carrots, blending well. Pour into a well-greased 9 x 9-inch cake pan or loaf tin. Bake for 35 to 45 minutes or until top springs back when pressed lightly and edges pull away from the side of the pan. If icing is desired, use the following:

NUT ICING

2 T. softened butter or margarine
3 oz. cream cheese (room temperature)
2 to 3 T. honey (to taste)
½ t. vanilla
¼ c. raw wheat germ
¼ c. non-instant powdered milk
¾ c. chopped walnuts

Blend butter and cream cheese until smooth. Add honey and vanilla. Stir in wheat germ and powdered milk. If frosting is too thick, add a little more honey. Spread onto cooled cake and pour walnuts over evenly.

KATHY'S APPLE-DATE PIE

Yield: 8 servings

2 eggs
½ c. brown sugar
2 t. whole wheat flour
¼ t. salt
1 t. grated lemon rind
1 t. lemon juice
1 c. sour cream
⅓ c. finely chopped dates
  (or raisins or currants)
3 c. sliced, tart apples
1 9-inch, unbaked, deep-dish pastry crust

Preheat oven to 400°. Beat the eggs until frothy and stir in sugar, flour, salt, lemon rind, and lemon juice. Fold in sour cream. Finally fold in dates and apples. Mix well and pour into pastry crust. Bake for 10 minutes. Sprinkle Topping onto pie and continue baking 30 to 35 minutes or until topping is lightly browned and filling is set. Chill until served.

TOPPING

⅓ c. brown sugar
½ c. whole wheat flour
½ t. grated nutmeg
1 T. butter

Combine dry ingredients. Cut in butter until mixture is crumbly.

Photograph opposite:
Carrot Cake

PEPPERNUTS

Yield: 7 dozen cookies

- 1 c. old-fashioned molasses
- 1 c. brown sugar
- 1 c. non-hydrogenated lard or shortening
- 2 t. cloves
- 1 T. cinnamon
- 1 T. anise seed (crushed with a rolling pin)
- 1 c. chopped nuts
- 2 t. baking soda, dissolved in 1 t. water
- ½ c. soy flour
- 1 T. nutritional yeast
- 2 c. whole wheat flour
- 1½ c. unbleached flour

Preheat oven to 300°. Thoroughly cream molasses, sugar, and lard. Mix in spices, then the rest of the ingredients until thoroughly blended. If dough is not stiff enough, add more flour. With floured hands, roll into balls approximately 1-inch diameter. Bake for 10 minutes or until lightly browned. Cool thoroughly on wire rack.

YOGURT APPLE PIE

Yield: 6 to 8 servings

- 3-4 apples (enough to fill an 8″ pie plate) Soft apples such as McIntosh or Jonathan work well
- 1 T. whole wheat pastry flour
- 2 T. non-instant powdered milk
- 1 T. raw wheat germ
- ¼ c. brown sugar
- ½ c. yogurt or sour cream
- 1 egg, beaten

Preheat oven to 350°. Wash and cut apples into eighths, removing core. Mix milk, flour, wheat germ, and sugar together. Add yogurt and stir well. Mix in egg, then apples. Pour into an 8-inch pie plate. Pour Topping evenly over top of pie, dot with butter. Bake for 45 minutes or until custard is set.

TOPPING

- ¼ c. brown sugar
- 1 T. whole wheat pastry flour
- 2 T. raw wheat germ
- ½ t. cinnamon

With a fork, mix together all ingredients.

RAISIN YEAST CAKE

Yield: 1 large or 2 small loaf cakes

- 2¼ t. or 1 pkg. active dry yeast
- 1⅓ c. lukewarm water
- 1 t. honey
- 2½ c. whole wheat pastry flour
- ¼ t. salt
- ¼ c. honey
- ½ t. cinnamon
- ½ t. ginger
- ½ t. nutmeg
- 1 c. raisins (or a mixture of currants and raisins)
- 1 t. grated orange rind
- ½ c. melted butter or margarine
- 2 eggs, slightly beaten

Mix yeast, water, and 1 teaspoon honey together and let stand for 15 minutes. Mix flour and salt together; stir into the yeast mixture. Cover the bowl with a towel, leave in a warm place (80°) for 1½ hours to rise. Stir into the dough the additional honey, spices, and fruit. Add the rind and butter and beat well. Finally, beat in the eggs. Divide in half, if desired. Place batter into two, small, well-greased bread tins or a 1-pound coffee can or larger tin. Cover and let rise for 30 minutes or until doubled. Preheat oven to 350°. Brush the top with milk and bake for 45 minutes or until done. Larger loaf will take longer. Remove from tins to cool.

DOUBLE PIE CRUST

Yield: Two 9 or 10-inch crusts

- 1½ c. whole wheat pastry flour
- ¼ c. raw wheat germ
- ½ t. salt
- ¾ c. margarine
- 2 T. (approximately) water

Have all ingredients cold. Mix together flour, wheat germ, and salt in a large mixing bowl. Cut in margarine with a pastry blender until mixture resembles fine crumbs. Add the water and stir gently with a fork until dough forms. Divide dough in half and roll out on a well-floured pastry cloth. Bake according to recipe specifications. If you want an unfilled, baked pie crust, prick crust with fork several times and bake in a 425° oven for about 10 minutes or until crust is done.

Note: Unbaked pastry shells freeze well. Just thaw before baking.

CAROB BROWNIES

Yield: Approximately 3½ dozen

1 c. margarine
2 c. honey
1 c. carob powder
½ t. salt
4 eggs
2 t. baking powder
2 T. soy flour, sifted
2 T. raw wheat germ
2 c. whole wheat pastry flour
1 t. vanilla
1 c. chopped nuts

Preheat oven to 350°. In a small pan over medium heat, melt margarine. Remove from heat and stir in honey, carob powder, and salt. In a large mixing bowl, beat eggs well. Stir in baking powder, soy flour, and wheat germ. Add carob mixture and beat well. Stir in flour and vanilla. Stir in nuts. Pour mixture into a well-greased 10 x 14-inch cake pan. Bake about 40 minutes or until toothpick inserted in center comes out clean.

BANANA-MIXED GRAIN COOKIES

Yield: 4 to 5 dozen cookies

¾ c. margarine
¾ c. brown sugar
1 egg
1 c. mashed ripe banana
1 t. lemon or vanilla extract
1 t. salt
1 t. baking powder
½ t. nutmeg
¾ t. cinnamon
1¼ c. whole wheat flour
¼ c. raw wheat germ
1½ c. raw mixed-grain cereal or oatmeal
½ c. chopped walnuts or other nuts or raisins

Beat margarine, sugar, and egg until light and fluffy. Stir in banana and flavoring until smooth. Add salt, baking powder, and spices and stir thoroughly. Slowly mix in dry ingredients until well combined, adding nuts last. Chill for at least 1 hour. Preheat oven to 375° Drop batter by teaspoonfuls onto lightly greased baking sheets. Bake 10 to 12 minutes or until done. Cool on wire rack.

CHRIS'S OATMEAL-RAISIN COOKIES

Yield: Approximately 6 dozen

1 c. margarine or shortening
1 c. brown sugar, firmly packed
¾ c. honey
3 eggs
2¾ c. whole wheat pastry flour
½ c. raw wheat germ
1 t. baking soda
1 t. baking powder
1 t. cloves
2 t. cinnamon
1 t. allspice
1 t. apple pie spice
1 t. nutmeg
1 t. vanilla
1 c. thick, unsweetened applesauce
8 c. oatmeal
4 c. raisins (or more, as desired)

Preheat oven to 350°. Cream together margarine and sugar; add honey and eggs, and blend thoroughly. In a separate bowl, mix together all the dry ingredients except oatmeal and raisins. Stir into the egg mixture. When thoroughly mixed, add vanilla, applesauce, oatmeal, and raisins. (Portions of the dough can be frozen at this point; thaw when ready to bake and proceed with recipe.) Drop dough from a teaspoon onto ungreased baking sheets. Bake 8 to 10 minutes or until done; remove immediately from tins and allow to cool on wire racks.

Glossary

Agar-agar: an edible seaweed gelatin; available in flakes, bars, and granules.

Braise: to cook by browning in vegetable oil and then simmering, covered, with a small amount of added liquid.

Bran: outer coating of the wheat kernel; high in B vitamins.

Buckwheat: also called kasha; not a wheat but from a hardy herb.

Bulgur or bulghur: cracked wheat.

Carob: a chocolate substitute made from the St. John's plant. It does not produce the allergic reactions that chocolate does, is low in fat, and contains no caffeine. It does not taste like chocolate.

Graham flour: another name for whole grain or whole wheat flour. The best graham flour is stone ground because this process does not generate the heat that kills many of the nutrients.

Mince: to cut up into very fine pieces.

Non-hydrogenated: preferable to hydrogenated foods and includes oils which are processed with hydrogen to produce a solid fat.

Non-instant powdered milk: has more nutrients than instant; is usually more satisfactory in baking.

Nutritional yeast: another name for brewer's yeast and can be consumed raw, unlike baking or active yeast. Can be added to foods to add protein and the vitamin B complex.

Old-fashioned molasses: unsulphured, dark molasses.

Organically grown: foods which are grown without chemical fertilizers or pesticides.

Purée: mashed into a pulp after cooking, usually in a blender or sieve.

Sauté: to cook quickly in a small amount of oil, turning frequently.

Simmer: to cook just at or below boiling point; bubbles rise gently to the surface.

Tamari: a soy sauce concentrate available in natural food stores. Commercial soy sauce is not really a substitute.

Tempura: deep-fried, battered foods.

Tofu: soybean curd. Made from soy products, it is very bland and blends well with seasonings. Some people call it soy cheese.

Unbleached flour: creamy white flour which has not been bleached with chemicals.

Wheat germ: the part of the grain from which the new plant can grow. Raw wheat germ should be used when possible, because some of the nutrients in toasted wheat germ have already been harmed by heat. Wheat germ contains a high quality protein and B vitamins.

Whole wheat flour: flour ground from the whole grain, containing the endosperm, bran, and germ; it is milled from hard wheat.

Whole wheat pastry flour: more finely ground than plain whole wheat flour; it is milled from soft wheat. Unfortunately, it differs from mill to mill.

SUBSTITUTIONS	
1 cup buttermilk or sour cream	= 1 cup yogurt
¼ cup cocoa	= ¼ cup carob powder
1 cup granulated sugar	= 1 cup honey in yeast breads; ⅞ cup honey in cookies and cakes; reduce liquid in recipe by 3 tablespoons. or 1 cup firmly packed light brown sugar or 1 cup maple syrup; reduce liquid in recipe by ¼ cup
1 cup all-purpose flour	= ⅝ cup oat flour plus ⅜ cup rice flour or ⅞ cup whole wheat flour or 1 cup unbleached flour or 2/3 cup whole wheat flour plus 1/3 cup wheat germ or ¾ cup whole wheat flour plus ¼ cup bran or ⅞ cup whole wheat flour plus 2 tablespoons soy flour (reduce baking temperature about 25° when adding soy flour)
2 cups water plus 1 T. unflavored gelatin	= 2 cups water plus 2 to 3 tablespoons agar-agar
1 T. fresh herbs	= 1 teaspoons dried herbs
1 cup white, enriched, or converted rice	= 1 cup brown rice

Photograph opposite:
Chris's Oatmeal Raisin Cookies, p. 61

Book II Index

Book III

Family
COOKBOOK

CONTENTS

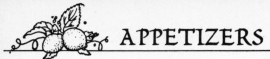

Crab Stuffed Mushrooms

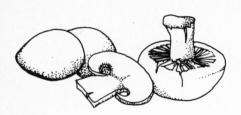

3 dozen large whole fresh mushrooms
1-7½ ounce can crabmeat, drained and
   flaked
1 tablespoon snipped parsley
1 tablespoon pimiento, chopped
1 teaspoon chopped olives
¼ teaspoon dry mustard
½ cup mayonnaise

Wash and dry mushrooms. Remove stems.
Mix all ingredients. Fill each cap. Bake 8
to 10 minutes at 375°

Millie Kusnier

Fried Cheese Puffs

Mix together 3 cups grated cheese, 2
tablespoons flour, ¾ teaspoon salt, and
dash of pepper. Add 4 egg whites beaten
stiffly. Form into balls, roll in cracker
crumbs. Fry in deep fat.

These can be made ahead and stored in
refrigerator, ready to be deep fat fried.

Mrs. Paul A. Beam

Ham-Cheese Ball

3 packages cream cheese (8 ounce packages)
1 cup diced ham bits
2 tablespoons horseradish
2 tablespoons mustard
2 cups finely chopped nuts

Combine first four ingredients and form in 3
or 4 inch balls. Roll in nuts. Delicious with
crackers.

Mary Jane Ricks

Glazed Meatballs

1 pound ground beef
½ cup dry bread crumbs
⅓ cup minced onion
¼ cup milk
1 egg
1 tablespoon snipped parsley

1 teaspoon salt
⅛ teaspoon pepper
½ teaspoon Worcestershire sauce
¼ cup shortening
1 bottle (12 ounce) chili sauce
1 jar (10 ounce) grape jelly

Mix ground beef, crumbs, onion, milk, egg and next four seasonings.
Gently shape into 1 inch balls. Melt shortening in large skillet; brown
meatballs.

Remove meatballs from skillet; drain off fat. Heat chili sauce and
jelly in skillet until jelly is melted; stirring constantly.

Add meatballs and stir until coated. Simmer 30 minutes. Serve hot in
chafing dish. You may put toothpicks in a few of the meatballs and
place a dish of toothpicks beside chafing dish for guests to use.

This recipe makes 5 dozen meatballs.

Nancy W. Burns

4

Shrimp Mold

Melt in top of double boiler, and cool:
    1 can condensed tomato soup
    1-8 ounce package cream cheese

Add:
    2 envelopes gelatin, diluted
       in ½ cup cold water
  ½ cup minced onion
  ½ cup chopped celery }Chop fine
  ½ cup chopped green pepper
  1 cup mayonnaise
  3 cans (small) shrimp (tiny size)

Mix well and pour in greased mold. Chill at least 24 hours. Serve unmolded with flavored crackers or rye bread rounds (cocktail size).

Mrs. John F. Allen

Chicken Livers Paté

½ pound chicken livers	2 tablespoons cream
2 hard-cooked eggs	2 tablespoons butter
⅛ teaspoon pepper	1 teaspoon salt
½ teaspoon Worcestershire sauce	⅛ teaspoon celery salt

Cut livers in small pieces and cook in butter in skillet until lightly brown. Put livers and eggs through food chopper using fine blade. Add remaining ingredients and mix until smooth.

Dorothy Piepmeyer

Parsley Tomatoes

Cut tomatoes in generous slices. Chill and marinate in oil and vinegar dressing. Sprinkle with minced parsley.

Smoked Beef Dip

Soak 1 teaspoon minced onion in
    1 tablespoon sherry until soft.

Add:
  1 large package cream cheese
  2 tablespoons mayonnaise
  ¼ cup stuffed olives, minced
  1-3 ounce package smoked beef, minced

Delicious served with crackers or potato chips.

Mrs. Roger C. Wilder

Hot Shrimp Dip

  1 can cream of shrimp soup
  1 cup shredded sharp cheese
  ¾ cup shrimp, cut up
    (baby or broken shrimp)
  ¼ teaspoon tabasco sauce

In a saucepan, combine all ingredients and heat slowly, stirring until blended and mixture bubbles. Pour into fondue dish and serve as a hot dip with melba rounds. Makes 2 cups.

Ginger Williams

Chive Cheese and Almond Dip

  6 ounce package chive cream cheese
  ¼ cup milk
  ¼ teaspoon salt
  1 teaspoon prepared mustard
  ½ cup chopped toasted almonds

Soften cheese with milk. Mix in rest of ingredients.

Serve with raw green pepper, radishes, carrots, celery and cauliflower.

Millie Kusnier

JAMS AND JELLIES

Tomato Preserves

Transparent flame, gold flecked,
Imprisoned in glass!

In a steel or enamelware kettle put:
  4 cups of red-ripe tomatoes, peeled and finely cut

Heat slightly, pouring off a generous cupful of the juice that forms. (Save this juice to use as a vitamin-rich, low-calorie soup or spaghetti sauce base.)

To the tomatoes add:
  1½ teaspoons pickling spices, these tied in a square of cheesecloth or muslin.
  ¼ teaspoon powdered ginger
  2 cups sugar
  1 lemon, thinly sliced.

Simmer slowly, stirring often, until tomatoes become transparent . . . about 20 minutes. Set kettle off heat. Cover and let stand.

12 to 18 hours later:
  Reheat and simmer slowly for 30 minutes. Stir frequently, as it scorches easily.

After removing the sack of pickling spices, pour mixture into small jars, sealing each with paraffin. This recipe makes three cups of preserves and a lot of happiness for those to whom it is served with dark bread or graham rolls.

Mrs. A. R. Bergantine

Peach-Orange Marmalade

1 dozen large or 15 small peaches
1 orange (whole orange, including rind)
  Medium sized jar of maraschino cherries
  Sugar

Cut peeled peaches in small pieces and grind cherries and orange (also rind). Mix together and for every cup of fruit mixture add an equal amount of sugar. Cook one hour. Spoon into jars. Makes about 9 jars of marmalade.

"This is an old family recipe, usually made by my grandmother. The jars of marmalade disappear in a short period of time. This recipe is a blue ribbon winner at our county fair every year."

Patty Doarn

Rhubarb Jam

4 cups diced rhubarb
4 cups sugar

Stir above over low heat until dissolved. Bring to a rolling boil, then turn off heat.

Stir in 1 package cherry or strawberry Jello.

Let set 10 minutes. Seal in your jars.

Mary Biegel

Honey Jelly

2½ cups honey
¾ cup lemon juice
½ cup liquid pectin

Combine lemon juice and honey. Bring to full rolling boil. Add pectin, stir and boil for two minutes longer. Pour into sterilized jars and seal with paraffin.

Mrs. J. H. Blackburn

Summer to Keep

Lee Avery

Put up the best of summer . . . As you keep its vivid fruit-like jewels in a jar . . . Conserve the gull-fleet moments that soar by . . . Enclose the pine that held an evening star . . . The clean delight that swept a beach at dawn . . . The sky that lifted with the flashing wings . . . Gather them to you while they still are fresh . . . Store up each beauty as it lifts and sings!

Copyrighted. From INLAND GULLS AND OTHER POEMS. Also published in the CHRISTIAN SCIENCE MONITOR, June 11, 1958

Frozen Strawberry Jam

2 cups strawberries, crushed
1 box pectin plus ¾ cup water
4 cups sugar

Prepare jars. Prepare fruit. Measure sugar, add to fruit and mix well. Combine ¾ cup water and pectin in saucepan. Bring to boil and boil for 1 minute, stirring constantly. Stir into fruit mixture. Continue stirring 3 minutes. A few sugar crystals will remain. Quickly ladle into jars. Cover at once with tight lids (no paraffin necessary). Set at room temperature about 24 hours. Then store in freezer. Ready to eat in 3 weeks.

Lanita Fleischmann

Steak Soup

1½ cups steak, cut fine
1 cup carrots, cut fine
1 cup celery, cut fine
1 cup onions, cut fine
1 cup frozen mixed vegetables
2 tablespoons butter
1 can #303 tomatoes
1 cup flour
8 cups water
2 tablespoons beef base
1 teaspoon freshly ground coarse black pepper

Sauté steak in skillet until it is half done. Cook fresh vegetables in small amount of water until half done. Melt butter in large kettle, add flour and mix until smooth, add the 8 cups water and cook, stirring until done and smooth. Then add all ingredients together and simmer slowly for 1 hour. This is a good hearty soup.

Mrs. Floyd Olson

> There is no spectacle on earth more appealing than that of a beautiful woman in the act of cooking dinner for someone she loves.
>
> *Thomas Wolfe*

Tasty Garnishes On Soup

Grated cheese
Crumbled bacon bits
Toasted slivered almonds on creamed soups
Lemon slice on clear tomato
Minced parsley or chives on any cream or jellied soup
Cheese popcorn on tomato soup
Toasted garlic flavored croutons
Sprinkled paprika, nutmeg or cayenne pepper on cream soups

Chicken Corn Soup

Cut up and cook one whole chicken in enough water to cover it. After it is well-cooked, remove the chicken from the broth, remove the meat from the bones and cut it up fine and return it to the broth. Add 1 large, diced onion, 1 stalk of diced celery, 3 diced, hard-cooked eggs. Add as much whole-kernel corn as you want. (I use one large bag of frozen whole-kernel corn if I cannot get fresh corn.) Cook until celery, onion and corn are done. Then add small "rivvels" made by mixing 2 cups of flour, 1 egg, and salt and pepper. Mix together until mixture is crumbly and then drop these into the broth and simmer about 15 minutes more. This soup can be simmered as long as you wish and seems to improve when reheated.

Martha Cramer

Ham Bone Soup

1 or more trimmed ham bones
6 quarts water
1 medium can tomatoes
1 teaspoon dried parsley
2 sprigs cut celery
3 peppercorns
2 tablespoons barley
3 cut carrots
  Half a small head of cabbage, cut up
  Salt
2 large diced potatoes

Place ham bone in two-gallon pot, add water, tomatoes, parsley, celery, peppercorns, barley, carrots and salt to taste. Boil for 2 hours, add cabbage and potatoes and cook for another half-hour.

More carrots can be used, also more cabbage and a little catsup to improve the flavor. The ham bone does not need to be trimmed too much, as parts of ham add to the flavor of the soup.

Stanley R. Rempala

Autumn Soup

1 pound ground beef
4 cups hot water
1 cup cut up celery
2 teaspoons salt
1 teaspoon meat extract
6 whole fresh tomatoes, stems removed
1 cup chopped onions
1 cup cut up carrots
1 cup cut up potatoes
½ teaspoon pepper
1 bay leaf, pinch of basil

Brown beef slowly in hot fat in a heavy skillet. Add onions and cook 5 minutes. Loosen meat from bottom of kettle. Add remaining ingredients, except tomatoes; bring to boil, cover and simmer 20 minutes. Add the tomatoes; simmer 10 minutes more.

Nutritious for dieters; add a hearty dessert for others. Serves 6.

Edith Borne

Peanut Butter Soup

3 tablespoons onion, minced
1 tablespoon butter
¼ cup peanut butter (chunky style)
1 can cream of chicken soup
1 soup can of water
¼ cup milk

Sauté onion in butter. Blend in peanut butter. Stir in soup, a little at a time to blend. Stir in water and milk. Heat but do not boil. Serves 3.

Maysie Newsom

Mormon Whole Meal Soup

1 tablespoon butter
2 pounds ground beef
2 quarts hot water
2 cups diced potatoes
1 cup diced celery
2 cups tomatoes
1 cup corn
1 cup diced carrots
2 cups shredded cabbage
2 onions, diced
1½ teaspoon salt
¼ cup rice

Melt butter, add meat and brown. Add water and bring to a full rolling boil. Add vegetables. Bring back to a boil. Add rice and seasonings. Simmer 1 to 1½ hours.

Leslie Epperson

Fruit Salad

1 pkg. vanilla pudding
1 pkg. orange or lemon tapioca pudding
1 can mandarin oranges
1 can pineapple chunks
1 banana sliced.

(You may substitute vanilla tapioca pudding and one heaping tablespoon of frozen concentrated orange juice in place of the orange or lemon tapioca pudding.)

Cook puddings together with 3 cups liquid. (Use liquids from canned fruits and add water to make remainder 3 cups.) Cool slightly then add fruits. Refrigerate.

Beverly J. Saleske

Maple Nut Salad

1½ cup crushed pineapple (#2 can) drained
2 packages cream cheese
½ cup chopped dates
¼ cup maple syrup
1 cup cream, whipped
½ cup chopped nuts

Fold all ingredients together, and set in refrigerator.

Velda Block

Georgia Nut Salad

Beat in a heavy saucepan, 2 eggs until foamy. Add ½ cup sugar and a scant ½ cup vinegar. Cook until thick, stirring slowly with a wooden spoon. Take from heat and beat until smooth, then let cool. When cool add 2 tablespoons of cream and beat again. Set aside and pare and dice about 6 large apples. Pour cooled sauce over apples then gently fold in 1 cup pecans. Serve at once.

"This delicious salad came from a gracious Georgia plantation. A family recipe traditional for their Christmas menu."

Mozelle Hotchkiss

Cherry Coke Salad

1 can (1 pound) bing cherries
1 can (1 pound, 4 ounces) crushed pineapple
1 large package (6 ounce) cherry gelatin
2 bottles (6½ ounces each) cola

Drain juice from fruit; add water if necessary to make 2 cups. Heat juice to boiling; add gelatin, stir until dissolved. Cool; add cola and fruit. Pour into 1½ quart mold. Chill until set. Serve with salad dressing, cream cheese dressing or whipped cream.

Florence Howard

Use a Variety of Salad Greens

Head lettuce   Leaf lettuce
Bibb lettuce   Boston lettuce

Romaine   Escarole   Watercress
            Celery lettuce
Curly endive   Spinach

Unusual Additions to Salads

Sliced water chestnuts
Tiny croutons browned in garlic butter
Chopped raw asparagus tips
Artichoke hearts
Crisp bacon
Sliced mushrooms
Ripe or stuffed sliced olives
Anchovies
Sliced hard-cooked eggs

Pink Applesauce Mold

Add a dash of salt and ⅓ cup red hots to 1 can applesauce. Heat slowly until red hots are melted. Add 1 package lemon gelatin, dissolve. Then add 1 small bottle of 7-Up. Mold. Good with ham.

Irene Moyle

Eggnog Holiday Salad

1 can (1 pound) fruit cocktail
2 envelopes plain gelatin
1 can (11 ounces) mandarin oranges, cut in half
1 cup flaked coconut
2½ cups dairy eggnog
Dash of nutmeg

Drain fruit, saving juice. Soften gelatin in juice and melt over hot water. Combine with rest of ingredients. Turn into 5-cup mold and chill until firm.

"This is very good to serve from Thanksgiving to New Years when eggnog is available. Has a delicious taste. When serving at Christmastime, a few extra maraschino cherries cut in half may be added. The extra red color makes it look more festive."

Maysie Newsom

Crab Louis

Louis Dressing:

- 1/4 cup chili sauce
- 1/2 pound sour cream
- 1/4 cup finely chopped green pepper
- 1/4 cup finely chopped green onion
- 1 cup mayonnaise
- 1 teaspoon lemon juice
- Salt to taste

Ingredients:

- 1 head lettuce
- 1 cup crabmeat (more if desired)
- 2 avocadoes
- 1 small can string beets
- 1 small can pitted olives
- 2 boiled eggs
- 2 tomatoes

Use remaining green pepper and green onion from dressing. Cut the green pepper in thin strips and onion in bite-size pieces.

Cover plates with bite-size pieces of lettuce. Put remaining ingredients in desired arrangement on top of lettuce. Pour dressing over top, or serve to the side in a small pitcher.

Note: This dressing can be used on green salads if any is left over. Yield 6.

Suzanna C. Bascochea

Tuna Crunch Salad

- 1-6 ounce can tuna, drained
- 1/4 cup chopped sweet pickles
- 1 tablespoon minced onion
- 1 to 2 tablespoons lemon juice
- 3/4 cup salad dressing
- 1 1/2 cups shredded cabbage
- 1 1/4 cups crushed potato chips

Combine first 5 ingredients. Cover and chill until ready to serve, then add cabbage and toss. Add 1 cup of crushed potato chips and toss. Heap in bowl and sprinkle remaining chips on top. Yield 5-6.

Ruth Lovaasen

Macaroni-Ham Salad

- 2 cups cooked and cooled macaroni (Remember — use 1/2 amount uncooked)
- 1 cup diced cucumber
- 1 cup diced ham
- 1 tablespoon grated onion
- 1 tablespoon minced parsley
- 3/4 cup mayonnaise
- 1/2 teaspoon salt
- 1/4 teaspoon pepper

Combine all ingredients. Toss together until blended. Put in tomato cups and sprinkle with grated cheese. 4-6 servings.

Mary Reiner

Hearty Lunch Salad

- 1 cup carrots grated
- 2 tablespoons minced onion
- 1/2 cup diced celery
- 1/2 cup salad dressing
- 2 tablespoons cream or milk
- 2 tablespoons salad mustard
- 1 can salmon
- 1 can shoestring potatoes

Mix the first 7 ingredients together. Top salad with potatoes just before serving.

Frances Langbecker

Chinese Chicken Salad

- 4 cups cooked chicken (cut up)
- 1 can bamboo shoots (5 ounces, drained)
- 1 can water chestnuts (5 ounces, drained)
- 2 cans mandarin oranges (drained)
- 1 cup slivered almonds
- 2 tablespoons dehydrated onions (minced)
- 2 cups mayonnaise
- 2 cans Chinese noodles

Combine first 7 ingredients and chill. Serve on the Chinese noodles. Yield 6-8.

Mrs. Robert C. Sauer

Holiday Relish

1 package whole cranberries, raw
2 apples (unpeeled)
2 oranges (unpeeled)
1 small can crushed pineapple
1 cup chopped pecans
2¾ cups sugar
1 teaspoon red food coloring

Place cranberries and 2 cups of water in blender. Chop finely and drain. Place cored and quartered apples (unpeeled) and 2 cups water in blender. Chop finely and drain. Quarter oranges (unpeeled), remove seeds, and chop finely in blender. Do not add water. Use only juice from oranges. Mix all ingredients together in glass bowl and refrigerate overnight to enhance flavor. Yields approximately 1½ quarts

LaVada Whiteley

Rosy Applesauce Relish

1 #2 can applesauce
½ cup diced celery
½ cup (or less) raisins
½ cup red-hot cinnamon candies
2 teaspoons of prepared horseradish
(about, or to taste)

Combine and stir. Chill in refrigerator overnight. Stir before serving. Keeps well. Yield 4 cups.

Mrs. Don L. Jacobs

Quick Pickled Beets

1 #2 can or jar sliced beets
¼ cup vinegar
1 teaspoon salt
¼ teaspoon cinnamon
⅛ teaspoon cloves
Dash of pepper

Drain juice from beets. Add remaining ingredients to juice and bring to boiling. Pour over beets and sprinkle caraway seeds over top. Chill overnight.

Harriet Myles

Russian Dill Pickles

1 cup water
2 cups vinegar
1½ cups sugar
Cook to boiling.

Select thin cucumbers about 5 inches long. Wash and cut lengthwise in quarters. Put 1 head of dill, 1 small red pepper, ½ teaspoon salt and 2 teaspoons of mixed spice in each quart jar. Pack cucumbers in jars and pour hot liquid over cucumbers. Seal jars.

Edith Shaska

Sweet Dill Pickles

1 quart dill pickle chips
2 cups sugar
½ cup tarragon or apple cider vinegar
1 teaspoon celery seed
1 teaspoon mustard seed (optional)

Rinse and drain cucumber chips. Mix all other ingredients and bring to a boil. Remove from stove, let cool 10 minutes. Pack chips into jars and pour syrup over them. Seal jars and let set about a week.

Mrs. C. E. Mathews

Spiced Peaches

7 cups sugar
1 pint cider vinegar
1 pint water
Boil together for 20 minutes.

Add peeled fruit and boil until tender. To each jar add 3 whole cloves and 3 small sticks cinnamon. Fill jars with fruit. Cover with syrup and seal. This is enough for 6 quarts. Process for 20 minutes in canner in hot water bath.

This recipe can be used for spicing pears, watermelon rind, apricots and pineapples. The juice from spiced fruit is good for seasoning ham or pork.

Mrs. Chester A. Cramer

13

Potato Soufflé

4 tablespoons chopped onion
3 tablespoons melted butter
1 cup milk
2 tablespoons flour
  Salt and pepper
2 eggs separated
3 cups leftover mashed potatoes

Brown onion in butter, add flour and then milk. Add yolks and sauce to potatoes and mix well. Then fold in beaten egg whites. Bake in greased oven dish about 25 or 30 minutes at 350°F.

Mrs. Hugh Morenz

Green Beans, Cream Style

1-10 ounce package frozen green beans
1-3 ounce package cream cheese, softened
1 tablespoon milk
¼ teaspoon celery seed
¼ teaspoon salt

Cook beans according to package directions, drain.

Combine remaining ingredients, blend thoroughly. Add to beans to heat through. 4 servings.

Mrs. John Allen

Vegetable Platter Combinations

1. Pile whole kernel corn with green pepper in center of platter; surround with broiled tomato halves.
2. Mound of mashed squash surrounded with baked potatoes and buttered asparagus, topped with grated cheese.
3. Cauliflower head with buttered almonds, surrounded with glazed sweet potatoes and creamed green beans.
4. Buttered green lima beans surrounded by small creamed onions and glazed carrots.
5. Baked acorn squash halves filled with pineapple and brown sugar.
6. Broccoli spears topped with toasted almonds, surrounded with buttered whole kernel corn.

Beets Royale

1 #2 can pineapple chunks
2 tablespoons cornstarch
1 #3 can diced beets or can
    of very small beets
1 tablespoon vinegar
3/4 teaspoon salt

Blend cornstarch with 1/2 cup pineapple juice. Add beet juice and cook until thickened. Add vinegar, salt, and pineapple and beets. Heat thoroughly.

Mrs. C. F. Frederick

Elegant Corn

1-16 ounce can corn
1 cup cracker crumbs
1/3 cup diced celery
1/4 cup onion
3/4 cup American cheese, cut
    in small pieces
1 teaspoon salt
2 eggs, well-beaten
2 tablespoons melted butter
1/4 teaspoon paprika
1 cup milk

Combine all the ingredients and pour into a greased casserole. Bake in 350° oven for 50 minutes. 4-6 servings.

Mrs. Walter Weichert

Swedish Red Cabbage

1 medium head red cabbage, sliced
1/4 cup butter
3 tablespoons brown sugar
1/4 cup chopped onion
2 firm tart apples, sliced
2 tablespoons vinegar
1/2 teaspoon caraway seeds
1/2 teaspoon salt
1/4 teaspoon pepper
1/2 cup grape juice

Sauté cabbage in butter for about 5 minutes, stirring occasionally. Add brown sugar, onions and apples; continue cooking for another 5 minutes. Add remaining ingredients; cover and simmer slowly for 30 or 35 minutes, stirring occasionally. Serve hot with meat course.

Mina Morris Scott

Scalloped Cabbage

1 small head cabbage   1 can cream of chicken
1/2 soup can milk   soup
1 cup bread crumbs   1/2 cup grated cheese
                      Butter for topping

Cut cabbage in small wedges. Cook in salted water until tender. Drain thoroughly. Into greased casserole place alternate layers of cabbage and soup-milk-cheese mixture. Top with bread crumbs and dot generously with butter. Bake about 30 minutes at 350°. Yield 4-6 servings.

Mrs. Claud J. Mustain

Eggplant, Pizza Style

1 medium eggplant   1 teaspoon oregano
1 beaten egg   2 tablespoons chopped parsley
1/3 cup fine dry bread crumbs   1/4 cup grated Parmesan cheese
    Salad or olive oil   4 to 6 slices (about 6 ounces)
    Salt, pepper   Mozzarella cheese
1-8 ounce can (1 cup)
    seasoned tomato sauce

Pare eggplant, cut in 1/2 inch slices. Dip in beaten egg, then coat well with bread crumbs; let dry a few minutes. Brown lightly on both sides in hot oil. Overlap slices in a lightly buttered 10 x 6 x 1 1/2 inch baking dish. Then sprinkle with salt, pepper, oregano, parsley and Parmesan cheese. Top with Mozzarella cheese. Pour tomato sauce over all. Bake in moderate oven (350°) for 20 minutes or until sauce is bubbly and cheese melts. Makes 5 or 6 servings.

Alberta Dredla

 # CASSEROLES

String Bean Casserole

2 medium cans string beans
1 medium can Chinese vegetables
1 can condensed cream of mushroom soup
1 medium can French fried onion rings
1 cup grated cheddar cheese

Drain beans and vegetables. Add condensed soup as it comes from can (do not add water.) Top with fried onion rings. Bake for 25 minutes at 325°. Sprinkle cheese over top and bake an additional 5 minutes. Add salt and pepper to taste.

Stephanie Meisch

Recipe for a Good Day

Take two parts UNSELFISHNESS and one part of PATIENCE and work together. Add plenty of INDUSTRY. Lighten with good spirits and sweeten with KINDNESS. Put in SMILES as thick as raisins in plum pudding and bake by the warmth which steams from a LOVING HEART. If this fails to make a good day, the fault is not with the recipe but with the cook.

submitted by Mrs. V. M. Miller

Asparagus Almondine

1 can cream of chicken soup
¼ cup of milk
3 hard-cooked eggs cut in
    ⅛ inch thick slices
1 cup cubed American cheese
1 package frozen cut asparagus
1 cup sliced almonds
½ cup bread crumbs
2 tablespoons butter

Combine milk and soup. Stir in eggs, cheese and asparagus (which has been cooked until tender). Turn mixture into buttered casserole. Cover top with almonds, then crumbs. Dot with butter. Bake at 350° for 30 to 40 minutes, until bubbly and slightly brown on top.

Marian Butterbaugh

Yuletide Scalloped Onions

2 pounds small white onions
¼ cup butter or margarine
¼ cup flour
2 cups milk
½ teaspoon salt
¼ teaspoon pepper
1 cup grated sharp cheese
¼ cup chopped pimiento
¼ cup chopped parsley
½ cup bread crumbs

Peel onions, cook in salted water 15 minutes until just tender; drain. Place in baking dish.

Melt butter, add flour and blend until smooth, cook 3 minutes.

Heat milk, add to flour mixture slowly, stirring. Bring just to boil and cook about 5 minutes, stirring constantly with wire whip. Add salt and pepper.

Stir in cheese until melted; add pimiento and parsley, mix. Pour over onions. Mix crumbs with 1 tablespoon softened butter. Sprinkle as a border for pan. Brown in moderate oven (375°) for 15 minutes. Serves 8.

Florence W. Furgasan

Carrot Ring

¼ cup butter
2 tablespoons flour
½ teaspoon salt
⅛ teaspoon pepper
3 eggs, separated
2 cups cooked carrots, mashed and seasoned

Melt butter, add flour and seasoning. Add to slightly beaten egg yolks and blend smooth. Add cooled mashed carrots and mix well. Fold in stiffly beaten egg whites. Pour mixture into well-greased 1½ quart mold. Set mold in pan of hot water and bake ½ hour at 350°F oven.

Invert on large platter and fill center with buttered peas. Yield 8 servings.

Gladys Long

Lima Bean Supreme

1 pound lima beans, soak overnight. Drain, add water and boil 45 minutes, drain again.

Mix in baking dish:
   Beans
½ pound butter
½ cup brown sugar
1 tablespoon dry mustard
½ pint sour cream
1 teaspoon molasses

Bake 1 hour at 350°. Stir once during baking time. Yield—6 servings.

Arline Quier

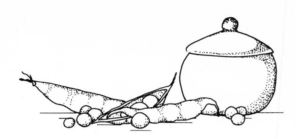

Barbecued Kraut

4 strips bacon
½ onion diced
½ cup brown sugar
1 #2 can tomatoes
   A-1 meat sauce
   Worcestershire sauce
   Barbecue sauce
2 #2 cans chopped kraut

Dice and brown bacon. Drain off excess grease and add onion, brown slightly. Add brown sugar and tomatoes and let simmer for 15 minutes. Add a dash of A-1 meat sauce, Worcestershire sauce and barbecue sauce to above. Drain sauerkraut and place in baking dish. Add cooked mixture. Toss lightly. Bake 1 hour at 350°. Serves 6.

Willabelle L. Wiley

Chicken and Yams

6 chicken breasts or 1 cut up fryer
¼ cup flour   ¼ teaspoon salt
¼ teaspoon paprika   Dash pepper
¼ cup oil
½ cup cut up celery and leaves
1 green bell pepper, sliced
1 medium clove garlic or garlic salt
⅛ teaspoon thyme   Dash rosemary
1 bay leaf
1 can condensed mushroom soup
½ cup liquid added to soup (use wine, broth, or water)
1 can whole white onions, drained
6 medium sweet potatoes cooked, or 1 can

Dust chicken with flour, salt, paprika, and pepper. Lightly brown in oil, then arrange in large casserole or pan.

Add to drippings celery, green pepper, garlic, bay leaf and rosemary.

Cook about 5 minutes, stir in remaining seasoned flour, gradually blend in soup and liquid.

Arrange onions and sweet potatoes around chicken in casserole. Pour seasoned soup over all.

Cover and bake at 375° about 30 minutes, then uncover and bake 30 minutes longer.

Marian Hunter

Helen's Vegetable Casserole

2 cups cooked carrots
2 cups green beans
2 cups celery
½ cup onions
½ cup green pepper
1 can tomatoes
4 teaspoons tapioca
1 teaspoon sugar
   Salt and pepper

Bake 2 hours at 350°
Makes 6 to 8 servings.

Helen Williams

17

Macaroni Mousse

Heat together ½ cup milk and 2 tablespoons butter. Add 6 slices white bread cut into ½-inch squares (remove crusts).

1 cup cut up cheese	2 cups cooked
½ can pimiento (cut up)	elbow macaroni
½ medium green	
pepper (cut up)	2 eggs beaten
1 tablespoon minced onion	Salt to taste

Place in buttered casserole. Sprinkle crushed cornflakes and paprika on top and dot with butter or margarine. Bake in 300° oven for ¾ hour. Serves 7.

Sauce for mousse

Mix together:
    2 tablespoons butter
    2 tablespoons flour
    2 cups milk

Cook and add 1 can shrimp, lobster or salmon.

Mrs. Wallace W. Morse

Baked Seafood Salad

½ cup chopped green pepper
¼ cup finely minced onion
1 cup chopped celery
1 cup cooked or canned crabmeat
1 cup cooked or canned shrimp
1 cup mayonnaise
½ teaspoon salt
1 teaspoon Worcestershire sauce
2 cups cornflakes crushed or
   1 cup dry bread crumbs
Paprika
2 tablespoons butter

Combine green pepper, onion, celery, crabmeat, shrimps, mayonnaise, salt and Worcestershire and mix lightly. (If using canned seafood, rinse shrimps well in plenty of cold water and drain. Look crabmeat over for shell bits.)

Place mixture in individual shells or a shallow baking dish. Sprinkle with crumbs and dot with bits of butter. Bake at 350° for 30 minutes. Serve with lemon wedges. Serves 6 or 8.

Mrs. J. Davidson

Yummy Casserole

1 can chow mein noodles
1 can cream of mushroom soup
1 cup shredded turkey or chicken
½ cup water
1 small can salted cashews
1 teaspoon grated onion
1 cup celery, cut fine

(Reserve ½ cup noodles for top.) Mix together and add noodles over top. Bake at 325° for 40 minutes.

Louise Hanicker

Rice Casserole

Use with a main meal dish instead of potatoes.
   1 can beef consommé
   1 can French onion soup
   ⅓ cup Parmesan cheese
   1 cup (8 ounce can) mushrooms and juice
   ¼ pound butter
   1½ cups raw converted rice

Bake 1 hour at 350°. Stir every 20 minutes. Yield 6 servings.

Audrey Mondloch

Quickie

1 can chicken rice soup
1 can cream of chicken soup
1 small can chicken
1 small can evaporated milk
1 small can mushrooms
1 small jar pimiento
1 can chow mein noodles

Mix and put in casserole. Top with crushed potato chips. Bake 1 hour at 350°.

Lois I. Typer

Broccoli

6 whole chicken breasts
4-10 ounce packages frozen broccoli
2 cans cream of chicken soup
1½ cups mayonnaise
⅔ cup half-and-half (half milk, half cream)
1½ cups grated cheddar cheese
2 teaspoons lemon juice
¼ teaspoon curry powder
1 cup fine dry bread crumbs, buttered

Cook chicken and let cool in liquid. Bone and cut in strips. Cook broccoli only until crisp tender. Mix together mayonnaise, half-and-half, cheese, lemon juice, curry and chicken soup. Pour over chicken and broccoli. Cover with bread crumbs. Bake at 350° for 40 minutes.

Mrs. Walter Rentsch

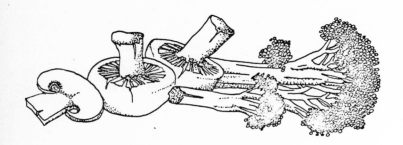

Cashew Beef

Brown in 1 tablespoon fat, 1 pound ground beef and 1 onion (minced). Add 1 can of cream of mushroom soup, 1 can cream of chicken soup and ½ cup milk, ¼ cup chopped green pepper, ½ cup chopped celery, 1 small can mushroom pieces, ½ cup cashew nuts, and 1 eight ounce package noodles cooked in boiling salted water and drained. Pour into greased casserole and top with potato chips or crumbs.

Bake 1½ hours at 350°F. Makes 10 servings.

Mrs. Lester V. Smith

Tuna Buffet

2 cans (6½ or 7 ounces each) tuna
    in vegetable oil
2 tablespoons finely chopped onions
1 cup sliced celery
1 medium green pepper, cut in strips
1 tablespoon curry powder
½ teaspoon ginger
1 teaspoon salt
1 can (14 ounces) pineapple chunks
1 can (10½ ounces) condensed cream
    of mushroom soup, undiluted
2 tablespoons raisins
1 tablespoon lemon juice
3 cups hot cooked rice

Drain oil from tuna into saucepan. Add onion, celery and green pepper, cook until crisp-tender. Stir in curry powder, ginger and salt. Drain syrup from pineapple and measure ½ cup. Add pineapple syrup, mushroom soup and raisins to saucepan. Bring mixture to boil, stirring constantly. Add lemon juice, pineapple and tuna. Heat to serving temperature. Serve with rice. Serves 6.

Mrs. D. C. Lemmon

Tamale Pie

Brown together:
    1 pound ground beef
    ½ pound salt pork, ground
    1 large onion, chopped
Add:
    1 large can tomatoes
    1 large can cream-style corn
    ½ cup olive oil

Cook slowly 10 minutes. In a separate pan heat 2 cups milk and add slowly 1½ cups yellow cornmeal. Stir until thick, then add:
    2 beaten eggs
    1 tablespoon salt
    1 tablespoon chili powder

Mix together with meat and add 1 can pitted ripe olives. Bake in a large casserole for 1 to 1½ hours. Serves at least 6. 300°

Mrs. John Bugbee

El Dorado

1 bag corn chips (medium size)
1 pound ground beef, browned
2 tablespoons onion, chopped
½ teaspoon garlic
2 cans tomato sauce (small)
    Mix last four ingredients together.
1 cup cottage cheese
1 cup sour cream
1 cup sliced olives
1 can Ortega chilies (diced)
    Mix last four ingredients together.

In oiled casserole place layer of chips, layer of meat mix, layer of cottage cheese mix. Sprinkle with grated cheese. Repeat layers and bake at 350°F. for 40 minutes.

Leila Teter

Contents of Cans

Size	Average Contents
#300	1¾ cups
1 tall	2 cups
303	2 cups
2	2½ cups
2½	3½ cups
3	4 cups
10	12-13 cups

Gourmet Omelet

8 garden onions   9 eggs
½ cup grated mellow cheese   ¼ cup milk
⅛ teaspoon salt   ⅛ teaspoon paprika
¼ cup melted butter or margarine

Cut onions finely, including green tops. Place in skillet with the heated butter or margarine. Cover with hot water, and cook slowly over medium heat until water is cooked out. Let onions brown slightly. Whip eggs until light, mix in cheese, add milk. Pour over the onions, and scramble. Serve with toast wedges. Serves 6. May be dusted with pepper instead of paprika if preferred.

Virginia K. Oliver

Yorkshire Hot Pot

4 shoulder lamb chops   2 teaspoons salt
1 garlic clove, minced   Pepper
4 small whole onions   1 can cream of mushroom soup
4 medium potatoes, halved, pared   ½ can water
    Paprika
1 package frozen cut beans
¼-½ teaspoon ground cloves

1. Brown chops in heavy skillet with garlic. Tuck onions and potatoes around and under chops. Add beans, cloves, salt, pepper, soup and water.
2. Cover, cook slowly 1 hour. Thicken and sprinkle with paprika.

Mrs. H. Kunnemann

St. Paul's Rice

1 pound bulk sausage   1 cup regular uncooked rice
1 bell pepper, chopped fine   4½ cups water
1 onion, chopped   ½ cup slivered almonds
1 cup chopped celery   Chopped parsley
1 package instant chicken noodle soup

Cook sausage in skillet, stirring through and cutting up to break into small bits. Drain off excess grease. Remove sausage. Sauté onion, pepper and celery. Mix the soup in water. Add rice and cook for seven minutes. Mix all ingredients together and put in a large baking dish; sprinkle almonds on top. Bake at 300° for 1 hour. Remove from oven and sprinkle a border of chopped parsley around the edge just before serving. Serves 4.

Fay Broyhill Edmonds

Veal Almondine

2 tablespoons butter
2 cups chicken stock or bouillon
2 tablespoons cornstarch
½ cup pineapple syrup
2 cups cubed cooked veal
½ cup drained canned crushed pineapple
½ cup toasted slivered almonds
½ cup chopped celery
1½ teaspoon salt.

Melt butter, add stock or bouillon, bring to a boil and reduce heat. Blend cornstarch and pineapple syrup and add to stock mixture until thickened. Boil 2 minutes. Add veal, pineapple, almonds, celery and salt. Heat thoroughly. Serve over chow mein noodles. 6 servings.

Mrs. Steven Frame

Spareribs With Caraway Kraut

2½ to 3 pounds spareribs, cut in pieces
2 teaspoons salt
¼ teaspoon pepper
1 #2½ can (3½ cups) sauerkraut
2 medium carrots, shredded
1½ cups tomato juice
2 tablespoons brown sugar
2 to 3 teaspoons caraway seed
1 unpared apple, finely chopped

Season ribs with salt and pepper. Combine kraut (including liquid) with remaining ingredients; place in Dutch oven. Place ribs, meaty side up, atop kraut. Bake, covered, in 350° oven 2½ to 3½ hours or until ribs are done, basting kraut with juices several times during the last hour. Makes 6 servings.

Nancy Watts

Swiss Steak in Sour Cream

Dredge round steak with flour, season with salt and pepper. Brown well on both sides in hot shortening. Add 2 sliced onions, 1 cup of sour cream (commercial), ½ cup grated cheese. Sprinkle paprika over all. Cover pan tightly and let simmer 2 hours at 300°.

Mrs. David Gruis

Hearty Ham Supper

2 cups cubed cooked ham
1 can whole kernel corn (drain)
1 cup diced cooked potatoes
¼ cup minced parsley
1 tablespoon finely chopped onion
¼ teaspoon paprika
¼ cup butter or margarine
¼ cup flour
2 cups milk
1 cup shredded American cheese

Make sauce of butter, flour and milk. Combine other ingredients in baking dish. Pour sauce over ham mixture and top with cheese. Bake 350° for ½ hour. 4-6 servings.

Iris Garrison

Wanted ... Time

Grace Allard Morse

Time to have my close friends in
    to drink a cup of tea;
Time to read the book of verse
    my sister sent to me.
Time to sort my linens out
    and stack them in neat rows;
Time to look my scrapbook o'er
    and work with rhyme and prose.
Time to bake some muffins
    for the boy who mows our lawn;
Time to listen to the lark
    at morning's early dawn.
Time to cut pink roses
    for a neighbor living near;
Time to plan the garden
    I have wanted for a year.
Time to breakfast leisurely
    and scan the paper through ...
Time, just to do the things
    I really want to do.

*Our sincere thanks to the author
whose address we were unable to locate.*

22

Stuffed Green Peppers

6 green peppers

Stuffing:

1½ to 2 pounds ground meat
 ½ cup grated onions
  1 cup raw rice
 ½ cup finely chopped celery
  3 eggs
  1 teaspoon salt
  1 tablespoon fresh-ground pepper
 ½ cup bread crumbs
  1 cup tomato juice and milk to make quite moist

Sauce:

4 cups tomato soup
1 cup tomato juice
1 can tomato sauce

Remove tops, membranes and seeds from peppers. Mix all ingredients for stuffing and fill peppers. If any mixture remains form into 2 inch balls and place all in baking dish or small roaster pan. Cover with sauce. Spoon sauce over peppers during baking period. Bake 2½ hours at 325°. Serves 6-8.

Arlene Steelman 23

Parmesan Chicken

2 frying chickens (cut up)
2 eggs well beaten with 2 tablespoons water
1½ cups cornflake crumbs
½ cup grated Parmesan cheese
1½ teaspoons salt
1 teaspoon onion salt
1 cup butter

Rinse chicken and pat dry. Dip in egg and water mixture. Combine crumbs with cheese, salt and onion salt. Drain chicken and coat heavily with the crumb mixture. Place in a foil lined pan which has been coated with half of the butter. Dot chicken with the remaining butter. Cover over with foil. Bake in a preheated oven 375° for 1 hour or until crisp and tender.

Mrs. Vernon Harter

Chicken Newburg

⅓ cup butter
¼ cup flour
2 cups milk
¾ cup shredded cheddar cheese
1 tablespoon chopped pimiento
1 teaspoon salt
½ cup toasted slivered almonds
½ cup sliced fresh mushrooms
1½ cups cooked sliced chicken
¼ cup cooking sherry
1 teaspoon minced onion
¼ teaspoon pepper

Melt butter and sauté mushrooms for 2 minutes in chafing dish. Stir in flour until smooth. Add milk, stirring constantly. Add chicken and all other ingredients except almonds. Top with almonds just before serving. Serve with rice or patty shells.

Mitzie Turck

Broiled Chicken

Select broiler chicken (1½ to 2 pounds). Split lengthwise. Brush with melted butter and season with salt and pepper.

Broil slowly, skin side down, about 8 inches from heat. Turn every 15 minutes, brushing each time with butter and lemon juice.

Broil 45 to 60 minutes or until nicely browned.

Mrs. James Turner

Roast Chicken

Select roasting chicken. Wash and pat dry. Sprinkle 1 teaspoon salt inside cavity. Stuffing may be made ahead of time but never placed in chicken until time for roasting. Make 1 cup stuffing for each ready to cook pound of chicken. Stuff body and neck cavities lightly. Close cavity with a skewer and string. Rub skin with chicken fat. Place breast side up in shallow roasting pan. Insert meat thermometer so that bulb is in the center of the inside thigh muscle. A thin cloth moistened with melted fat may be placed over chicken to help uniform browning. Keep cloth moist with fat in pan. Roast at 325° until meat thermometer registers 190°-200°

Stuffing:
Ingredients for 5 pound chicken

½ cup butter
½ cup chopped onion
½ cup chopped celery
4 cups dry bread cubes
1 tablespoon minced parsley
1 teaspoon salt
⅛ teaspoon pepper

Sauté onions and celery in butter until tender. Add other ingredients and toss lightly. Add bouillon, stock or water if moist stuffing is desired (stock made from cooking giblets).

Mrs. Boris Zielinski

Party Chicken

4 whole chicken breasts (boned)
8 slices of bacon
1 4-ounce jar of dried beef
1 cup sour cream
1 can mushroom soup

Separate beef and place in a layer on bottom of a greased 8-inch square pan. Wrap bacon around chicken breasts and lay on beef slices. Mix undiluted soup and sour cream. Pour over chicken breasts. Refrigerate overnight. Bake at 350° for 2 hours.

Bea White

Yugoslavian Paprikash

¼ cup butter
1 frying chicken (cut up)
½ cup chopped onion
¼ cup flour
2 tablespoons paprika
2 teaspoons salt
¼ teaspoon pepper
1 can chicken broth
2 cups sour cream
1 tablespoon Worcestershire sauce
1-8 ounce package medium noodles
    cooked and drained.

Melt butter in large frypan. Sauté chicken until lightly brown. Remove chicken, add onion. Blend in flour, paprika, salt and pepper. Add chicken broth and cook, stirring constantly until thick and smooth. Stir in sour cream and Worcestershire sauce.

Mix ½ of sauce with cooked noodles and pour into 3 quart baking dish. Arrange chicken on top of noodle mixture and pour remaining sauce over chicken. Bake at 325° for 1 hour. 6 servings.

Mary Novak

Baked Chicken

4 cups diced cooked chicken
¾ cup mayonnaise
¾ cup canned cream of chicken soup
2 cups chopped celery
4 hard-cooked eggs, sliced
1 teaspoon salt
1 teaspoon finely minced onion
2 tablespoons lemon juice
2 pimientos, cut up
1 cup crushed potato chips
⅔ cup finely shredded sharp cheddar
⅓ cup chopped almonds

Mix first 9 ingredients. Put in large shallow 1½ quart baking dish. Combine potato chips with cheese and almonds and sprinkle on top. Chill several hours or overnight. Bake in hot oven (400° F.) 25 minutes, or until heated.

Mrs. Leo Waters

Chicken Creole

1 stewing chicken (5-6 pounds)
1 cup chopped celery
2 green peppers, chopped
2 onions, chopped
½ pound thin spaghetti, broken
1 tablespoon Worcestershire sauce
1 can pimiento, chopped
1 can mushrooms, chopped
1 pound American cheese
Salt and pepper to taste

Boil chicken until very tender. Remove from broth, (about 2 quarts broth needed). Boil celery, peppers and onions in broth for 20 minutes. Add broken spaghetti, and boil 20 more minutes. Then add Worcestershire sauce, salt and pepper, pimientos and mushrooms. Dice chicken; and add to above. Grate cheese and mix well in above mixture. Put in baking dishes and leave in refrigerator for 24 hours. Just before serving time, place in 400° oven until warmed all through, at least ½ hour. Serves 10.

Lucille Pearce

Orange-Glazed Rack of Lamb

1 rib rack of lamb
½ cup orange marmalade
1 tablespoon brown sugar
2 teaspoons prepared mustard
3 tablespoons lemon juice
  Orange slices and maraschino cherries
    for garnish

Place lamb on rack in roasting pan. Roast in 350° oven 1¼ hours, or until meat thermometer registers 175 to 180°. Meanwhile combine marmalade, brown sugar, mustard and lemon juice in small saucepan and heat, stirring constantly until blended. Baste lamb with mixture during last half hour. Garnish with orange slices and cherries.

Gladys Biesik

Greek Meat Loaf

½ cup chopped onion
2 tablespoons butter
½ cup shredded carrot
½ cup shredded raw potato
1 small eggplant (about 1 pound)
    trimmed, pared and shredded
    (About 2½ cups)
2 cloves of garlic, thinly sliced
2 pounds meat loaf mixture (beef, veal, pork)
2 eggs

2 medium size tomatoes, peeled
    and finely diced (1 cup)
1½ cups fine dry bread crumbs
3 teaspoons salt
½ teaspoon ground cinnamon
¼ teaspoon pepper
4 tablespoons lemon juice
2 tablespoons sugar

Sauté onion in butter or margarine in a medium size skillet, remove from heat; stir in carrot, potato, eggplant, and garlic, tossing to coat well. Cover. Cook 5 minutes or until wilted but still crisp.

Combine meat loaf mixture, eggs, tomatoes, bread crumbs, salt, cinnamon, pepper, 2 tablespoons of lemon juice and the cooked vegetables in a large bowl, mixing lightly. Form into loaf and put into a lightly greased shallow baking pan.

Bake in moderate oven (350°) for 45 minutes. Mix remaining 2 tablespoons of lemon juice and sugar in a cup, stirring until sugar is dissolved. Brush over loaf. Continue to bake 15 minutes longer, or until brown and glazed. Lift to heated platter with 2 wide spatulas. 8 servings.

Mrs. Nick Costas

Barbecue Sauce

Suitable for any kind of meat or fowl. Brush on with a pastry brush as the meat is cooking.

1 pint cider vinegar
½ cup salt
1¼ cup granulated sugar
1 teaspoon celery seed
1 tablespoon red pepper
2 tablespoons black pepper
    Unstrained juice and pulp of 4 lemons
1 large grated onion

Mix all ingredients. Bring to boil in saucepan. Remove immediately from fire (do not overcook) and cool. Store mixture in a covered quart jar and let season for at least a week, occasionally shaking the jar. No need to store in refrigerator. It will keep perfectly on the pantry shelf.

Beatrice Branch

Veal Cutlets Cordon Bleu

12 veal cutlets
    Pepper
6 slices swiss cheese
6 slices boiled ham
½ cup flour
¼ teaspoon nutmeg
¼ teaspoon cloves (ground)
3 eggs, beaten
1 cup dry bread crumbs
¾ cup butter

Pound veal. Sprinkle with salt and pepper. Place 1 slice of cheese and 1 slice of ham on each patty. Cover with remaining patties. Roll in flour and spice mixture, dip in eggs and then into crumbs. Brown 5 minutes on each side. White sauce with mushrooms may be poured over before serving.

Mrs. Harvey Knoll

Pepper Steak

1½ pounds boneless round steak
1 garlic clove, minced
2 large tomatoes, skinned
    and chopped
4 medium green peppers,
    seeded and cut into strips

¼ teaspoon ground black pepper
1¼ teaspoons ground ginger
¼ cup olive oil
¼ cup soy sauce
½ teaspoon sugar
1¼ cups beef bouillon or stock
2 tablespoons cornstarch

Cut meat across the grain into thin strips. Heat the oil and brown the meat and garlic in it quickly. Then stir in tomatoes and peppers. Add soy sauce, pepper, sugar, ginger and ¾ cup of stock. Cover and cook 20 minutes or until meat strips are tender. Blend cornstarch with remaining stock. Stir into meat mixture, bring to boil and simmer for two minutes, stirring constantly. Serve over bed of rice.

Ruth Guidi

Swedish Glottstek

4 pounds rolled beef chuck
1 tablespoon salt
½ teaspoon allspice
½ teaspoon pepper
4 tablespoons butter
1 tablespoon oil
2 large onions, minced

1 teaspoon anchovy paste
2 bay leaves
2 tablespoons vinegar
2 tablespoons molasses
2 tablespoons flour
4 tablespoons water
½ cup heavy cream, whipped

Rub the salt, pepper and allspice on the meat and brown in the butter and oil. Add the onions, anchovy paste, bay leaf, vinegar and molasses. Cover and simmer 2 to 3 hours until meat is tender. Slice the meat thin and surround with vegetables. Make the gravy with flour dissolved in cold water then fold in the whipped cream. Serves 8.

Mrs. Peter Gaber

Crown-of-Gold Meat Loaf

1½ cups fine, soft bread crumbs
4 egg yolks
1½ teaspoons salt
1½ tablespoons prepared horseradish
2 tablespoons minced onion

1½ pounds ground lean
    chuck beef
2 tablespoons mustard
3 tablespoons finely diced
    green pepper
⅓ cup catsup

Topping:
4 egg whites
4 tablespoons mustard
¼ teaspoon cream of tartar

Mix bread crumbs with meat. Combine remaining ingredients. Blend into meat-bread mixture. Pack lightly into a 9-inch casserole and bake at 325° for 30 minutes. To make topping, beat egg whites until foamy; add cream of tartar and beat until very stiff. Fold into mustard gently. Swirl on hot meat. Return to oven and bake 20 to 25 minutes longer or until tipped with brown. Makes 6-8 servings.

Sister Mercedes SCC

Sauerbraten

1½ pounds beef cubes
1 tablespoon fat
1 envelope brown gravy mix
2 cups water
1 tablespoon minced onion
2 tablespoons white wine vinegar
2 tablespoons brown sugar
½ teaspoon salt
¼ teaspoon pepper
½ teaspoon ginger
1 teaspoon Worcestershire sauce
1 bay leaf
Hot buttered noodles

Cut meat into 1-inch pieces. Brown in hot fat. Remove from skillet. Add gravy and water to skillet and bring to boil, stirring constantly. Stir in remaining ingredients except noodles. Return meat to skillet and simmer 1½ hours. Stir occasionally. Remove bay leaf. Serve over hot, buttered noodles. Serves 6.

Faye Wheatley

Spanish Steak

1¼ pounds round steak
1 tablespoon vinegar
1 teaspoon salt
¼ teaspoon pepper
2 tablespoons chopped onion
1 tablespoon chopped parsley
2 tablespoons chopped celery leaves
½ cup chopped green pepper
1 #2 can tomatoes

Pound steak on both sides with edge of sturdy saucer. Cover with mixture of the remaining ingredients. Let stand for 1 hour. Lift meat out and drain. Save all of juice. Brown meat in 2 tablespoons meat drippings on both sides. Place in shallow baking dish and add tomato mixture in which meat was soaked. Cover. Bake 2 hours at 325°. Serves 6

Judy O'Connell

Roast Beef
(flavored with "trimmings"!)

Take vegetable trimmings that you usually throw out such as celery leaves, carrot peelings and ends, lettuce leaves (anything except vegetables with starch content). Line the bottom of the roast pan with them, using plenty of the trimmings. Place roast on top of this and put a piece of beef fat on top of the roast and put about half an inch of water in the pan to keep them moist. Place your roast in the oven in an uncovered pan. Roast in 300° oven. Baste the roast every half hour with juice from the bottom of the pan. If it evaporates, add water to the half-inch level. Continue with the basting until the roast is done.

Mrs. Wiley Seward

Lasagne

Brown together:

2 pounds ground beef
1 large onion, chopped
1 or two tablespoons olive oil
1 teaspoon Worcestershire sauce
  Garlic salt, salt, and pepper to taste

Add:

2 cans tomato sauce
1 can tomato paste
1 can tomatoes
1 teaspoon oregano
2 bay leaves

Simmer, covered, at least 2 hours or until cooked down. Stir often. Boil 1 package lasagne noodles, blanch, and drain. Grease a large 9 x 13-inch casserole. Mix 1 pint cottage cheese with 2 raw eggs. Place one layer noodles in casserole and cover with meat sauce; add ½ the cottage cheese mixture. Cover with grated Parmesan. Add a layer of Mozzarella or Provolone cheese. Repeat. Usually only about 2 layers are possible and it is best to end with the cheese on top. About 6 slices of Mozzarella or Provolone cheese are needed. Bake at 350° about 30 minutes or until cheese is melted and the sauce is bubbly.

Mrs. John H. Bugbee

Spice Sauce for Ham

2 tablespoons red wine garlic vinegar
2 tablespoons prepared mustard
½ teaspoon ground cloves
½ teaspoon cinnamon
1 cup apple jelly

Place ingredients in pan over low fire. Stir until jelly is smooth. Remove from fire. Sauce will jell when cold. Re-heat and serve over ham.

Mrs. W. S. McFarlane

Sour Cream Scalloped Potatoes and Ham

2 slices smoked ham (½ inch thick)
8 medium potatoes (sliced thin)
1 can cream of mushroom soup
1 cup sour cream
1 teaspoon salt
1 cup sliced onions
  Dash of pepper
1 cup shredded cheddar cheese.

Cut ham into 8 serving pieces. Slice potatoes. Combine soup, sour cream, salt and pepper. In greased 3 quart casserole alternate layers of ham, potatoes and onions with sour cream mixture. Top with shredded cheese. Cover casserole loosely with foil. Bake at 325° for 2½ hours. Yields 8 servings.

M. Neacy

Horseradish Dressing

Combine ½ teaspoon salt, ⅛ teaspoon white pepper, dash of cayenne pepper. Whip 1 cup heavy cream. Add seasonings to cream. Combine ½ teaspoon sugar, 2 tablespoons cider vinegar, ½ cup drained horseradish. Add this mixture to the seasoned cream.

Singapore Pork and Cabbage

(A one-dish meal)

1 pound pork shoulder, cut in strips or use leftover pork
2 quarts shredded cabbage
1 cup (8 ounce can) water chestnuts, drained, sliced
1 cup sliced mushrooms
2 tablespoons chopped pimiento
1 cup water
¾ cup Italian dressing
½ cup soy sauce
4 tablespoons cornstarch

If using raw pork, brown meat; cover and cook 15 minutes. Drain. If using leftover pork, slice and set aside while preparing vegetables. Mix vegetables, water, and Italian dressing; cook 8 to 10 minutes. Add meat, stir till heated. Add soy sauce combined with cornstarch; stir until thickened. Serve over rice, if desired. Makes 6 servings.

Evelyn L. Jenney

Crown Roast of Pork

Place crown roast of 16 ribs (about 4½ pounds) on rack in a shallow pan. Season the meat to your own tastes with salt and freshly ground pepper. Insert meat thermometer into the fleshiest part of the meat, making sure that it is not touching a bone. Cover exposed rib ends with foil. Place in 350° oven and cook for 1½ hours. Then remove it and fill the crown with your favorite stuffing. Return to oven for another hour or until the thermometer reads 185°. Serves 8.

Mrs. L. Bolerud

Stuffed Pork Chops

6 rib or loin chops, ¾ or more inches thick with pockets cut.
  Trim off excess fat. Prepare a dressing of:
1 cup bread crumbs
¼ cup chopped celery
¼ cup chopped onion
2 tablespoons chopped parsley
¼ teaspoon salt
⅛ teaspoon paprika
  Enough milk to moisten dressing

Fill pockets with dressing and sew together or fasten with toothpicks. Sear in hot skillet, then place in 9 x 13 inch baking dish. Dilute 1 can cream of mushroom soup with ⅓ can milk and cover the chops with the soup. Cover pan with foil and bake at 350° about 1 hour. Serves 6.

Mrs. John Bugbee

GAME

Game Notes

Duck, Goose, Venison:

To remove wild flavor soak birds for 3 hours in water to which 1 tablespoon baking soda and 1 tablespoon salt has been added.

Try to remove all shot pellets from flesh of birds so there is no chance of biting into one while eating cooked fowl.

It is very important that venison be cleaned immediately and that all meat is clear of any hair particles. Cut off excess tallow as this will give meat a strong flavor.

Wild Duck With Apple Raisin Stuffing

6 cups dry bread crumbs
1 cup cubed apple
½ cup raisins
¾ cup butter, melted
2 teaspoons salt
½ teaspoon pepper
¼ teaspoon cinnamon
⅛ teaspoon ginger
3 ducks

Clean ducks thoroughly. Combine other ingredients in bowl and mix. Fill cavity of ducks and close opening with skewers or string.

Place in roasting pan (breast side up) and roast for 15 minutes uncovered at 450°, reduce heat to 325°. Cover ducks and bake at least another 2 hours. Serves 6.

Doris Milligan

Venison Teriyaki Style

2 pound venison steak
⅓ cup soy sauce
1 tablespoon sugar
1 tablespoon minced onion
2 garlic cloves, crushed
½ teaspoon ginger
2 bay leaves
⅓ cup cooking oil

Cut meat into 6 equal pieces. Place in baking dish. Combine remaining ingredients and pour over venison. Cover and refrigerate overnight.

Drain. Place on broiler rack about 5 inches from heat. Broil 10 minutes brushing on marinade periodically. Turn steak and broil 5 minutes more. Serves 6.

Lisa Wainwright

Pheasant In Gourmet Sauce

2 pheasants
½ cup flour
1 teaspoon salt
1 teaspoon paprika
⅛ teaspoon pepper
⅛ teaspoon sweet basil
¼ cup shortening
1 clove garlic, crushed
¼ cup chopped olives
½ cup water
½ teaspoon Worcestershire sauce
½ cup white cooking wine

Clean pheasant well, removing all buckshot and pin feathers. Cut into serving pieces. Coat bird pieces with seasoned flour. Heat shortening in heavy skillet. Brown pheasant on all sides. Add garlic, olives, water and Worcestershire sauce. Cover and simmer 45 minutes. Turn pheasant and add wine. Recover and simmer another 45 minutes (longer if needed). Add additional water to make extra sauce.

Mrs. Bradford Williams

Hasenpfeffer

2½ pound rabbit, cut in pieces
1¼ cups water
¾ cup vinegar
1 onion sliced
3 bay leaves
10 whole cloves
2 teaspoons salt
½ teaspoon pepper
⅓ cup flour
⅓ cup shortening
2 tablespoons brown sugar
1 cup sour cream

Place rabbit (make sure it is well cleaned) in bowl and cover with water, vinegar mixture. Add onion, bay leaves, cloves, 1 teaspoon salt and pepper. Cover tightly and refrigerate 3 days. (Hold liquid for further use.) Remove rabbit, roll in flour and remaining salt. Melt shortening in heavy skillet and fry rabbit until golden brown, turn frequently. Add slowly 1 cup strained vinegar mixture and brown sugar. Cover and simmer for 1 hour. Add sour cream just before serving.

Anna Schultz

Baked Fish
With Lemon Mushroom Sauce

2 packages frozen haddock fillets
1 can undiluted cream of mushroom soup
½ cup milk
1 can sliced mushrooms
1 large onion, chopped
2 tablespoons lemon juice
1 teaspoon paprika
½ teaspoon salt
¼ teaspoon oregano
¼ teaspoon pepper
1 bay leaf, crushed

Place frozen fillets in shallow buttered baking dish. (9″) In saucepan combine rest of ingredients. Simmer 10 minutes. Pour over fillets.

Top with 1 cup buttered crumbs lightly seasoned with poultry seasoning (or 1 cup prepared stuffing mix). Dot with butter. Bake 45 minutes at 375°. Serves 6. Recipe may be halved easily.

Mrs. Roger C. Wilder

Baked Ocean Perch

¼ cup flour
½ teaspoon salt
¼ teaspoon pepper

2 pounds ocean perch fillets
2 tablespoons butter
⅓ cup grated onion
3 tablespoon lemon juice
½ cup minced parsley
1 cup sour cream
½ cup shredded American cheese
¼ cup buttered bread crumbs

Dip fish in flour, salt and pepper mixture. Place in a buttered 12 x 8 inch baking dish.

Melt butter in saucepan, add onion and sauté until tender. Remove from heat, add lemon juice, parsley, sour cream and cheese. Spread over fish. Sprinkle with crumbs. Bake 375° for 30 to 40 minutes. Serves 6.

Jody Petry

Baked Stuffed Pike

2 to 3 pound dressed whole fish
 Salt
2 cups stuffing
3 tablespoons melted butter for basting

Stuffing: Lemon Bread Stuffing

¼ cup butter
2 tablespoons grated onion
2 cups soft bread cubes (slightly moist prepared stuffing may be used. If so eliminate thyme in recipe).
2 tablespoons lemon juice
2 teaspoons grated lemon rind
¼ teaspoon thyme
¼ teaspoon salt
¼ teaspoon freshly ground pepper

Salt inside of fish. Melt butter for stuffing and sauté onions until tender. Add remaining ingredients.

Fill fish with stuffing securing edges with wooden picks. Place in shallow baking dish and brush with melted butter. Bake at 450° for 10 minutes. Reduce heat to 350° and continue baking for 30 to 40 minutes longer. Baste with butter during baking period. Remove picks and garnish with parsley and lemon wedges.

June Parson

Pan-fried Fish

2 pounds dressed fish pieces
½ cup milk
1 egg, slightly beaten
½ cup flour, cornmeal, pancake mix or cracker crumbs
¼ cup shortening
 Salt
 Pepper

Wash and dry fish. Dip in egg, milk mixture. Roll in dry ingredient used.

Salt and pepper to taste.

Heat shortening in heavy skillet. Fry fish about 5 to 7 minutes.

Turn fish only once and do not crowd in the pan. Serve with tartar sauce.

Marilyn Ross

33

BREADS

Banana Nut Bread

2 cups sifted flour
2 teaspoons baking powder
1 teaspoon salt
½ teaspoon baking soda
1 cup sugar
½ cup butter or margarine
2 eggs
1 cup mashed bananas
1 teaspoon lemon juice
1 cup chopped nuts

Sift together flour, baking powder, salt, soda, and sugar. Add shortening, eggs, bananas and lemon juice. Stir to combine ingredients, then beat 2 minutes at medium speed on electric mixer or 300 strokes by hand. Stir in ¾ cup nuts. Pour into greased loaf pan 5¼ x 9½ inches. Sprinkle ¼ cup nuts over top of batter. Bake in moderate oven 350° degrees 1 hour and 15 minutes. Makes one loaf.

Ruth Sprenkle

Apple Bread

Cream together:

½ cup butter
1 cup white sugar
2 eggs
1 teaspoon vanilla
½ teaspoon salt
1 teaspoon soda dissolved in
    2 tablespoons sour milk

Add:

2 cups diced apples
2 cups sifted flour

Turn into 2 small or 1 large bread tin. Greased and floured.

Topping: Mix together

2 tablespoons butter
2 tablespoons flour
2 tablespoons sugar
1 teaspoon cinnamon

Sprinkle on top of loaf and bake 1 hour at 325°.

Mrs. Gordon A. Luscher

Cranberry Orange Bread

2 cups flour
1 cup sugar
1½ teaspoons baking powder
½ teaspoon salt
1 egg beaten
2 tablespoons shortening
Grated rind and juice of 1 orange plus water to make ¾ cup, or use ¾ cup orange juice.
1 cup raw cranberries, cut in halves

Measure flour and blend dry ingredients. Mix in shortening, orange rind and juice and egg. Fold in cranberries. Bake one hour at 350°F. in a well greased 9x5x3-inch loaf pan. Cool thoroughly before slicing.

James F. Bennett

Saffron Bread

2½ cups milk
½ pound butter
1 package saffron
1 teaspoon salt
2 cakes yeast
1 cup sugar
2 eggs
8 cups flour
1½ cups seeded raisins

Heat milk, add butter to melt and cool to lukewarm. Dissolve saffron and yeast in 1 teaspoon milk. Add to milk with the sugar — blend in beaten eggs. Stir in flour until sticky and knead in rest of flour along with raisins.

Keep kneading until smooth, firm and glossy. Let rise in greased bowl until double in size. Place on board and shape into braided loaves. Let rise one hour after placing in bread tins. Bake 375° for 45 minutes. Makes 2 loaves.

Jill Susan Dalbey

Sour Cream Graham Bread

2 eggs, well beaten
1½ cups maple syrup
½ cup thick sour cream
2 cups white flour
1½ cup sour milk
2 cups graham flour
1½ teaspoon salt
2 teaspoons soda
2 teaspoons baking powder

Sift dry ingredients together. Beat eggs well, stir into cream, milk and syrup. Beat in dry ingredients. Batter should be stiff. Add more graham flour if necessary. Butter bread tins and line with heavy waxed paper. Fill ⅔ full. Bake at 375° for 1 hour, reduce heat the last part of time. Test with a toothpick.

Donna Kingsley

White Bread

2 packages active dry yeast
½ cup warm water
⅓ cup sugar
⅓ cup shortening
2 tablespoons salt
2 cups milk, scalded
1½ cup cold water
10 to 12 cups all purpose flour

Soften yeast in warm water.

In large mixing bowl blend well sugar, shortening, salt and hot milk until shortening is melted. Add cold water, cool. Stir in yeast. Gradually add flour to make a stiff dough.

Knead on floured board until smooth (5 to 10 minutes). Place in greased bowl, turn dough so all sides are greased. Cover with damp towel. Let rise until double in size (about 2 to 2½ hours).

Punch down dough by plunging your fist in center of dough. Turn upside down in bowl and let rise another 30 minutes.

Place on floured board and divide in fourths. Mold into balls, cover and let rise 15 minutes more. Shape into loaves. Place in well-greased loaf pans. Cover with damp towel. Let rise until dough is well above pan edges (about 1½ to 2 hours).

Bake at 375° for 40 to 50 minutes.

Remove from pan onto wire rack to cool. Makes 4 loaves.

Marianne Morgan

A Cook's Prayer

Lord, guide my willing hands
To bake my bread today,
To mix a little laughter
In what I do or say.

Help me to feed my family
With good food seasoned right,
With wisdom of a loving heart
Keep my kitchen shining bright.

Guide my erring thoughts to Heaven
When my spirit is sad and low,
Help me set my dinner table
With food for hearts that glow.

Polly Perkins

Apricot Bread

2 cups sifted regular flour
2½ teaspoons baking powder
¾ teaspoon salt
¾ cup crunchy nut-like cereal
⅔ cup chopped dried apricots
1 cup sugar
1 egg
1¼ cup milk
2 tablespoons shortening, melted

Sift flour, sugar, baking powder and salt into large bowl; stir in cereal and apricots. Beat egg well with milk in a small bowl; stir in shortening. Add to flour mixture all at once; stir until evenly moist. Pour in a greased loaf pan 9 x 5 x 3 inches. Bake at 350° 1 hour and 5 minutes or until toothpick comes out clean. Store, wrapped, overnight.

Fern Snyder

Pumpkin Bread

3½ cups flour
3 cups sugar
2 teaspoons soda
1 teaspoon each
  cinnamon, salt, nutmeg
4 eggs
2 cups pumpkin (#303 can)
1 cup cooking oil
⅔ cup water
1 teaspoon vanilla
1 cup nuts

Mix flour, soda, sugar and spice together. Make a well or hole in dry ingredients and add pumpkin, eggs, oil, and water. Beat until smooth, add nuts and vanilla. Pour into greased loaf pans and bake 1 hour at 350°.

This will make two 4 x 9-inch loaf pans or two 2-pound coffee cans or four 1-pound coffee cans. Makes a moist bread and is easy to mail in the coffee cans, as it keeps fresh a long time.

Betty Johnson

Oatmeal Bread

1 cup uncooked oatmeal (quick)
1 cup milk, scalded
½ cup boiling water
⅓ cup shortening (bacon drippings are good)
½ cup brown sugar, firmly packed
2 teaspoons salt
2 packages dry yeast
½ cup warm water
5 cups sifted flour

Put oatmeal in large bowl, stir in milk and boiling water. Add shortening, sugar and salt. Let stand until lukewarm. Sprinkle yeast into ½ cup of warm water. Stir until dissolved. Stir into oatmeal mixture, add ½ the flour, mix until smooth. Add remaining flour, a little at a time. Mix until dough leaves side of bowl. Turn out on board and knead 7 minutes. Place dough in greased bowl. Cover with damp cloth and let rise 1½ hours. Knead and shape into loaves. Bake at 400° for 10 minutes. Reduce heat to 350°, bake 40 minutes. Makes 2 loaves.

Thelma E. King

Soybean Bread

2 cups of water or milk
2 cups of soybean flour
2 cups of white flour (approximately)
1 tablespoon of shortening
1 tablespoon of sugar
1 teaspoon of salt
1 cake yeast

Prepare soft dough according to the usual method, using the soybean flour. Then add enough white flour to mix to a consistency for kneading. Let rise until double in bulk, mix, and let rise again.

Make into loaves and place in a pan. When double in bulk, bake at 375°F. Due to the composition of soybean flour, the mixture requires more kneading, and rises more slowly than white bread. This recipe makes 2 small loaves.

Della C. Pigg

French Bread

2½ cups warm water
1 tablespoon sugar
1 tablespoon salt
1 package active
    dry yeast

2 tablespoons soft shortening
½ cup water
½ teaspoon salt
1½ teaspoons cornstarch
    Sesame seed
8½ cups sifted flour

Combine first four ingredients; stir to dissolve yeast; let stand 5 minutes. Stir in flour and shortening, then work flour in with hands. Knead until smooth and elastic. Cover; let rise in warm place until doubled. Shape into 3 balls. Let rest 15 minutes. Shape each ball into a roll 15 inches long, tapered at each end. Place on baking sheet, cover with a towel; let rise until light. Meanwhile combine water, remaining salt and cornstarch. Cook and stir until thickened and clear. Brush over loaves; sprinkle tops with sesame seed. Make several diagonal gashes ½ inch deep in top of each loaf. Heat oven to 450°. Place a large pan of hot water on lower shelf. Place bread on upper shelf. Bake 10 minutes. Reduce heat to moderate, 350°; bake 50 to 60 minutes longer. Makes 3 loaves.

Jean Stephenson

Irish Bread

4 cups flour
4 teaspoons baking powder
¼ teaspoon baking soda
2 tablespoons shortening
1 tablespoon butter
½ tablespoon salt
    Buttermilk
2 eggs

Mix dry ingredients, add shortening and work in like biscuits. Add eggs and buttermilk (enough to moisten). Add raisins, citron, currants as desired. Bake in moderate oven about 1 hour.

"The above recipe was given to me by my mother-in-law, Cathrine Hegarty, when I was married 28 years ago. She is from Ireland and is 85 years young."

Helen C. Hegarty

Lemon Bread

3 tablespoons margarine
½ teaspoon salt
1 cup sugar
2 eggs (unbeaten)
1½ cups sifted flour
1 teaspoon baking powder
½ cup milk
    Grated rind of 1 lemon

Cream margarine, add salt and sugar gradually and one egg at a time, beating well. Add lemon rind, milk, flour and baking powder. Pour into greased loaf pan. Bake at 350° for 55 minutes. While loaf is still hot, spoon over bread the juice of one lemon and ½ cup sugar that has been brought to a boil enough to dissolve sugar. "This is delicious! And the secret is in performing the last operation while everything is hot!"

Mrs. Karyl Gadecki

Good Egg Bread

1½ cups scalded milk
½ cup butter
2 teaspoons salt
½ cup sugar

2 packages (or cakes) yeast
½ cup lukewarm water
2 beaten eggs
    About 9 cups sifted
    white flour

Pour scalded milk over butter, salt and sugar. Cool. Dissolve yeast in lukewarm water and let stand till it bubbles, about 5 minutes. Add yeast and beaten eggs to cooled milk. Gradually add flour, beating thoroughly. Do not use any more flour than necessary to make easily handled dough. Turn out on floured board and knead till smooth and elastic. Place in greased bowl and let rise till doubled (about 1½ hours.) Punch down and turn onto lightly floured board. Shape into 3 loaves and place in greased 8 inch loaf pans. Cover and let rise till dough is as high as pan. Bake at 425° for 10 minutes, then 350° for 40 minutes more. Makes 3 loaves.

Mrs. George Nordmann

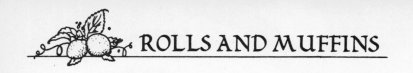

"Dieter's Breakfast Biscuits"

"If you're on a diet and you crave something sweet in the morning, take one slice of bread, spread with cottage cheese, sprinkle with cinnamon, and one packet of sugar substitute and bake in oven at 350° for three minutes or until the cinnamon is brown. It is very tasty and satisfies your craving for sweets".

Sheila Gracin Singer

Butter Pecan Rolls

½ cup shortening
¼ cup and 2 tablespoons sugar
½ cup cold water
1 cake yeast
½ cup boiling water
1 egg
½ teaspoon salt
3 cups unsifted flour

Filling
2 tablespoons melted butter
½ cup sugar
2 teaspoons cinnamon

Topping
½ cup brown sugar
¼ cup butter
1 tablespoon light corn syrup
⅓ cup pecans

Dissolve yeast in cold water. Cream the sugar and shortening. Add boiling water and cool to lukewarm. Add yeast, flour, salt and beaten egg. Mix well. Brush top lightly with soft shortening. Cover and let rise in warm place until double (1½–2 hours). Punch down. Turn out on lightly floured surface and divide dough in half. Roll each piece into a 12"x8" rectangle. Make the filling by brushing each rectangle with the melted butter. Combine sugar and cinnamon. Sprinkle half over each rectangle. Roll each rectangle as for a jellyroll, beginning with long side. Seal edge. Cut each roll in eight 1½" slices.

In each of two 9½" x 5" x 3" metal loaf pans, mix the topping by adding brown sugar, butter and corn syrup. Heat slowly, stirring frequently until blended. Remove from heat. Sprinkle pecans in each pan. Place eight rolls cut-side down in each pan. Cover and let rise in warm place until double (35–45 minutes). Bake in moderate oven (375°) for 25 minutes or until done. Cool two or three minutes; invert on rack and remove pans. Makes 16 rolls.

"This recipe won a Silver Spoon Award in a newspaper recipe contest."

Carol Anderson

Potato Refrigerator Rolls

1½ cups warm water
1 package yeast
⅔ cup sugar
1½ teaspoons salt
2 eggs
⅔ cup oil
1 cup mashed potatoes
7 to 8 cups flour

In large bowl dissolve yeast in water. Stir in sugar, salt, ⅔ cup oil, eggs and potatoes. Mix in flour and knead on lightly floured board until smooth and elastic. Place in greased bowl and cover with damp cloth. Place in refrigerator. Punch down occasionally as it rises. Shape dough into two inch rolls and place each in well-greased muffin cup. Cover and let rise until double in size. Bake in 400° oven 12 to 15 minutes.

Donna Moul

Spoon Biscuits

1 cup self-rising flour
½ cup sweet milk
2 tablespoons mayonnaise

Combine the flour and milk. Stir well. Add the mayonnaise and stir well. Butter small muffin tins. Spoon the dough into tins about ½ to ⅔ full. Bake at 400° for 20 minutes. Makes 9 two-inch biscuits.

Mrs. Coy D. Wilcoxson

Hot Cross Buns

1 package dry yeast
2 tablespoons warm water
Soften yeast in water.
Combine the following:
1 cup milk, scalded
¼ cup sugar
1½ teaspoons salt
½ teaspoon cinnamon
¾ cup currants

Cool to lukewarm. Add yeast mixture and two well-beaten eggs. Add two cups of sifted flour and mix. Add 1/2 cup melted butter and beat well. Add two more cups of flour gradually. Mix but do not knead. Place in greased bowl and grease top of dough. Cover and chill until firm enough to handle. Divide dough into 18-20 portions and shape them into buns. Place on greased cookie sheet. Cover and set in a warm place until doubled in bulk. Bake at 400° 10-15 minutes. Form a cross on each bun with a powdered sugar frosting.

Raised Doughnuts

1 cup shortening
1 cup boiling water
1 cup cold water
2 eggs
1 cup sugar

2 teaspoons salt
Dash nutmeg
8 cups flour
2 yeast cakes
   (or package)

Dissolve 2 yeast cakes in ½ cup warm water. In mixing bowl put in shortening, boiling water and cold water. Add beaten eggs, sugar, salt and dash of nutmeg. Then add dissolved yeast and gradually mix in sifted flour into a smooth dough. Place in refrigerator overnight.

Roll out on floured board to about ½ inch thickness. Cut with cutter coated in flour. Let doughnuts raise for 1 hour.

Then place doughnuts in deep shortening and fry on each side until golden brown. Take them out of deep fat and place on paper toweling or brown paper.

May be eaten plain, rolled in granulated or powdered sugar. Makes about 4 dozen.

Virginia Nelson

Doughnuts

2 eggs
1 cup granulated sugar
4 tablespoons
   melted butter
3 teaspoons baking
   powder

3 cups sifted flour
1 teaspoon vanilla
1 cup sifted flour
1 cup milk
¾ teaspoon salt

Slightly beat eggs in a mixing bowl, add sugar and mix thoroughly. Melt butter, measure and add to mixture. Beat, add milk, mix. Sift flour, measure, sift dry ingredients together, add to mixture. Add vanilla, mix well, and add last amount of flour. Roll out dough and cut ½ inch thick. Dough is very soft and will stick easily to cutter and board. Keep dusted with flour at all times. Handle gently as dough will fall apart easily. Fry in hot deep fat until golden brown on both sides. Drain on absorbent paper to remove excess fat. Roll in granulated sugar or top with favorite icing.

Suzanna C. Bascochea

Funnel Cakes

2 beaten eggs
1½ cups milk
2 cups flour
1 teaspoon baking powder
½ teaspoon salt
2 cups cooking oil

In mixing bowl, combine eggs and milk. Sift together flour, baking powder and salt. Add to the egg mixture. Beat until smooth. Test mixture to see if it flows easily through funnel. If too thick, add milk; if too thin, add flour. Heat cooking oil to 360°. Covering the bottom of funnel with finger, pour generous ½ cup batter into funnel. Remove finger and release batter into hot oil in a spiral shape. Fry till golden, about 3 minutes. Turn cake carefully. Cook 1 minute more. Drain on paper toweling. Sprinkle with sifted confectioners' sugar. Serve hot with syrup.

Mrs. Lawrence Riggle

Bran Buttermilk Muffins

½ cup sugar
⅓ cup shortening
1 egg
1 cup flour
2 teaspoons baking
   powder

2 cups bran flakes cereal
   with raisins
1 cup buttermilk
½ teaspoon salt
½ teaspoon baking soda

Mix together.

Fill paper baking cups ⅔ full.
Bake at 400° for 18 to 20 minutes.

Vera Kremenak

Applesauce Muffins

½ cup oil
1 cup sugar
¾ teaspoon salt
½ teaspoon soda
½ teaspoon baking
   powder

1½ cup flour
½ cup applesauce
½ teaspoon nutmeg
½ teaspoon cinnamon
1 teaspoon allspice
1 egg

Put all into your mixing bowl and mix well. Bake in muffin pans at 400° for 15 to 20 minutes.

Ruth E. Payne

40

Double Quick Coffee Bread

Melt in ring mold ⅓ cup butter and ½ cup brown sugar. Decorate with nuts and maraschino cherries. Cool before spooning on the dough.

¾ cup warm water	1 package yeast
1 teaspoon salt	2½ cups flour
¼ cup soft shortening or butter	¼ cup sugar
	1 egg

Mix yeast in water, add sugar, salt and half flour. Beat thoroughly then add egg and shortening. Beat in rest of flour until smooth. Drop by spoonfuls over topping. Cover and let rise about 1 hour or until double in bulk. Bake at 375° for 30 to 35 minutes until brown. Immediately turn out of pan to avoid sticking. Serve warm.

Pat Philley

Notes

1 tablespoon = 3 teaspoons
1 cup = 16 tablespoons
1 pint = 2 cups
2 pints = 1 quart or 4 cups
4 quarts = 1 gallon
8 quarts = 1 peck
4 pecks = 1 bushel
16 ounces = 1 pound

Keep baking powder dry or it will lose its leavening power.

Nut Stollen

½ cake yeast
¼ cup lukewarm water
1 teaspoon sugar

Mix:

2 cups flour
¾ cup shortening (butter or margarine)
2 eggs (beaten)

Add yeast mixture.

Roll out like pie dough—2 sections, roll in a rectangle. Spread with poppy-prune filling or use your own favorite filling. Roll from long side, seal edges. Make 3 slashes crosswise or 1 long cut through center.

Bake at 350° for ½ hour. Makes 2.

Peg Hollaway

Sour Cream Twists

Sift 4 cups flour, 1 teaspoon salt into bowl. Cut in 1 cup shortening with blender as for piecrust. Soften 1 envelope Quick Dry Yeast in ¼ cup warm water according to directions on envelope. Beat 1 egg and 2 egg yolks together until light. Combine with 1 cup thick sour cream, the yeast, 1 teaspoon grated lemon rind and 1 cup currants. Stir into pastry base. Mix thoroughly. Let rise in refrigerator for 2 hours.

Measure out ⅔ cup sugar and cinnamon for rolling. Use all but no more. Sprinkle lightly over board. Place dough on board. Sprinkle over top and roll into 12 inch square. Fold dough from either side to make 3 layers. Roll out again and repeat the folding job, using a little more sugar on the board and dough to prevent sticking. Just remember to sprinkle lightly. Too much sugar and your dough will be too hard to handle. Cut into strips 1 inch by 4 inches. Shape into twists. Lay on ungreased baking sheets. Sprinkle remaining sugar on. No additional rising needed. Bake at 375° for 18 minutes. Makes 3 dozen twists.

Mrs. R. B. Kirkby

Elephant Ears

(a delicious snack from my mother)

3 egg yolks	1 teaspoon salt
1 whole egg	2 cups flour
6 tablespoons cold water	Confectioners' sugar

Beat eggs until very fluffy (about 8 minutes). Beat in water and salt. Stir in flour working with hands if necessary. Roll dough out on well-floured cloth. Knead slightly until not sticky, but still soft. Divide dough into 12 equal portions. Roll each portion out on floured cloth to approximately 8 inch circles. (very thin) Heat liquid cooking oil to 375° in heavy skillet. (About 1 inch deep in skillet) Gently place one circle of dough at a time in hot oil, frying only about 10-15 seconds per side. When turning, and to remove, use tongs and be very careful as they break easily. They should not be brown, but a golden yellow when removed. Place confectioners' sugar in small strainer and gently sprinkle on both sides of elephant ears. They may be drained first on paper towels if desired. Happy eating!

Ruth H. Underhill

Sponge Cake

7 eggs separated
1¼ cups sugar
½ teaspoon vanilla
1 cup sifted flour

½ teaspoon almond extract
¼ teaspoon salt
1 teaspoon cream of tartar

Beat egg yolks until thick. Add ¼ cup sugar gradually and beat well. Add vanilla and almond extract and mix.

Add salt and cream of tartar to egg whites and beat until stiff. Add 1 cup sugar, very little at a time, beating often after each addition. Fold egg yolk mixture into egg whites. Add flour gradually and gently fold after each addition. Pour batter into ungreased tube pan. Cut batter with spatula in pan to prevent holes in cake. Bake at 325° for 70 minutes. Invert pan to cool before removing cake.

Merry Biever

Happiness Cake

1 cup of good thoughts
1 cup of kind deeds
1 cup of consideration for others
2 cups of sacrifice
2 cups of well-beaten faults
3 cups of forgiveness.

Mix thoroughly. Add tears of joy, sorrow and sympathy. Flavour with love and kindly service. Fold in 4 cups of prayer and faith. Blend well.

Fold into daily life. Bake well with the warmth of human kindness and serve with a smile, anytime. It will satisfy the hunger of starved souls.

Author Unknown

Caramel Frosting

2 cups dark brown sugar
1 stick butter
1/2 cup milk

Boil for 2 minutes. Cool to lukewarm, undisturbed. Add 1 teaspoon vanilla and beat until thick.

Mrs. Harold R. Kelly

Gram's Vanilla Sauce

2 cups boiling water
1/2 cup sugar
2 tablespoons cornstarch
4 tablespoons butter
1/2 teaspoon nutmeg
1/2 teaspoon vanilla

Put the water on to boil. Cream sugar, cornstarch, butter and nutmeg. Stir into the boiling water. Add the vanilla and serve warm as a sauce over apple dumplings or fruitcake. Serves 3 generously.

Patty Doarn

Almond Chiffon Cake

2 cups sifted all-purpose flour
1 1/2 cups sugar
1 tablespoon baking powder
1 teaspoon salt
7 egg yolks
1/2 cup salad oil
1 teaspoon lemon extract
1 teaspoon almond extract
3/4 cup ice water
7 egg whites (1 cup)
1/2 teaspoon cream of tartar

Sift first four ingredients four times. Set aside. Combine egg yolks, salad oil, extracts and ice water. Add dry ingredients. Beat 30 seconds and set aside. Beat egg whites and cream of tartar until stiff peaks form (about five minutes). Gradually pour egg yolks mixture over beaten egg whites. Pour into ungreased 10" tube pan. Bake at 325° for 55 minutes, increase temperature to 350° and bake 10 minutes longer. Invert to cool for 1 1/2-2 hours.

Ice with Double Boiler Frosting

2 egg whites
1 1/2 cups sugar
1/4 teaspoon cream of tartar
1/3 cup water
1 teaspoon vanilla

Combine egg whites, sugar, cream of tartar and water in top of double boiler. Beat on high for one minute with electric mixer. Place over boiling water and beat on high speed for seven minutes. Remove pan from boiling water. Add vanilla. Beat two minutes longer on high speed. Spread on cake and sprinkle sliced almonds on top.

My State Fair Second Prize Winner in October 1971.

Geneva Bratton

Carrot Cake with Pineapple

3 beaten eggs
2 cups sugar
1 1/3 cups cooking oil
3 cups flour
1 teaspoon salt
2 teaspoons vanilla
2 teaspoons baking soda
2 teaspoons cinnamon
2 cups grated carrots
1 cup chopped walnuts or pecans
1 cup drained crushed pineapple

Blend eggs, sugar and cooking oil. Sift together flour, salt, soda and cinnamon. Stir in, with the flour mixture, the grated carrots, chopped nuts, pineapple and vanilla. Pour the batter into a 10" tube pan, ungreased, and bake at 350° for one hour and 15 minutes (75 minutes). Cool cake right-side up 25 minutes, then loosen around sides. Ice with a lemon glaze. Winner of three ribbons.

Mrs. B. G. Troutman

Strawberry Shortcut Cake

Generously grease bottom only of 13 x 9 inch baking pan
Sprinkle evenly over bottom of greased pan:

1 cup miniature marshmallows.

Thoroughly combine and set aside the following:

2 cups (2 10 oz. packages) frozen sliced strawberries in syrup, completely thawed.
1 package (3 oz.) strawberry flavored gelatin

Combine in large mixer bowl:

2¼ cups flour — all purpose
1½ cups sugar
½ cup shortening
3 teaspoons baking powder
½ teaspoon salt
1 cup milk
1 teaspoon vanilla
3 eggs

Blend at low speed until moistened; beat 3 minutes at medium speed, scraping sides of bowl occasionally. Pour batter over marshmallows in pan. Spoon strawberry mixture evenly over batter. Bake at 350° for 45 to 50 minutes until golden brown or when a toothpick inserted in center comes out clean.

Mrs. Fred J. Dolaway

Lemon Cheese Cake

18 graham crackers
½ stick butter, melted
1 package lemon gelatine
1 cup boiling water

1-8 ounce package cream cheese
1 cup sugar
1 teaspoon vanilla
1 large can evaporated milk, chilled

Crush graham crackers; combine with butter. Line a 9 x 13 inch pan with half the mixture. Mix gelatine and boiling water. Mix cream cheese, sugar and vanilla. In a large bowl, whip evaporated milk until stiff. Add gelatine; then cheese mixture; blend well. Pour into graham cracker crust; sprinkle reserved crust mixture over top. Chill 12 hours.

Note: May be topped with cherry or strawberry preserves when served. This cheese cake may be frozen.

Marie H. Giddings

Orange Fruit Cake

1⅔ cups sifted flour
1½ teaspoons baking powder
⅓ cup butter or other shortening
1 cup sugar
2 eggs (unbeaten)
½ cup milk
1 teaspoon vanilla extract
    Candied cherries and other candied fruits, amount to suit taste
2 fresh oranges
¾ cup raisins
¾ cup walnut meats

Squeeze juice from oranges, add sugar to fill large glass (8 ounces or more), set aside. Grind orange rinds, raisins and nutmeats together. Sift flour once, measure and add baking powder. Then sift them three times. Cream butter thoroughly gradually adding sugar and cream together until light and fluffy. Add eggs, one at a time, beating well after each. Add flour alternately with milk, a small amount at a time, beating after each addition until smooth. Fold in candied cherries and mixed fruit with flour. Add flavoring. Add ground walnuts, raisins and orange rind. Mix thoroughly. Spoon into large greased tube pan, bake in 350° oven, one hour and fifteen minutes or until done. Let hang, upside down until cool. Remove from pan and pour orange, sugar mixture over cake.

Mrs. W. J. Demerly

> Spice a dish with love, and it pleases every palate.
>
> *Plautus*

Graham Cracker Cake

½ cup butter
1 cup sugar
3 eggs
1 scant cup milk

23 graham crackers
1 teaspoon baking powder
1 cup broken walnuts
½ teaspoon salt

Cream butter and sugar together. Beat egg yolks until they are light and add to butter and sugar mixture. Then add milk. Roll or crumble crackers until fine. Add baking powder, nuts and salt to cracker crumbs. Now add this to first mixture. Last add the well-beaten egg whites. Bake in a moderate oven about ½ hour.

Marjorie L. Barker

Oatmeal Cake

2 cups oatmeal (regular or quick cooking)
2 cups boiling water. Pour over oatmeal, mix, let stand 20 minutes.

Mix the following ingredients in the order given:
  2 cups brown sugar
  4 eggs (beaten)
  1 cup shortening

Sift together:
  2 cups flour
  1 teaspoon soda
  2 teaspoons cinnamon
  ½ teaspoon salt

Mix together. Add 1 cup chopped dates or raisins, 1 cup chopped nuts. Bake 45 minutes to 1 hour at 350°. Makes a large cake.

Mary Beth Hollaway

Chocolate Cream Cheese Frosting

2 cups confectioners' sugar
1 small package cream cheese
2 tablespoons cream
3 squares chocolate, melted
1 teaspoon vanilla

Beat cream cheese, add cream. Gradually add confectioners' sugar and melted chocolate. Beat well, stir in vanilla.

Donna Kingsley

Chocolate Mayonnaise Cake

1 cup sugar
4 tablespoons cocoa
1 cup cold water
2 teaspoons baking soda
2 cups flour
1 teaspoon vanilla
½ teaspoon salt
1 cup mayonnaise

Combine sugar and cocoa. Add soda to cold water and combine with sugar mixture, along with salt and vanilla. Then add flour and mix. It will be quite heavy. Fold in mayonnaise and bake in a 350° oven for 30 minutes. Cool and frost.

Mrs. George V. Nelson

Coconut Cake

1 cup butter	1 teaspoon vanilla
2 cups sugar	½ teaspoon salt
3 cups flour	½ cup buttermilk
4 eggs	½ cup water
3 scant teaspoons baking powder	

Cream butter and sugar. Add eggs one at a time, beating thoroughly as each egg is added. Add dry ingredients, sifted together alternately with the buttermilk and water which have been mixed together. Add vanilla and beat well. Pour batter into three round or square pans that have been greased and floured and lined with wax paper. Bake in 375° oven for about 20 minutes. Don't overbake.

Filling for Coconut Cake

1 large coconut grated (reserve milk from coconut)
2 cups sugar
2 tablespoons cornstarch
1 cup coconut milk (use sweet milk to make up difference if there is not enough from coconut)

Mix all ingredients in the order given in a large boiler. Place over heat and cool until thick or about the consistency of mayonnaise. Stir while cooking. Cool slightly. Spread between layers and on sides and top of cooled cake. Reserve enough grated coconut to sprinkle on top of cake. The cake batter is excellent even when used with another filling or icing.

Martha Lindsey

Mocha Cake

2 eggs	1 cup cold coffee
1 cup brown sugar	1 cup raisins and nuts
½ cup butter	2 teaspoons baking powder
1 square of unsweetened chocolate	½ teaspoon soda
	1½ cups all purpose flour
1 teaspoon each of cinnamon and cloves	1 teaspoon vanilla

Mix ingredients. Bake at 350° for 30 minutes. Makes 2 layers.

This cake has been our birthday cake for over fifty years and is always enjoyed. A cup of cooked dates may be placed between layers. Ice to suit.

Edna Jaques

Cream Cheese Refrigerator Torte

Crust

    2 cups graham crackers (crushed)   ½ cup melted butter or margarine
    ⅓ cup sugar   1 teaspoon cinnamon

Combine all ingredients and pat into a buttered 9″ or 10″ spring form and bake in 425° oven for 5 minutes. Cool.

Mixture for Torte

    1-8 ounce cream cheese package   ¼ cup pineapple juice
    ½ cup sugar   1 #2 can crushed pineapple
    1 pkg. lemon gelatin   1 large can evaporated milk (chill overnight)
    1 cup hot water   2 teaspoons vanilla

Mix hot water with gelatin, add pineapple juice, let cool until it begins to congeal. Mix cream cheese with the sugar. Whip chilled milk in large cold bowl until it is stiff. Add cheese mixture and whipped milk to gelatin and fold in gently, add vanilla and pineapple. Pour mixture into graham cracker crust and chill for 8 hours in refrigerator. When serving top with prepared cherry or pineapple pie filling. Serves 12 to 14.

Marie Bruner

Pumpkin Torte

Crust:

    24 crushed graham crackers
    ½ cup margarine or butter
    ½ cup sugar

Mix and pat lightly in a 9 x 13 inch pan.

Beat the following:

    2 eggs
    ¾ cup sugar
    2-8 ounce packages cream cheese (soft)

Put on top of crust.
Bake 20 minutes at 350°. Cool.

Mix and cook:

    1 can pumpkin, size number 1
    3 egg yolks
    ½ cup sugar
    ½ cup milk
    ½ teaspoon salt
    ½ teaspoon cinnamon

Cook until thick, about 3 or 4 minutes. Remove from heat, add 1 envelope gelatin dissolved in ¼ cup cold water. Cool well.

    Beat 3 egg whites until stiff.
    Add ¼ cup sugar

Fold into pumpkin mixture. Pour into baked crust. Let set. Top with whipped cream.

Mary Lavota

Orange Juice Torte

⅛ pound butter
24 graham crackers, rolled

Warm butter in pan, add crumbs. Pat into 9″ square pan, saving ⅓ cup for later.

Filling

1 cup fresh orange juice
1 pound marshmallows

Melt marshmallows in juice (use large kettle as mixture will foam up).

Cool this mixture.

Whip 1 pint heavy cream. Fold the cooled marshmallows into whipped cream. Pour over crumbs. Sprinkle remaining crumbs on top.

Chill at least 2 hours.

Mrs. David Bullard

Cherry Squares

1 cup sugar	1 egg
1 cup flour	1 cup chopped nuts
1 teaspoon cinnamon	1 #2½ can bing cherries
1 teaspoon soda	2 tablespoons melted butter

Drain cherries — save juice.
Mix in order given.
Bake in 9 x 9 inch pan at 325° for 45 minutes.

Topping

Heat cherry juice. Add ⅓ cup sugar, 1 tablespoon cornstarch mixed with cold water. Add little butter. Cool until thickened. Serve squares topped with dollop of whipped topping or cream and sauce poured over.

Mary Turck

Date-Nut Torte

1 cup sifted cake flour	1 cup sugar
¼ teaspoon salt	½ teaspoon vanilla
1 teaspoon baking powder	2 cups cut, pitted dates
3 eggs, separated	2 cups chopped walnuts

Mix and sift flour, salt, and baking powder. Beat egg yolks until thick. Add ¾ cup sugar and beat well. Add vanilla and mix.

Add dry ingredients and mix well. Fold ¼ cup sugar into stiffly beaten egg whites. Fold into egg yolk mixture. Fold in dates and nuts.

Bake in 9-inch square pan at 350° for 50 minutes. Serve with sweetened whipped cream.

Lois Balerud

Mallow Lemon Torte

1 can condensed milk (chilled)	1 cup marshmallow bits
1 pint whipping cream	½ cup lemon juice

Put lemon juice in milk and beat until stiff. Fold into whipped cream and marshmallows.
Put in 9 x 13 inch graham cracker crust.
Chill.

Jean Crowley

Frozen Lemon Torte

¾ cup vanilla wafer crumbs
3 eggs, separated
4 teaspoons grated lemon rind
¼ cup lemon juice
⅛ teaspoon salt
½ cup sugar
1 cup heavy cream, whipped

Line refrigerator tray with ½ of wafer crumbs. Combine egg yolks, lemon rind, lemon juice, salt and sugar in top of double boiler. Cook over boiling water stirring constantly until thick. Cool. Beat egg whites until stiff, fold in lemon mixture. Fold whipped cream into lemon mixture. Spoon into pan, top with remaining crumbs. Freeze. Thaw slightly in refrigerator prior to serving.

Patricia Drake

Ladyfinger Dessert

1 package ladyfingers (split)
7 — 10¢ size Heath bars
 (chilled and broken into small pieces)
1 pint whipping cream (whipped)

Line a 13 x 9 x 2 inch baking dish with ladyfingers. Fold Heath bars into whipped cream. Place over ladyfingers and refrigerate 24 hours in advance.
Cut in serving pieces. Serves 8 to 10.

Gretchen Handrich

Spring Green Torte

Dissolve:

 1 package lime gelatin in
 ½ cup water

Add:

 ¼ cup lemon juice
 ¼ cup sugar

Cool until slightly jelled.
Beat 1 large can evaporated milk (chilled)
Add gelatin and green coloring.
Line springform with 12 whole chocolate wafers.
Put wafer crumbs on bottom and reserve a few for the top.

Alice Moore

Vienna Torte

3 eggs	1½ teaspoon baking powder
1½ cups sugar	¼ teaspoon salt
¾ cup milk	1 teaspoon vanilla
1 tablespoon butter	½ teaspoon lemon extract
1½ cups flour	

Beat eggs until very thick and lemon colored. Gradually add sugar and beat until sugar is completely dissolved. Add flavoring. Bring milk and butter to a boil and add it to the egg mixture. Then fold in the flour which has been sifted with the baking powder and salt. Bake in three 9" layer cake pans which have been greased and floured. Bake at 350° for 15 to 20 minutes until lightly browned and the cake springs back at touch. Cool and split in half crosswise. Spread filling on the cut side each time.

Filling

2½ cup milk, scalded
½ cup flour
¼ teaspoon salt   } Blend — add hot milk, slowly
½ cup powdered sugar

Cook in double boiler until thick; cool and add 1 teaspoon of vanilla. Cream 1 cup butter, add 1 cup powdered sugar. Blend into the cold milk mixture and divide in half. Add 1 square of melted baking chocolate to one portion.

Spread the filling between the split layers, alternating the white and the chocolate mixture ending with the chocolate. Sprinkle chopped nuts on top of the cake. Refrigerate until ready to serve.

Caroline Rossabo

Pineapple Torte

2 cups flour
3 tablespoons sugar
1 teaspoon baking powder
1 cup butter (or ½ cup butter,
    ½ cup margarine)

Mix like pie crust and then add 4 egg yolks (beaten). Mix all. Line springform on sides and bottom. Cook together one #2½ can of crushed pineapple and 2 tablespoons cornstarch. Pour into lined springform. Bake at 325° for 45 minutes. Then beat 4 egg whites until they hold a peak. Add 1 cup sugar and ¼ cup ground almonds. (Do not blanch.) Spread over pineapple and bake another 15 minutes, or until lightly brown. Serve with whipping cream.

Frieda Brott

Cranberry Torte

3 cups graham cracker crumbs
½ cup butter
2 cups sifted confectioners' sugar
1 egg
1 medium sized apple, ground
1 cup raw cranberries, ground
1-12 ounce can crushed pineapple, drained
1 cup granulated sugar
1 teaspoon vanilla extract
1 pint heavy cream, whipped

Pat the graham cracker crumbs into a 12" x 7½" pan. Reserve ½ cup of the crumbs for later. Cream butter, add confectioners' sugar gradually and continue creaming until fluffy. Add egg and mix well. Place over crumbs in pan. Then combine apple, cranberries, pineapple and sugar and spread over butter mixture. Chill well. Makes 12 servings.

R. Hansen

Frost on the Pumpkin Pie

Crust —

1½ cups graham cracker crumbs
¼ cup margarine, melted
½ cup powdered sugar

Mix contents, then press into a 10″ pie plate and bake at 325 degrees for 10 minutes. Allow to cool.

Set aside, 1 tablespoon unflavored gelatin dissolved in ¼ cup cold water.

Filling —

3 egg yolks
⅓ cup sugar
1 pound can pumpkin
½ cup milk
½ teaspoon salt
1 teaspoon cinnamon
½ teaspoon allspice
¼ teaspoon ginger
¼ teaspoon nutmeg

Mix well and cook until it boils about 2 minutes. Remove from heat and add the gelatin. Stir until mixed well and cool.

Make meringue of the 3 egg whites and ¼ cup powdered sugar. Fold into cooled pumpkin mixture.

Whipped Cream Filling —

1 cup whipping cream, whipped
1¼ cups powdered sugar
½ teaspoon cinnamon
½ teaspoon vanilla

Put half of pumpkin mixture into the baked graham cracker crust. Top with half of the whipped cream mixture, and top off with the remaining pumpkin. Chill 2 hours to set.

Before serving, top with remaining whipped cream.

Mrs. De Jonge

Butterscotch Pie

2 egg yolks
3 tablespoons flour
¼ cup white sugar
¾ cup brown sugar
3 tablespoons water
1½ cups milk
1 teaspoon vanilla
3 tablespoons butter

Cream sugar, flour and egg yolks, add water, milk, vanilla and butter. Stir together and cook until thickened and fill baked pie shell. Use egg whites for meringue.

Iris Crosser

German Sweet Chocolate Pie

1 pkg. German sweet chocolate
¼ cup butter
1⅔ cups (14½ ounce can evaporated milk)
1½ cups sugar
3 tablespoons cornstarch
⅛ teaspoon salt
2 eggs
1 teaspoon vanilla
1 unbaked 10 inch pie shell
1⅓ cups angel flake coconut
½ cup chopped pecans

Melt chocolate with butter over low heat, stir until blended. Remove from heat. Gradually blend in milk. Mix sugar, cornstarch and salt thoroughly, beat in eggs and vanilla. Gradually blend in chocolate mixture, pour into pie shell. Mix coconut and nuts, sprinkle over filling. Bake at 375° 45 to 50 minutes or until top is puffed and browned. (Filling will be soft but will set while cooling). Cool 4 hours or more.

Virgie Edwards

Sour Cream Raisin Pie

Pastry for 2 crust pie
2 egg yolks
1 cup dairy sour cream
1 tablespoon vinegar
2 cups seedless raisins
1 cup dark brown sugar
2 tablespoons flour
1 teaspoon cinnamon
½ teaspoon nutmeg
¼ teaspoon salt

Prepare pastry using recipe for double crust. Beat eggs, stir in sour cream, vinegar and raisins. Mix dry ingredients. Stir into raisin cream mixture. Pour into unbaked pastry crust. Cover with lattice crust strips. Bake 450° for 10 minutes. Lower heat to 350° and bake for 20 to 25 minutes, until filling is set and crust is brown. Serve warm.

Donna Kingsley

Summertime Peach Pie

4 tablespoons of cornstarch
1 cup sugar
3 medium sized peaches

Mix cornstarch and sugar together and sprinkle half of the mixture into the bottom of an un-baked pie shell. Arrange fresh, peeled peach halves with their cut sides up in the pie shell and sprinkle the rest of the cornstarch and sugar mix over them. Then fill the pie shell with half & half cream until it covers the peaches. Bake for about 50 to 60 minutes in a 375°–400° oven. Serve with ice cream.

Sue Harenchar

Coconut Delight

To 4 beaten eggs

Add: 2 cups sugar
2 cups milk, gradually
½ cup plain flour
Pinch of salt
½ tablespoon baking powder

Sift flour, salt and baking powder together before adding:

1 stick melted margarine
1 teaspoon vanilla
1 small can flake coconut

Pour into two pie tins that have been generously greased. Bake at 350° approximately 30 minutes or until set. Makes own crust as it bakes.

Lois Martinec

No-Weep Meringue

½ cup water
¼ cup sugar
1 tablespoon cornstarch
Dash of salt

Combine and cook over low heat until it turns white—*cool*. Beat 3 egg whites very stiff, then fold in cooled mixture. Spread on pie and brown in oven at 350° for 12-15 minutes.

Mrs. Emil Koch

Rhubarb Meringue Pie

1 tablespoon butter
4 cups rhubarb (inch pieces)
1¼ cups sugar
2 tablespoons cornstarch
Pinch of salt
2 eggs
¼ cup cream
1 9-inch baked pie shell
¼ cup sugar

Melt butter in heavy saucepan. Add rhubarb and 1 cup sugar. Cook, stirring constantly until rhubarb is tender, about 10 minutes. Combine remaining ¼ cup sugar, cornstarch, salt, egg yolks and cream. Add to rhubarb and continue to cook, stirring constantly, until thick. Cool and turn into pastry shell. Beat egg whites stiff, add ¼ cup of sugar and place over filling. Bake in 400 degree oven to brown meringue.

Leona A. Howell

Tropical Ice Cream Pie

Pie crust: 1 cup vanilla wafers
2 tablespoons sugar
⅓ cup melted margarine

Mix together and press into a 9″ pie tin and bake at 400° for about 10 minutes.

Pie filling: 1 cup milk
1 package vanilla *instant* pudding mix
1 pint vanilla ice cream, slightly soft

Beat slowly until well blended (1-2 minutes). Pour into crust. Refrigerate while making glaze.

Glaze: 1½ cups (#2 can) crushed pineapple
¼ cup sugar
1 tablespoon cornstarch

Combine all ingredients in small heavy saucepan. Cook over low heat, stirring constantly, until thick. Cool. Spoon over pie. Chill overnight.

Mrs. Tommy Cochran

New Method Custard Pie

4 eggs
3 cups milk
¾ cup sugar
1 teaspoon vanilla
⅛ teaspoon salt

Beat eggs slightly, add sugar, milk, vanilla and salt. Place over low heat, stirring constantly. When steam shows, remove from heat and pour into a 9-inch unbaked pie shell. Sprinkle with nutmeg. Bake at 450° for 10 minutes. then at 350° for 15 minutes or until firm. (This custard pie never gets watery or soaks crust.)

Mrs. Fred Wilson

Puff Pastry

1 stick of margarine
½ cup sour cream
1½ cups of flour

Cream margarine. Add flour like you do to pie crust. Fold in sour cream. Divide in 2 pieces, wrap and store in refrigerator for at least 8 hours. Leave out one hour before using. Roll out ½ inch thick. Cut in 3-by-3-inch squares.

Fill with apple or cherry filling. Fold edges and moisten. Put on ungreased sheet. Brush with a glaze of 3 tablespoons powdered sugar and 1 tablespoon of water mixed. Bake in 350° oven for 15 to 20 minutes.

Eleanor Steffen

Pink Lemonade Pie

1 baked 9" pie crust
1 envelope unflavored gelatin
¼ cup cold water
1 can (6 ounces) frozen lemonade concentrate
¾ cup sugar
1 cup evaporated milk, chilled
3 drops red food coloring

Soften gelatin in cold water, add lemonade and sugar. Stir constantly over low heat until completely dissolved. Then chill. Beat the chilled milk until stiff and then fold the cooled gelatin mixture and food coloring into it. Pour into pie crust. Chill 3 to 4 hours before serving.

Alice Morgan

Swedish Apple Pie

2 cups sliced apples, cooked
2 tablespoons flour
¾ cup sugar
Pinch salt
1 egg
1 teaspoon vanilla
1 cup commercial sour cream
9" unbaked pie shell

Mash apples slightly, add flour, sugar and salt. Beat egg and vanilla, add to apple mix. Beat sour cream until stiff and fold in apple mixture. Pour into pie shell. Sprinkle over pie a mixture of 1½ tablespoons sugar and 1 teaspoon cinnamon. Bake at 350° for 35-40 minutes.

Mrs. Alvin J. Yoder

Southern Pecan Pie

3 eggs
½ cup sugar
1 cup white syrup
¼ cup butter
1 cup pecans (ground or chopped)
⅛ teaspoon salt
1 teaspoon vanilla

Beat eggs and add sugar, syrup, salt, vanilla and butter. Line a 9" pie tin with pastry. Pour pecans into crust and add mixture. Bake in 350° oven for 50 or 60 minutes. Pecans will rise to top to form a crust.

Mrs. Austin M. Kay

Fresh Strawberry Pie

1 baked pie shell

Filling: 4 heaping tablespoons cornstarch
1 cup sugar
Pinch salt
1 cup water

Cook above ingredients until thick. Add several drops of red food coloring. Cool a little and then fold in about a quart of strawberries into glaze. Pour into pie shell. Top with whipped cream.

Joan Glass 53

 # DESSERTS

Lemon Fluff

1 — 15 ounce can evaporated milk
1 — 3 ounce box lemon gelatin
¼ cup lemon juice
¾ cup sugar
2½ cups graham cracker crumbs

Chill milk 3 hours.
Dissolve gelatin in 1½ cups hot water —
chill until thick and then beat until fluffy.
Add lemon juice and sugar.
Beat milk until thick — add first mixture.
Sprinkle ½ of crumbs into 13 x 9 x 2 inch
pan. Pour in mixture and cover top with
other ½ of crumbs. Chill until firm.

Elaine Nelson

Angel Pineapple Icebox Pie

1 cup (small can) crushed pineapple
1 cup sugar
1 cup water
3 heaping tablespoons cornstarch
  Dash of salt
¼ teaspoon cream of tartar
2 teaspoons vanilla (one is for topping)
½ pint whipping cream
½ cup sugar
¼ cup chopped pecans
1 9-inch baked pie shell
2 egg whites.

Combine pineapple, sugar, cornstarch, water and
salt. Mix well in a heavy pan or double boiler. Cook
over medium heat until thick and clear. Cool.

When completely cool, beat egg whites with cream
of tartar until very stiff. Fold into cool mixture,
add vanilla and pour into cool crust.

Topping

½ pint whipping cream whipped, add ½ cup sugar
and 1 teaspoon vanilla. Cover pie and sprinkle the
¼ cup chopped nuts over whipping cream. Chill in
refrigerator several hours.

Very easy and most delicious!

Helen I. Haupt

Peach Delight

Prepare crust:

Beat 2 whole eggs till light and airy.
Add ¾ cup sugar, 2 tablespoons at a time.
Fold in 18 soda crackers crushed.
Add 1 teaspoon vanilla and ¼ cup chopped nuts.
Butter a 9-inch pie tin.
Pour in mixture.
Bake at 350°, 20 to 25 minutes.
Do not overbake. Bake till a light tan.

Drain a 13½ ounce can sliced peaches.
Arrange peaches in crust.

Put this topping over the peaches:

Combine: ½ pint cream whipped
          1 cup miniature marshmallows
            Sugar to taste
          ½ teaspoon almond extract
          ⅓ cup chopped nuts
          ⅛ cup maraschino cherries, cut

Chill at least two hours in refrigerator.

Mrs. Craigen Thom

Baked Devil's Float

½ cup sugar
1½ cups water — boil together 4 minutes and
                pour over
12 quartered marshmallows in casserole
½ cup sugar
2 tablespoons shortening
½ cup milk
1 teaspoon vanilla
1 cup flour
½ teaspoon salt
1 teaspoon baking powder
3 tablespoons cocoa
1 egg
½ cup chopped nuts (optional)

Cream together shortening, sugar, egg and vanilla;
add flour sifted with salt, baking powder and cocoa
alternately with milk, then nuts if desired. Drop by
spoonfuls over marshmallow mix. Cover. Bake at
350° for 45 minutes. Serve warm with a little milk.
(If baked uncovered the cake is a little crusty, which
is the way we've come to prefer it.)

This is an old family favorite, the origin of which has
long been forgotten.

Pollyanna Sedziol

Company Squares

Crush 12 to 16 crisp chocolate wafers with rolling pin to make 1¼ cupfuls of coarse crumbs.

Cream until light and fluffy 3 tablespoons butter or margarine. Add 2 tablespoons powdered sugar and cream.

Gradually work crumbs into creamed mixture. It will still be crumbly.

Spread ½ the buttered crumbs on the bottom of a refrigerator ice tray.

Spread 1 pint of ice cream over the crumbs and sprinkle the rest of the crumbs on top, pressing down gently.

Freeze until firm in the refrigerator.

Cut in squares and lift out with wide spatula.

To dress it up, put 2 tablespoons whipped cream and a maraschino cherry on top of each square.

Kate M. Ownly

Hot Fudge Sauce

½ cup margarine
2½ cups sugar
½ teaspoon salt
3 squares chocolate
1 large can evaporated milk
1 teaspoon vanilla

Melt margarine in top of double boiler.
Drop in chocolate and melt.
Add sugar very gradually (4 tablespoons at a time — stirring).
Add salt.
Add milk very gradually — Water in double boiler must keep boiling.
Last add vanilla.

Cook until desired thickness — about 1 hour, 10 minutes. Can be stored in refrigerator for a long time and reheated. Makes 1 quart.

Mrs. John F. Allen

Recipe Saver

I clip them from the magazine
And from newspapers too,
I gather them from neighbors, friends . . .
And this is nothing new.
I take them down from radio
And file them all away,
From TV cooking schools I find
New dishes day by day.
What fancy menus do I plan
From all the recipes;
O I'll bake this and I'll cook that . . .
The family will I please.
And yet somehow I find myself
Repeating, so it seems,
The same old meals I've done for years . . .
The rest are in my dreams.

Hilda Butler Farr

Sugar Plum Ring

1 package yeast	¼ cup melted butter
¼ cup water	¾ cup sugar
½ cup milk, scalded	1 teaspoon cinnamon
⅓ cup sugar	½ cup whole blanched
⅓ cup shortening	almonds
1 teaspoon salt	⅓ cup dark corn syrup
3¾ cups flour	½ cup whole candied
2 beaten eggs	red cherries

Soften yeast in warm water. Combine scalded milk, the ⅓ cup sugar, shortening, salt, and cool to lukewarm. Stir in 1 cup flour. Beat well. Add yeast and eggs. Add remaining flour or enough to make soft dough. Place in greased bowl turning once to grease surface. Cover and let rise until double. Punch down. Let rest 10 minutes. Divide dough into 4 parts. Cut each part into 10 pieces and shape into balls. Dip balls in ¼ cup melted butter then ¾ cup sugar into which 1 teaspoon cinnamon has been blended. Arrange ⅓ of the balls in well-greased tube pan. Sprinkle with part of ½ cup whole blanched almonds and part of ½ cup whole candied red cherries. Repeat with 2 more layers. Mix ⅓ cup dark corn syrup with butter left from dipping balls; drizzle over top. Cover and let rise till double. Bake 350° for 35 minutes. Cool 15 minutes.

Helen Elaine Boring

Heavenly Rice Pudding

½ cup raw white rice
1 can (8¾ ounces) pineapple tidbits
1 cup miniature marshmallows
10 maraschino cherries, halved (⅓ cup)
1 package (2⅛ ounces) whipped topping mix
½ cup cold milk
½ teaspoon vanilla extract
2 tablespoons maraschino cherry juice

Cook rice as package label directs for softer rice. Refrigerate until well chilled. Drain pineapple, reserving syrup. In large bowl, combine chilled rice, drained pineapple, marshmallows and cherries; stir until well combined. Refrigerate, covered overnight with the pineapple syrup stored separately.

Next day, prepare whipped topping mix with milk and vanilla as package label directs. Stir reserved pineapple syrup and the cherry juice into rice mixture. Fold in whipped topping just until combined. Refrigerate about one hour before serving. Makes eight servings.

Mrs. John Baker

Bread Pudding

Scald 2 cups milk
Pour over 4 cups soft bread crumbs – cool.

Add ½ cup melted butter
2 eggs, slightly beaten
¼ teaspoon salt
½ cup raisins
1 teaspoon cinnamon
½ cup sugar

Pour into greased ½ quart casserole.
Set in a pan of hot water.
Bake at 350° for 1 hour.
Serve hot with hard sauce:

Mix and chill 1 hour:

½ cup butter
1 cup confectioners' sugar
1 teaspoon vanilla

Barbara A. Clark

Flaming Peaches

Sprinkle brown sugar in hollows of peach halves in baking dish. Dot with butter.

Broil slowly until sugar crusts. Put in center of each peach half a lump of sugar that has been soaked for 20 minutes in lemon extract. Light lump and bring to table flaming.

Flo Miller

Schaum Torte

8 egg whites
¼ teaspoon salt
1 teaspoon vanilla
2 cups sugar
1 tablespoon vinegar

Beat egg whites and salt about 10 minutes, until stiff but not dry. Add sugar gradually and vinegar. Beat 10 to 15 minutes longer. Add vanilla. Bake in spring torte pan. Place in preheated oven – 400°. Turn off and leave torte in oven until cool. (2 to 3 hours)

Serve with fresh or frozen berries and whipped cream.

Gladys Biesik

Horns-of-Plenty

2 cups flour
1 tablespoon sugar
1/8 teaspoon salt
3/4 cup butter (part shortening may be used)
  Mix all together like pie crust.

1 package fresh yeast dissolved in
  5 tablespoons warm water
2 egg yolks, beaten
  Mix together.

Then mix first mixture with second mixture lightly with a fork.

Filling:

2 egg whites stiffly beaten
1/2 cup sugar. Add to egg whites
Cinnamon, chopped pecans, raisins

Form dough into ball; cut in four equal parts. Roll 1 part at a time on well-floured board to form a 9" circle. Spread with 1/4 of egg white mixture, sprinkle with cinnamon, nuts and raisins. Cut into 8 pie shaped pieces. Roll as for butterhorns, starting at wide end. Bake on greased cookie sheet at 375° for about 15 minutes. Frost while warm with powdered sugar icing. (Powdered sugar, vanilla and milk).

Note: Although you use yeast, you do not let them rise, it gives them a delicious tenderness.

Mrs. Alton W. Cheney

Cheese-Apple Crisp

6 medium apples (2 pounds)
1/4 cup water
2 teaspoons lemon juice
1 1/2 cups sugar or
    2 cups white corn syrup
1 teaspoon cinnamon
1 cup flour
1/3 teaspoon salt
1/2 cup butter
3/8 pound grated
    cheese
    (1 1/2 cups)

Peel, quarter, core, slice apples. Arrange slices in a shallow greased baking dish. Add water and lemon juice. Mix sugar, cinnamon, flour and salt. Work in butter to form a crumbly mixture. Grate cheese. Add to topping mixture and stir lightly. Spread mixture over apples and bake in a moderate oven at 350° F. until apples are tender and crust is crisp (about 30-35 minutes). Serve with lemon sauce or garnish with whipped cream.

Lemon sauce:

1/2 cup sugar
1 tablespoon cornstarch
2 tablespoons lemon juice
2 tablespoons butter
1 cup boiling water
1 tablespoon grated
    lemon rind
Salt

Mix sugar and cornstarch. Add the boiling water and a pinch of salt. Boil until thick and clear. Continue cooking in double boiler for 20 minutes. Remove from stove. Stir in butter and lemon rind. A pinch of nutmeg may be added if desired.

Mrs. Lester Smith

Grandmother's Baked Custard

4 eggs, slightly beaten
1/2 cup sugar
1/4 teaspoon salt
1 1/2 teaspoon vanilla
3 cups scalded milk

Mix eggs, sugar, salt and vanilla until sugar isn't grainy. Slowly add scalded hot milk. Place in baking dish and set in a pan of hot water. Sprinkle with nutmeg before placing in oven. Bake 35 to 40 minutes in a 325° oven, until a knife inserted in center comes out clean. Serve warm or cold.

Mabel White Epling

Strawberry Marlow

1 12-ounce package frozen strawberries
24 marshmallows
1 teaspoon grated lemon rind
1 cup heavy cream, whipped

Defrost the strawberries and drain well. Place the juice and marshmallows in the top of a double boiler. Heat until the marshmallows are melted. Chill. Add the strawberries and lemon rind. Fold in the whipped cream. Pour into refrigerator trays and freeze.

This is a delightful luncheon or after-dinner dessert.

Nana Beck

Memee's Sweetheart Cookies

"This is an old recipe from France, given to me over 30 years ago by a dear little French lady we called 'The Little Grandmother.'"

  1 cup butter
  2 cups granulated sugar
  4 eggs
  5 cups sifted flour
½ teaspoon salt
  3 teaspoons baking powder
    Juice and grated rind of 1½ lemons

Cream together well, butter and sugar until fluffy. Add unbeaten eggs, one at a time, beat well between each. Add lemon juice and rind. Add dry ingredients sifted together, flour, salt and baking powder. Mix well. Chill for an hour or two. Roll out ¼-inch thick, cut with heart-shape cookie cutter. Slightly grease cookie sheets. Sprinkle cookies with granulated sugar. Bake 375°—about 10 minutes. The fresh lemon juice gives a real lemon flavor.

Mrs. William N. Robey

Spice Bars

Bring to a boil:

    1 cup water
    1 cup sugar
    1 cup raisins
  ½ cup butter
    Pinch salt

And let cool while you mix:

    2 cups flour
    1 teaspoon soda
    1 teaspoon cinnamon
  ½ teaspoon nutmeg
  ½ teaspoon clove

Combine the mixtures well and add:

  ½ cup chopped dates
  ½ cup English walnuts, chopped

Spread on greased cookie sheet and bake in a 350° oven 25 minutes. Glaze with a thin powdered sugar icing while warm.

Mrs. Wade A. Bauer

Grandma's Cookie Jar

When I went to visit Grandma
I was always thrilled
For I knew she kept
A cookie jar well-filled.

Quickly I removed my wraps
And Grandma led the way
Into a pungent kitchen
With treasures on display.

Peanut butter cookies,
Gumdrops tart and sweet,
Macaroons and gingersnaps
And brownies for a treat.

With a glass of buttermilk
I tasted everything,
Grandma looking on at me
As though I were a king.

I love to visit Grandma,
It's a trip I most enjoy
Though manhood's now replaced
That eager little boy.

Bernice Peers

Snow-Covered Gingersnaps

¾ cup shortening
1 cup sugar
4 tablespoons molasses
1 egg
2 cups unsifted all-purpose flour
2 teaspoons soda
1 scant teaspoon salt
1 teaspoon cloves
1 teaspoon cinnamon
1 teaspoon ginger

Cream shortening, add sugar gradually, creaming well after each addition. Add molasses. Mix well, add egg. Beat. Measure flour before sifting, add soda, salt, and spices. Sift together, stir in dough. Roll into balls the size of a walnut. Roll balls in powdered sugar. Place on ungreased cookie sheet. Bake at 350° for 10-12 minutes about 2 inches apart. Sprinkle with powdered sugar before removing from cookie sheet.

Eleanor Cultice

Molasses Cookies

1 cup shortening
1 cup sugar
1 cup molasses
1 teaspoon ginger
1 teaspoon salt
½ cup coffee
2 teaspoons baking soda
5 cups flour

Cream shortening and sugar, add molasses, sift flour and add ginger, salt and baking soda. Add the dry ingredients to the shortening, sugar and molasses gradually, alternating with the coffee, and ending up with the flour mixture. Bake at 400° temperature. If butter is used for shortening, do not grease cookie sheet.

Mrs. H. V. Sherman

Fudge Squares

2 squares unsweetened chocolate
½ cup shortening
1 cup granulated sugar
2 well-beaten eggs
½ cup sifted flour
¼ teaspoon salt
1 teaspoon vanilla
½ cup chopped walnuts

Melt chocolate and shortening. Blend in sugar, eggs, flour and salt. Stir well with spoon. And flavoring. Spread into 8″ x 8″ x 2″ pan. Sprinkle with nuts. Bake in moderate oven (350°) for about 12 minutes.

Pudding powder icing:

4 tablespoons butter
3 tablespoons milk
½ teaspoon vanilla
2 cups powdered sugar
2 tablespoons custard pudding powder

Combine ingredients and mix until smooth. Spread on cooled square. Melt 2 squares chocolate with 1 tablespoon butter. Dot icing with this mixture.

Winnie Donbrook

Chocolate Mint Wafers

Cream thoroughly:

⅔ cup butter
1 cup sugar

Add 1 egg and beat well.

Add the following sifted dry ingredients alternately with milk:

2 cups enriched flour
¾ cup cocoa
½ teaspoon salt
1 teaspoon baking powder
¼ cup milk

Mix thoroughly, chill. Roll ⅛ inch thick on lightly floured surface. Cut with floured 2 to 2½ inch cookie cutter. Bake on greased sheet 350° for 8 minutes.

When cool, put together with:

½ cup confectioners' sugar
2 drops peppermint
3 to 4 tablespoons light cream or milk
Salt

Beat until of spreading consistency.

Gladys Eborall

Chocolate Frosted Brownies

½ cup flour
¼ teaspoon baking powder
½ teaspoon salt
⅓ cup shortening
⅓ cup cocoa
1 cup sugar
¼ cup milk
2 eggs
1 teaspoon vanilla
½ cup chopped nuts

Sift flour, baking powder and salt. Melt shortening and cocoa together, add sugar and milk and let come to a boil. Remove from heat and add flour mixture. Beat eggs and add to other ingredients. Add vanilla and nuts. Bake in square pan for 25 to 30 minutes at 350°.

Frosting

1 package chocolate bits
½ cup sweetened condensed milk
1 teaspoon vanilla

Melt bits. Add condensed milk. (Do not use evaporated milk). Heat bits and milk thoroughly. Beat and add vanilla. Spread over brownies, cut in squares and serve.

Jane Shanck

Thimble Cookie

Mix thoroughly:

½ cup soft butter or shortening
¼ cup brown sugar
1 egg yolk
½ teaspoon vanilla

Stir in:

1 cup sifted flour
¼ teaspoon salt

Roll into balls. Dip in slightly beaten egg white, then in chopped nuts or crushed cornflakes. Place on lightly greased cookie sheet. Make a thimble-size print and fill with your favorite jam. Bake for 10 minutes at 375°.

Mrs. Muriel Hunter

Sugar Cookies

2 cups sugar
2 cups butter
4 eggs, well-beaten
5 cups flour
2 teaspoons soda
4 teaspoons cream of tartar
1 teaspoon salt
1 teaspoon nutmeg

Cream butter and sugar. Add remaining ingredients. Roll not too thin. Sprinkle with sugar. Use your favorite cookie cutter.

Bake at 375° for 10 minutes.

This is an old recipe. They are so delicious and crisp. I have been making them for 24 years for our family. They are so attractive in seasonal shapes plus colored sugars.

Mrs. Alvin J. Yoder

Lemon Bars

Base:

Cut together 2 sticks of margarine, 2 cups flour, ¼ teaspoon salt, ½ cup sugar. Press in 9 x 12-inch pan. Bake 20 minutes in 350° oven.

Filling:

Mix together by hand 4 eggs, 2 cups sugar, 4 tablespoons flour, ½ teaspoon baking powder, 7 tablespoons lemon juice. Pour filling over base. Return to oven and bake 20 minutes more. Sprinkle with powdered sugar.

Nancy McDonald

Coconut Dainties

1 cup butter or margarine
¼ cup sifted powdered sugar
2 teaspoons vanilla
1 tablespoon water
2 cups sifted flour
1 cup chopped pecans

Thoroughly cream butter, sugar and vanilla. Stir in water, add flour and mix well. Stir in nuts. Shape into 1" balls. Bake 1" apart on ungreased cookie sheet in slow oven (300°) about 20 minutes or until firm to touch. Cool thoroughly before removing from sheet. Dip cookies in powdered sugar and roll in tinted fine coconut. Makes about 4 dozen.

Mrs. Gerald C. Hasley

Drop Sugar Cookies

⅔ cup shortening
1⅔ cup sugar
2 teaspoons vanilla
2 eggs
3½ cups sifted flour
½ teaspoon soda
1 teaspoon salt
2 teaspoons baking powder
½ cup heavy sour cream

Cream sugar, shortening, eggs and vanilla until fluffy. Sift together flour, soda, salt and baking powder. Add alternately to creamed mixture—with the sour cream. Drop by teaspoonfuls on ungreased cookie sheet. Bake in 375° oven about 12 minutes.

Frieda J. Hawes

Civil War Applesauce Cookies

"This recipe has been handed down from Civil War times. Grandmother Selden got the recipe from her mother in 1880 and gave it to me on our first visit to the farm in 1925. The original recipe called for 'lard compound' for shortening, and sour cream instead of applesauce."

2¼ cups sugar	6 cups sifted flour
1⅓ cups shortening	1 teaspoon baking soda
3 eggs	2 teaspoons baking powder
2 teaspoons vanilla	2 teaspoons nutmeg
1 cup applesauce	1 teaspoon salt

Cream shortening, sugar, eggs and vanilla. Add applesauce and mix well. Add sifted dry ingredients and blend well. Drop by heaping tablespoons on greased cookie sheet, flatten, sprinkle lightly with sugar and bake 10 to 12 minutes at 375° (do not brown). Makes 44 four-inch cookies.

Mary A. Selden

Cream Cheese Cookies

1 small package cream cheese
¼ pound margarine
Yolk of 1 egg
1 cup flour
2½ tablespoons sugar
½ package chocolate chip bits

Mix ingredients together, adding flour last. Chill dough in refrigerator 2 hours or overnight. Use wax paper to form dough into roll. Chill again. Cut into ¼" slices to form cookies. Bake on ungreased cookie sheet in 350° oven for about 20 minutes or until light brown around edge of cookie.

Aurora Santerre

Mother's Butterscotch Cookies

½ cup butter
2 cups brown sugar
½ teaspoon baking soda
⅛ teaspoon salt
½ cup chopped pecans or hickory nuts
2 teaspoons vanilla

2 eggs
3 cups flour
2 teaspoons baking powder

Cream butter and sugar. Add unbeaten eggs and stir. Add vanilla and sifted dry ingredients and nuts. Mix well. Knead into a roll and let stand in the refrigerator several hours or overnight. Cut in very thin slices and bake about 15 minutes or less in a 375° oven.

Mrs. Stewart Brawn

Chocolate Fudge

4½ cups sugar
  Dash salt
  1-14½ ounce can (1⅔ cups)
    evaporated milk (undiluted)
  2 tablespoons butter
  1 package (12 ounces) semisweet
    chocolate chips
  3 packages (¼ pound each) sweet
    cooking chocolate
  1 pint jar marshmallow cream
  2 tablespoons vanilla
  2 cups nutmeats

In a large heavy saucepan stir together sugar, salt, evaporated milk and butter. Stirring constantly, bring to a boil. Boil 7 minutes, stirring occasionally.

Pour boiling hot syrup over both kinds of chocolate and marshmallow cream. Stir vigorously until chocolate melts. Add vanilla. Stir in nutmeats.

Turn into buttered pan (9 x 9 x 1¾). Let stand in cool place to set. Refrigerate if necessary to keep firm, or store in tightly covered metal box.

Mrs. Charles W. Bailey

Most Wonderful Toffee

  1 cup butter
  1 cup sugar
  3 tablespoons water
½ cup chopped almonds
  1 package chocolate chips

Cook together butter, sugar and water until mixture turns caramel color or 300 degrees on candy thermometer. Remove from heat and stir in ½ amount of nuts. Pour into a buttered 13 x 9 x 2 baking dish. Sprinkle on ½ package of chocolate chips, and let stand for a few minutes until chips melt. Spread chips and cover with wax paper. Turn dish over and spread remainder of chocolate chips and nuts over top.

Let cool until mixture is hard, then break into pieces.

Helen Rogowski

Christmas Pudding Candy

  3 cups sugar
  1 cup light cream
  1 heaping tablespoon butter
  1 teaspoon vanilla
  1 pound dates, chopped
  1 pound figs, chopped
  1 pound raisins
  1 pound coconut
  2 cups nuts, chopped

Cook sugar, cream, and butter to a soft ball. Beat until creamy then beat in fruit and nuts. If coconut is coarse, grind it. When well mixed, roll as for meat loaf. Wrap in wet cloth, then in wax paper and put away to ripen two weeks, or longer, in refrigerator.

"This has been a family favorite for over forty years."

Virgie Edwards

Book III Index

Lasagne, 29
Orange-Glazed Rack of Lamb, 26
Pepper Steak, 28
Roast Beef, 29
Sauerbraten, 29
Singapore Pork and Cabbage, 31
Sour Cream Scalloped Potatoes and Ham, 31
Spanish Steak, 29
Spice Sauce for Ham, 30
Stuffed Pork Chops, 31
Swedish Glottstek, 28
Veal Cutlets Cordon Bleu, 27

Pies
Butterscotch Pie, 50
Coconut Delight, 50
Fresh Strawberry Pie, 53
Frost on the Pumpkin Pie, 50
German Sweet Chocolate Pie, 50
New Method Custard Pie, 53
No-Weep Meringue, 52
Pink Lemonade Pie, 53
Puff Pastry, 53
Rhubarb Meringue Pie, 52
Sour Cream Raisin Pie, 50
Southern Pecan Pie, 53
Summertime Peach Pie, 52
Swedish Apple Pie, 53
Tropical Ice Cream Pie, 52

Relishes
Holiday Relish, 13
Quick Pickled Beets, 13
Rosy Applesauce Relish, 13
Russian Dill Pickles, 13
Spiced Dill Pickles, 13
Sweet Dill Pickles, 13

Rolls and Muffins
Applesauce Muffins, 40
Bran Buttermilk Muffins, 40
Butter Pecan Rolls, 38
Dieter's Breakfast Biscuits, 38
Double Quick Coffee Bread, 41
Doughnuts, 40
Elephant Ears, 41
Funnel Cakes, 40
Hot Cross Buns, 38
Nut Stollen, 41
Potato Refrigerator Rolls, 38
Raised Doughnuts, 40

Sour Cream Twists, 41
Speedy Rolls, 38
Spoon Biscuits, 38

Salads
Cherry-Coke Salad, 11
Chinese Chicken Salad, 12
Crab Louis, 12
Eggnog Holiday Salad, 11
Fruit Salad, 10
Georgia Nut Salad, 11
Hearty Lunch Salad, 12
Macaroni-Ham Salad, 12
Maple-Nut Salad, 11
Pink Applesauce Mold, 11
Tuna Crunch Salad, 12

Soups
Autumn Soup, 9
Chicken Corn Soup, 8
Ham Bone Soup, 9
Mormon Whole Meal Soup, 9
Peanut Butter Soup, 9
Steak Soup, 8
Tasty Garnishes on Soup, 8

Tortes
Cherry Squares, 48
Cranberry Torte, 49
Cream Cheese Refrigerator Torte, 47
Date-Nut Torte, 48
Filling, 49
Frozen Lemon Torte, 48
Ladyfinger Dessert, 48
Mallow Lemon Torte, 48
Orange Juice Torte, 47
Pineapple Torte, 49
Pumpkin Torte, 47
Spring Green Torte, 48
Vienna Torte, 49

Vegetables
Beets Royale, 15
Eggplant, Pizza Style, 15
Elegant Corn, 15
Green Beans, Cream Style, 14
Potato Soufflé, 14
Scalloped Cabbage, 15
Swedish Red Cabbage, 15
Vegetable Platter Combinations, 15

1
2
3
4
5
6
7
8
9
0
1